Antonio Kleber Zea Cobo

Tracking Extended Objects with Active Models and Negative Measurements

Karlsruhe Series on Intelligent Sensor-Actuator-Systems

Volume 21

ISAS | Karlsruhe Institute of Technology
Intelligent Sensor-Actuator-Systems Laboratory

Edited by Prof. Dr.-Ing. Uwe D. Hanebeck

Tracking Extended Objects with Active Models and Negative Measurements

by

Antonio Kleber Zea Cobo

KIT Scientific Publishing

Dissertation, Karlsruher Institut für Technologie
KIT-Fakultät für Informatik

Tag der mündlichen Prüfung: 26. Januar 2018
Erster Gutachter: Prof. Dr.-Ing. Uwe D. Hanebeck
Zweiter Gutachter: Prof. Umut Orguner

Impressum

KIT Scientific Publishing

Karlsruher Institut für Technologie (KIT)
KIT Scientific Publishing
Straße am Forum 2
D-76131 Karlsruhe

www.ksp.kit.edu

Print on Demand 2019 – Gedruckt auf FSC-zertifiziertem Papier

ISSN 1867-3813
ISBN 978-3-7315-0877-9
DOI 10.5445/KSP/1000088267

Acknowledgements

This thesis is the culmination of several years of work at the chair of Intelligent Sensor-Actuator-Systems (ISAS) of the Karlsruhe Institute of Technology (KIT). It was a journey that started as an internship, then as a job as a student assistant, continuing during my Diplom thesis, and finally as a research assistant. Throughout these years, I had the fortune of meeting many generous people that helped me in several ways. I would like to dedicate this book to them.

First, I would like to thank my advisor, Prof. Dr.-Ing. Uwe D. Hanebeck, for his unconditional support and the opportunities he has offered me. He patiently helped me during my time as a student assistant, entrusted me with responsibilities at the Holodeck laboratory, and taught me the value of focus. I know for sure that I owe a large part of my career success to his counsel. I would also like to thank my second advisor, Prof. Umut Orguner, for his insights and suggestions on how to improve my work.

Second, I would like to give special thanks to two of my former colleagues, with whom I shared my office for a long time. Even if they no longer work at ISAS, their presence will always be felt, especially because of all the plants they left here. First, I would like to thank Florian Faion, for being my supervisor during my Diplom thesis, and for being a personal and close friend after that. His unwavering support guided me during difficult times, and I hope we get the chance to work together once more. Second, I would like to thank Jannik Steinbring, a friend and colleague who never failed to give me support when I needed it. May the three of us drink a lot more beer, eat more Wurstsalat, and throw a lot more little plastic balls at each other.

Finally, I would also like to thank my family back in Ecuador, for always being by my side, even if they are physically a long distance away. Special thanks go to my parents, Esmirna and Antonio, and to my sister Ennie, with her three kids Emiliana, Cristian, and little Santi. I hope one day to be able to return all the kindness they have given me during my life.

Once more, thanks for everything. This book is for all of you.

Karlsruhe, November 2018

Contents

Notation

General Notation

$\mathbb{R}$	Set of real numbers
$\mathbb{R}_+$	Set of positive real numbers
$\mathbb{N}$	Set of natural numbers
$\mathbb{N}_+$	Set of positive natural numbers
a	Scalar
$\underline{a}$	Column vector
$\mathbf{A}$	Matrix
$\|\underline{a}\|$	Euclidean norm of vector $\underline{a}$
$\det(\mathbf{A})$	Determinant of matrix $\mathbf{A}$
$(\mathbf{A})^{-1}$	Inverse of matrix $\mathbf{A}$
$\mathbf{I}_N$	Identity matrix of dimension N
$(\,\cdot\,)^\top$	Transpose of a vector/matrix
$\delta(\underline{a})$	Dirac-δ distribution of vector $\underline{a}$

Probability Theory

$\hat{s}$	Mean of a random variable s
$\hat{\underline{s}}$	Mean of a random vector $\underline{s}$
σ_s^2	Variance of random variable s
$\mathbf{C}^s$	Covariance matrix of random vector $\underline{s}$
$\underline{s} \sim f$	Random vector $\underline{s}$ distributed according to PDF f

State Estimation

$\underline{x}_k$	System state at time step k
$\hat{\underline{x}}_k$	State mean at time step k
$\mathbf{P}_k$	State covariance matrix at timestep k
$\underline{y}_k$	Measurement at timestep k
$\underline{z}_k$	Source of the measurement at timestep k
$\underline{p}_k$	A point in the same space as $\underline{y}_k$
$\mathbf{C}_k^w$	System noise covariance matrix at timestep k
$\mathbf{C}_k^v$	Measurement noise covariance matrix at timestep k

Zusammenfassung

Beim Tracking von ausgedehnten Objekten (auf Englisch 'extended object tracking', kurz EOT) geht es darum, die Form und Lage eines Zielobjekts anhand von verrauschten Punktmessungen zu schätzen. Im Gegensatz zu traditionellen Trackingverfahren, die das Zielobjekt als punktförmig betrachten, modellieren wir das Objekt als ausgedehnte Form, deren Parameter ebenfalls geschätzt werden. Diese Aufgabe ist nicht einfach, da sie die folgenden Herausforderungen beinhaltet.

- Erstens liefern Sensoren stets verrauschte Messungen, und oft kann nur Teil der ganzen Form beobachtet werden, zum Beispiel wegen Verdeckungen oder Artefakten.
- Zweitens ist es möglich, dass nur wenig Vorwissen über das Zielobjekt zur Verfügung steht, zum Beispiel über die Formkomplexität oder die Bewegung. Die verwendeten Modelle sollen deshalb flexibel genug sein, eine große Vielfalt an potentiellen Formen zu beschreiben, gleichzeitig aber robust und nicht anfällig für Overfitting.
- Drittens ist in vielen Fällen der Sensor nur in der Lage, wenige verrauschte Messungen des Zielobjekts aufzunehmen, weil das Objekt sich oft in großer Entfernung befindet.

Wegen diesen drei Faktoren ist es im Allgemeinen schwer, robuste und präzise Lösungsansätze zu entwickeln, die gleichzeitig effizient und leicht zu implementieren sind. Die Bewältigung dieser Herausforderungen ist die Kernaufgabe dieser Arbeit.

EOT wird traditionell zur Verfolgung von Großobjekten wie Flugzeugen, Schiffen, oder Autos verwendet. Allerdings ermöglichen Technologiefortschritte bei Tiefenkameras wie Microsoft Kinects mittlerweile sogar Laien, Punktwolken aus ihrer Umgebung aufzunehmen. Das stellt eine neue Herausforderung für EOT-Ansätze dar, die in modernen Anwendungen, wie z.B. Objektmanipulation in Augmented Reality oder in der Robotik, Zielobjekte mit vielen möglichen Formen anhand von Messungen unterschiedlicher Qualität verfolgen müssen. In diesem Kontext ist die Auswahl der Formmodelle ausschlaggebend, denn sie bestimmen, wie robust und leistungsfähig der Schätzer sein wird, was wiederum eine sorgfältige Betrachtung der Modalitäten und Qualität der verfügbaren Informationen erfordert. Solch ein Informationsparadigma kann als ein Spektrum visualisiert werden: auf der einen Seite, eine große Anzahl an genauen Messungen, und auf der anderen Seite, nur wenige verrauschte Beobachtungen. Allerdings haben sich die Verfahren in der Literatur traditionell auf einen schmalen Teil dieses Spektrums konzentriert. Einerseits assoziieren 'gierige' Verfahren, die auf der Methode der kleinsten Quadrate basieren, Messungen mit der nächsten Quelle auf der Form. Diese Verfahren sind effizient und liefern sogar für komplizierte Formen akkurate Ergebnisse, allerdings nur solange das Messrauschen niedrig bliebt. Ansonsten kann nicht gewährleistet werden, dass der nächste Punkt immer noch eine passende Approximation der wahren Quelle ist, was zu verzerrten Ergebnissen führt. Andererseits sind probabilistische Modelle wie Raumverteilungen präzise für einfache Formen, sogar bei extrem hohem Messrauschen, allerdings werden sie schon für wenig komplexe Formen unlösbar oder numerisch instabil. Die Schwierigkeit besteht darin, dass in vielen modernen Trackingszenarien die Menge an verfügbarer Information sich drastisch mit der Zeit ändern kann. Das unterstreicht den Bedarf an Ansätzen, die nicht nur die Stärken beider Modelle kombinieren, sondern auch alle Bereiche des Spektrums und nicht nur dessen Grenzfälle abdecken können.

Das Ziel dieser Arbeit ist es, diese Lücke zu füllen und somit die drei oben angesprochenen Herausforderungen zu lösen. Dazu schlagen wir vier Beiträge vor, die den aktuellen Stand der Technik signifikant erweitern. Zuerst schlagen wir *Level-set Partial Information Models* vor, einen probabilistischen Ansatz zur erwartungstreuen Formschätzung für Szenarien mit Verdeckungen und hohem Messrauschen. Zusätzlich führen wir *Level-set Active Random Hypersurface Models* ein, die von Konzepten aus EOT und Computervision inspiriert sind, eine flexible Formparametrisierung für konvexe und nicht-konvexe Formen ermöglichen, und die auch mit wenig Information umgehen können. Darüber hinaus machen *Negative Information Models* sogenannte 'negative' Information nutzbar, indem Messungen verarbeitet werden, die uns sagen, wo das Zielobjekt nicht sein kann. Schließlich zeigen wir eine einfach zu implementierende Erweiterung von diesen Beiträgen, *Extrusion Models*, um dreidimensionale Objekte mit realen Sensordaten zu verfolgen.

Der erste Beitrag dieser Arbeit betrachtet die erste Herausforderung, und beschäftigt sich mit Shape Fitting in Szenarien mit niedriger Messqualität und Verdeckungen. Die Schwierigkeit in diesem Kontext besteht darin, dass es im Allgemeinen wegen des Sensorrauschens nicht möglich ist, zu wissen, von welcher Quelle auf der Form eine gegebene Messung generiert wurde. Inkorrekte Assoziationen verursachen wiederum verzerrte Schätzungen, die verringerte Genauigkeit oder sogar Divergenz bei hohem Messrauschen zur Folge haben. Um dieser Herausforderung zu begegnen, stellen wir **Level-set Partial Information Models** vor. Kernidee hier ist die Herleitung eines probabilistischen Terms zur Verzerrungskorrektur, der durch eine Analyse der Formfunktion in der Nachbarschaft einer approximierten Messquelle entsteht. Durch eine Neuinterpretation dieses Terms als eine Integral über einer Niveaumenge der Formfunktion, lässt sich die Korrektur mit beliebiger Genauigkeit und in geschlossener Form berechnen. Diese Formulierung führt zu hoher Robustheit gegenüber Rauschen und Verdeckungen, sogar in Szenarien, wo andere state-of-the-art Verfahren divergieren.

Für die zweite Herausforderung brauchen wir eine geeignete Formparametrisierung, die mit wenig a-priori Information umgehen kann. Insbesondere soll sie für alle möglichen Zielobjekte präzise Ergebnisse liefern, unabhängig von der Konvexität der Form, dem Startwert, oder wo sich die Messquellen im Objekt befinden, da unter Umständen der Sensor auch Messungen aus dem Inneren der Form beobachten kann. Obwohl in der Literatur bereits mehrere Algorithmen existieren, die beliebige nicht-konvexe Formen mit hoher Genauigkeit approximieren können, basieren diese meistens auf sternkonvexen Parametrisierungen. Diese erfordern jedoch die Existenz eines sogenannten 'Zentralpunkts', der sich mit allen Punkten auf der Oberfläche verbinden lässt, ohne die Oberfläche zu schneiden. Leider führt die Verwendung dieser Ansätze bei Zielobjekten, die nicht sternkonvex sind, zu fehlerhaften und vergrößerten Formschätzungen, die eine akkurate Berechnung der Pose schwierig machen. Um diese Probleme zu beseitigen, werden Ideen des etablierten Konzepts von Random Hypersurface Models erweitert zu **Level-set Random Hypersurface Models**. Die Hauptidee hier ist, die Formoberfläche durch eine polygonale Parametrisierung zu beschreiben, die keinerlei Restriktionen über die Konvexität erfordert, und dazu das Forminnere durch Niveaumengen der Formfunktion zu modellieren. Diese Flexibilität erhöht allerdings das Risiko von Overfitting und niedriger Robustheit, das wir durch einen Regularisierungmechanismus reduzieren, der von Active Contours aus der Computervision inspiriert wurde. Unser Beitrag ist nicht nur flexibel und einfach zu implementieren, sondern erlaubt auch den leichten Einbau von zusätzlichen dynamischen Modellen wie Shape Morphing.

Allerdings kann die Verwendung von erwartungstreuen und flexiblen Formmodellen allein nicht zu akkuraten oder robusten Ergebnissen führen, wenn die Menge an Information nicht ausreichend ist. Daher ist es nötig, um die dritte Herausforderung zu behandeln, alle möglichen Informationsmodalitäten eines Sensors einzubauen. Beispielsweise nehmen Sensoren wie RGB- oder Tiefenkameras auch Messungen von der Umgebung des Zielobjekts auf. Diese 'negativen' Messungen enthalten ebenfalls wertvolle Information, denn sie teilen uns mit, wo das Zielobjekt nicht sein kann. Aus diesem Grund sind sie in Szenarien besonders wertvoll, in denen es nur wenige bis gar keine 'positiven' Beobachtungen des Objekts gibt. Um beide Arten von Messungen verwenden zu können, führen wir **Negative Information Models** ein, die Ideen von probabilistischer Formschätzung und Shape Fitting kombinieren. Es ist allerdings zu beachten, dass negative Messungen zwar ähnlich, aber nicht identisch zur Idee von 'negativer Information' sind. Dort geht es darum, Wissen aus dem Event abzuleiten, dass überhaupt keine Messung aufgenommen wurde, während es in dieser Arbeit um Beobachtungen geht, die von anderen Objekten stammen. Wir zeigen, dass unser Ansatz in Szenarien mit viel Information ähnliche Ergebnisse wie Vergleichsverfahren aus der Literatur liefert. In Szenarien mit Ausreißern oder Clutter kann unser Ansatz aber dramatisch bessere Ergebnisse erzielen.

Die Untersuchung der Anwendbarkeit dieser Beiträge in realen Szenarien ist in diesem Forschungsfeld von besonderem Interesse. Aus diesem Grund wollen wir sicherstellen, dass unsere Konzepte sich auch mit dreidimensionalen Daten verwenden lassen, wie sie bei z.B. in der Robotik oder autonomer Navigation zur Verfügung stehen. Es werden daher für unsere Modelle Erweiterungen zu 3D hergeleitet, die zusätzlich die Eigenschaften von realen Sensormessungen beachten, um Overfitting zu vermeiden oder mögliche Artefakte zu kompensieren. Ein einfacher Mechanismus, um dieses Ziel zu erreichen, ist durch **Extrusion Models**. Dabei ist die Grundidee, eine dreidimensionale Form durch die vertikale 'Verschiebung' einer planaren Grundform zu konstruieren, analog zur Konstruktion eines Zylinders durch die Verschiebung eines Kreises. Zusätzlich können wir die Grundform während der Verschiebung größer oder kleiner machen, um komplexere Formen wie Flaschen, Dosen, oder Teekannen darzustellen. Da diese Formulierung von Extrusionen kompatibel zu allen anderen in dieser Arbeit vorgestellten Beiträgen ist, lässt sich die praktische Anwendbarkeit dieser Modelle mit einer umfassenden Evaluierung zeigen, in welcher die Form und Lage eines Objekts in Bewegung anhand realer Sensordaten geschätzt wird.

Abstract

Extended object tracking (EOT) deals with estimating the shape and pose of an object based on noisy point measurements. In contrast to traditional tracking approaches, which assume that the target is a single point, we model the target as a shape whose parameters also need to be estimated. This task is not straightforward, in particular because we are faced with the following three challenges.

- First, the sensor only provides noisy measurements, and may not even be observing the entire shape, for example due to occlusions and artifacts.
- Second, we may have little a priori information about the target, in particular about the shape complexity or its motion. This means that the shape model needs to be flexible enough to represent a large variety of shapes while retaining robustness and avoiding overfitting.
- Third, in many circumstances the sensor may only be able to provide a small amount of low-quality measurements from the target, for instance when sensor and target are far from each other.

These three factors make it difficult to develop robust, accurate estimators that are also efficient and simple to implement. Addressing these challenges is the main task of this thesis.

Traditionally, EOT has concerned itself with large objects such as planes, ships, or cars, but with modern advances in depth cameras such as Microsoft Kinect sensors, even laymen can capture point clouds of their daily-life surroundings. This raises new challenges for EOT approaches, as modern applications in fields ranging from robotics to augmented reality are now required to track targets with many different possible shapes, while incorporating measurements whose quality may change in time. In this context, the selection of appropriate shape models is crucial, as it determines how robust and performant the estimator can be, and requires a careful consideration of the amount of information available. This paradigm can be visualized as a spectrum, with a high amount of accurate measurements on one side, and few noisy observations on the other. State-of-the-art approaches, however, have traditionally focused narrowly on a single part of this spectrum. On the one hand, 'greedy' algorithms, such as those based on least squares methods, associate measurements to the nearest source on the shape. These approaches work efficiently even with very complex shapes, but only as long as the measurement noise remains low, otherwise they yield biased estimates as the nearest point ceases to be an appropriate approximation of the true source. On the other hand, probabilistic techniques such as Spatial Distribution Models are accurate for simple shapes, even with extremely high noise, but become intractable or numerically unstable as soon as the shape becomes moderately complex. The problem is that, in many modern practical tracking scenarios, the amount and the quality of available information may change drastically over time. This raises the need for new approaches that combine the strengths of these models, but can work suitably in any part of the information spectrum, not just on the edges.

This thesis aims to bridge this gap, and presents four contributions to the state-of-the-art which address the previously introduced challenges. First, *Level-set Partial Information Models* present a probabilistic mechanism for unbiased shape fitting that can handle situations with occlusions and high measurement noise. Second, *Level-set Active Random Hypersurface Models* provide a flexible shape representation for convex and non-convex shapes, capable of dealing with scenarios with little a priori knowledge by combining ideas from EOT and computer vision. Third, *Negative Information Models* aim to increase the amount of available information by incorporating knowledge about where the target cannot be, exploiting measurements usually discarded as clutter. Finally, we develop a straightforward extension of these contributions, called *Extrusion Models*, that allows them to estimate three-dimensional targets in real-world scenarios.

The first contribution is aimed towards the first challenge, and focuses on shape fitting scenarios with low measurement quality and occlusions. The main difficulty in this context is the fact that, due to measurement noise, it is generally not possible to know which source on the shape generated the received measurements. Incorrect associations, in turn, cause issues of estimation bias, leading to lack of accuracy and even divergence if the noise is high enough. In order to address this, we introduce **Level-set Partial Information Models**, which derive a bias correction term by analyzing how the distance function behaves around a potential source. This probabilistic correction term can be evaluated with arbitrary accuracy by reinterpreting it as an integral over a level-set, which can be calculated in closed form. This formulation leads to high robustness against noise and occlusions even in scenarios where state-of-the-art approaches diverge.

For the second challenge, we need an appropriate shape representation that can handle situations with little a priori knowledge. In particular, it must able to yield accurate results for arbitrary targets, independent of the shape convexity, the initial value of the estimator, or whether the sensor also receives measurements from the interior of the shape. While state-of-the-art approaches have developed techniques capable of closely approximating non-convex shapes, they have focused on star-convex representations, which require a 'center' that can be connected to all points in the boundary without intersecting it. Unfortunately, applying these techniques on shapes that are not star-convex yields inappropriate, oversized estimates that make it difficult to obtain an accurate pose. In order to address this, we present **Level-set Active Random Hypersurface Models**, which extend ideas from Random Hypersurface Models from previous work. The key idea is to describe the shape boundary using a polygonal representation, which does not impose any demands of convexity, and model the interior using level-sets of the distance function. This increased flexibility, however, raises the risk of overfitting and reduced robustness, which we avoid by introducing *active models*, a regularization mechanism inspired from ideas of active contours. This approach is not only flexible and easy to implement, but can also easily incorporate additional dynamic models such as shape morphing.

Even if we employ unbiased and flexible shape models, the estimate cannot be accurate or robust if there is little information to work with. Thus, in order to address the third challenge, we need to be able to incorporate every piece of information provided by the sensor. It is useful to take into account that when sensors such as depth or RGB cameras observe a target, they also capture measurements from its surroundings. These 'negative' observations carry important information that tells us where the target cannot be, and become extremely valuable in situations where there are few 'positive' measurements from the target. In order to incorporate both types of information, we introduce **Negative Information Models**, which combine ideas from probabilistic models and shape fitting. Note that negative measurements are the result of actively observing an object that is not the target being tracked, and thus, they differ conceptually from the traditional idea of 'negative information', which represents knowledge gained from the event that no measurement was received at all. We show that our contribution works similarly to state-of-the-art in situations with high-quality information, but conclusively surpasses them in cases of outliers and clutter.

As usual in EOT, it is extremely important to take into account how the proposed theoretical contributions can be used in real-life scenarios. In particular, we are interested in potential applications that work with three-dimensional data, for example in the fields of robotics or autonomous navigation. This requires an extension of the previously explored ideas into 3D, while taking into account the sensor characteristics and the measurement quality in these scenarios, in order to compensate for artifacts and to avoid overfitting. A straightforward mechanism to achieve this is by using **Extrusion Models**, which construct a three-dimensional surface by 'shifting' a planar shape vertically, similarly to how a cylinder is constructed from a circle. Furthermore, by making the planar shape larger or smaller as it is being shifted, we can obtain even more detailed shapes such as bottles, cans, or teapots. Given that this formulation of extrusions encapsulates all the previously explored ideas, we demonstrate their applicability in real scenarios through a comprehensive evaluation based on real-life captures of a moving object.

CHAPTER 1

Introduction

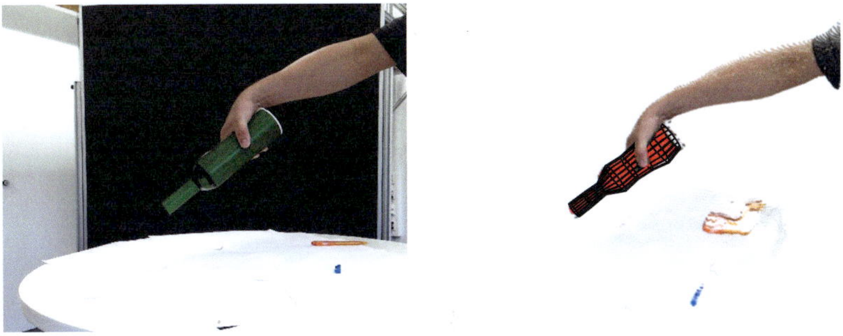

(a) Image of a person holding a bottle.

(b) 3D point cloud with segmented bottle.

Figure 1.1: Illustration of a moving bottle being observed by a Microsoft Kinect 2 depth camera. The segmented bottle is shown in bright red, and an example estimate is shown in black.

This thesis is concerned with estimating the shape and pose of an extended object based on point measurements observed from its surface. This is not a straightforward task, as illustrated by the scenario in Figure 1.1, where we are required to estimate the pose, i.e., the position and orientation, of the moving object. Applications such as this are relevant to a variety of disciplines, including robotics, human-machine interaction, telepresence, and augmented reality. We are faced with the following three challenges.

- First, the measurements captured by the sensor are noisy, and occlusions are usually present. In particular, we cannot guarantee at any moment that we are observing the entire target, as happens in Figure 1.1b where the sensor can only observe the bottle from one side.
- Second, we may have little a priori information available about the target shape, and we may not even know that we are observing a bottle. This imposes important requirements on the selected shape representation, as it needs to be flexible enough to describe a large variety of targets while surviving situations of overfitting and high uncertainty.
- Third, accurately tracking a moving target with an unknown shape requires a minimum of information to be available, due to the amount of parameters involved. However, under certain circumstances, such as the target being far from the sensor, only a low amount of noisy measurements from the target may be available. This motivates the derivation of approaches that optimally incorporate all the available sensor data.

The goal of this thesis is to provide reliable shape and pose estimation techniques, as seen for example in Figure 1.1b, that address these challenges.

1.1 Related Work

In order to appreciate in practical terms why this task can be difficult, it is useful to take into account the wide variety of scenarios in which tracking is applied, and the techniques that have been developed as solutions in the last years. Broadly speaking, the source of all the difficulties we face can be said to be *uncertainty*, which is an umbrella term that describes a lack of information or knowledge about the system. The properties of this uncertainty are critical, as they determine the assumptions that can be made, the models to be applied, and the type of estimators that should be employed. For illustration, we can consider the scenarios shown in Figure 1.2. Let us start with Figure 1.2a, which shows an example of an airborne synthetic-aperture radar scan used for maritime surveillance. In each scan, at most one single measurement becomes available for each ship, as a consequence of their small size and the immense distance between sensor and target. Because of this, it makes no sense to model the spatial extents, and instead, the 'small object' assumption is employed [1], where each target is described as a single point and their orientation is assumed to be the same as the motion direction [2, 3]. Due to their generality, low computational complexity, and wide applicability, single point targets are commonly used in a variety disciplines [4, 5], but especial attention has been given in literature to aircraft tracking [6, 7, 2, 5]. Even if they ignore the target extent, the mathematical concepts explored by these techniques have served as the cornerstone for the more complex models that followed.

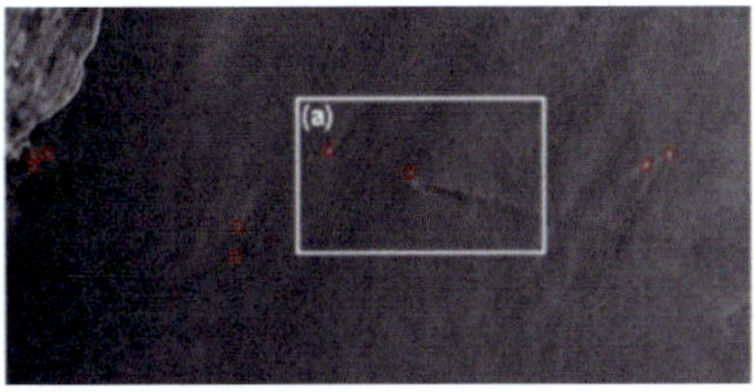

(a) SAR scan of maritime vessels [8], *©2011 IEEE.*

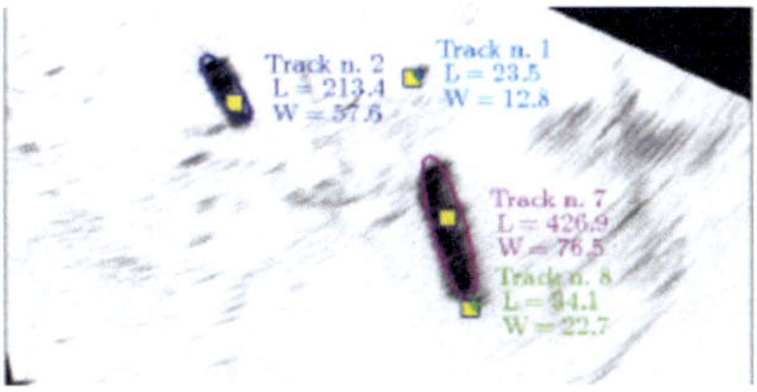

(b) X-band radar scan of maritime vessels [9], *©2016 IEEE.*

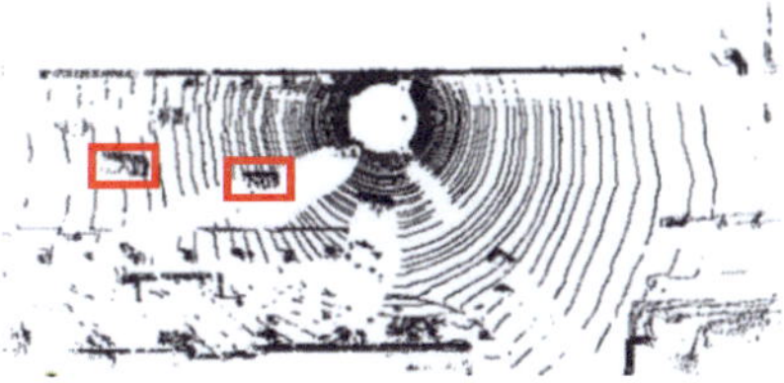

(c) LIDAR scan from autonomous car [10], *©2012 IEEE.*

(d) Kinect scan for reconstruction [11], *©2011 IEEE.*

Figure 1.2: Example practical tracking scenarios, sorted according to the information available.

In other scenarios, increased sensor quality allows for multiple measurements per target to become available in each scan. This is the case in Figure 1.2b, where marine X-band radar is being used to monitor the ships traversing a harbor. The received information is generally sufficient to detect the dimensions of the ship, which in turn can be used for classification. It can also serve to determine which measurements belong to clutter, such as the blurry gray lines produced by interference. Because of these factors, models which treat targets as single points become insufficient, raising the need to treat them as *extended* objects, i.e., possessing a non-zero area or volume. The discipline that deals with these targets, and the focus of this thesis, is called extended object tracking (EOT) [12, 13]. While there are several EOT works dealing explicitly with radar data [14, 15], it can be seen that the provided information is not sufficient to obtain a detailed reconstruction of the target. In cases such as this, approximations using simple shapes are preferred, such as ellipses [16, 17, 14, 15], rectangles [18, 19, 20], or line segments [147].

As sensor accuracy increases even further, much more information becomes available about the target's shape. This can be seen for example in Figure 1.2c, which shows a car using a rotating LIDAR to scan its surroundings. By segmenting objects above the ground, the car can detect and classify objects around it, allowing it to recognize which objects are static (such as walls and lamp posts), and which can be in motion (such as pedestrians, cars, or bicycles). This raises the need for more flexible models able to reasonably approximate arbitrary shapes. Approaches such as occupancy grids [21, 22, 23] can be used, which have the advantage that they can be extended into navigation maps. Also popular are parametric models, which describe knowledge about the shape using a fixed (usually small) amount of parameters. Literature for parametric estimation can be divided in two camps, based on whether the observed target is 'filled' or not. For reference, when we talk about filled shapes, we are referring to situations where observations stem both from the target boundary and its interior. This can happen, for example, in indoor navigation and autonomous driving (as in Figure 1.2c), where the scene is flattened by projecting measurements onto the floor [24], or in eagle-eye vehicle tracking, where targets are seen from above [1, 25].

In these cases, the task is to obtain the smallest (or 'tightest') approximation that contains all observed measurements. A commonly used mechanism to describe the interior is by using boundary representations such as Fourier series [26, 27, 28] or using ideas from Gaussian processes [29], and then scaling the boundary inwards [30]. Another consists of joining simple shapes together, such as ellipses, and ensuring spatial coherency through unified kinematic models [31, 32, 33, 34]. However, if the shape is not filled and we only observe its boundary, the task becomes simply to obtain an estimate that minimizes some sort of distance or metric to all measurements. In literature, this is known as shape fitting [35]. While related work has focused on conic fitting [36, 37, 38, 39], there are also works representing arbitrary shapes using polygons [40], Bézier curves [41], Fourier series [27, 28], and Gaussian processes [29]. In cases of occlusions, the missing information can be compensated using assumptions of symmetry [42, 149]. Furthermore, it may be necessary to correct for estimation bias caused by incorrect assumptions about the source [148, 43]. If the shape is known a priori, and only the translation, rotation and scaling need to be estimated, iterative closest point [44, 45] can be used.

A common feature of the sensors mentioned before is that, due to their high price, they have been out of reach to the layman. The arrival of affordable, off-the-shelf depth sensors such as Microsoft Kinect [46, 47] or Asus Xtion PRO changed this, which also allow for dense three-dimensional point cloud captures with high measurement quality. This, in turn, permits extremely detailed surface reconstruction in real time such as in Figure 1.2d. Non-parametric representations are highly popular in this context, in particular the KinectFusion application [11] and its extensions [48]. This approach is based on three-dimensional occupancy grids, a technique also used by [49, 50]. Other popular reconstruction techniques include [51, 52], and off-the-shelf libraries implementing all of these algorithms are also available [53]. Literature for parametric representations in these scenarios, however, is less extensive. Approaches that estimate three-dimensional shapes have been traditionally extensions of two-dimensional counterparts, such as going from ellipses to ellipsoids [54], or cubes to cuboids [55]. While parametric works that deal exclusively with three-dimensional shapes are scarce [1], exceptions include [56, 57] which propose approximating targets as extrusions.

There are also related disciplines that are not directly relevant to the main task of this thesis, but which are still worth mentioning for the sake of completeness. On the one hand, the field of multiple target tracking (MTT) [58, 59] deals with simultaneously estimating the position of several targets, usually modeled as points. Unlike EOT, where the sources have some spatial coherence in the form of a 'shape', in MTT the point targets may appear, disappear, form groups, or separate at any moment. In this case, managing hypotheses on which measurement belongs to what target is critical, and several approaches exist that address this task [60, 61, 62, 63, 64, 13, 16]. Others deal with a hybrid system, tracking multiple extended targets simultaneously combining ideas from MTT and EOT [65, 66, 67, 68]. On the other hand, it is also worth discussing works that focus on object tracking using raster images [69]. Unlike the main focus of EOT, which deals with separate point measurements with individual noise characteristics, raster images work with relative large pixel grids which can provide thousands or millions of observations in each frame. It is then necessary to extract, or segment [70, 71], the measurements that belong to the target, and then find a simpler representation that contains all the relevant information, usually in the form of a contour [69, 72] or a silhouette [73, 74]. The shape and pose of the target are then tracked across frames [75, 76] using dynamic models comparable to those employed in EOT and MTT. Note that, by interpreting individual pixels from the target as point measurements, EOT shape estimation techniques can also be used with raster images. This approach is extremely useful in situations where a high amount of gaps or measurement noise is expected, as is the case in depth images from sensors such as Kinects or LIDARs, including the scenario illustrated in Figure 1.1. Works that combine EOT with raster images include [57, 56, 77, 147, 78].

1.2 Contributions

As mentioned in the previous section, uncertainty in the system is a key characteristic to take into account when choosing an estimation procedure and the associated models. With this in mind, let us revisit the scenario introduced at the beginning of this chapter, and its corresponding three challenges. On the one hand, we saw that there is often very little a priori information about the target, and thus, we may not know how much measurement information will be available. This, in turn, makes the selection of an appropriate shape representation, and its initialization, extremely difficult. On the other hand, factors such as measurement quality and the amount of observations may change in time. For example, a target far from the sensor will yield sparse, extremely noisy measurements, while another close to the sensor may produce enough information for an accurate estimate in a single scan. This means that in modern target tracking scenarios with rapidly moving targets, as seen in disciplines such as robotics, indoor navigation, or even augmented reality, the level of uncertainty in the system is constantly changing. Thus, as modern applications begin covering wider ranges of the uncertainty spectrum, categorizations based on which kind of measurement quality an approach focuses on, as we did in Figure 1.2, are quickly becoming less relevant. Taking this into account, in the following we enumerate the contributions of this thesis and how they address these three challenges.

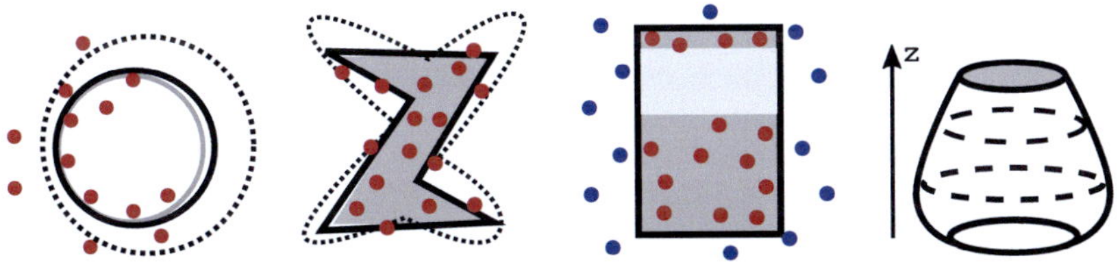

(a) Level-set PIMs. **(b)** Level-set ARHMs. **(c)** Negative Information Models. **(d)** Extrusion Models.

Figure 1.3: The four main contributions of this thesis.

For the first challenge, we will focus on shape fitting scenarios with low information quality, where it is important to retain an appropriate level of accuracy and robustness even if only a few noisy measurements are available. An important issue in this context is that it is difficult to associate a measurement to the part of the shape that generated it, as a consequence of the sensor noise. As an example, we observe that finding the exact points on the grey circle that generated the red points in Figure 1.3a is not straightforward. Inappropriate associations will in turn cause estimation bias, yielding shapes with incorrect extents and poses (such as the large circle with dotted line), raising the risk of divergence when the uncertainty becomes large enough. Previous work in literature alleviated this issue using multiple mechanisms [79, 43], which were generalized in the form of Partial Information Models (PIMs) [148]. The key idea for PIMs was to develop a probabilistic model of how the distance function behaves around an assumed source, and use this information to derive a bias correction term, which could in turn be easily incorporated into an estimator. In this thesis, we introduce an extension of this idea in the form of **Level-set Partial Information Models** [160], capable of calculating this bias correction term with arbitrary accuracy even in the presence of extremely high noise, as seen for example in the circle estimate shown in black. This is achieved by reinterpreting the calculation of the correction term as an integral over level-sets of the distance function. Based on this improved formulation, we show how our contribution is capable of robust, efficient, and accurate shape estimation even in scenarios where state-of-the-art alternatives produce invalid results.

The next challenge is to find an appropriate shape representation that can handle situations with little a priori knowledge. As mentioned before, shape complexity in literature can be described as a spectrum based on the amount of information available, ranging from single points to convex forms such as ellipses and rectangles, up to star-convex approximations. The latter, despite its flexibility, requires the shape to have a 'center' that can be connected to all points in the boundary [26, 27, 28]. If this is not the case, such as the gray shape in Figure 1.3b, the star-convex approximation will not be capable of describing the target appropriately (dotted line), losing vital information that can increase accuracy and robustness. In this thesis, we go even farther in the complexity spectrum by introducing **Level-set Active Random Hypersurface Models** (Level-set ARHMs) [156, 160] which extend ideas from Random Hypersurface Models (RHMs) [30] from previous work. The advantage of this contribution (shown in black) is that it can be used to estimate arbitrary non-convex shapes, and can be employed both for shape fitting or when the shape is filled. As an example implementation, we propose a polygonal representation to describe the boundary, and model the interior using level-sets of the distance function. While increased flexibility has traditionally brought issues of overfitting and lack of robustness, we avoid this problem by introducing a regularization mechanism inspired by ideas of active contours [75, 76], called *active models.* The key idea here is to model each vertex as a sort of spring, pulling each of its neighbors slightly at each timestep. We show how our proposed model is capable of not only describing non-convex shapes, but can also keep an accurate representation while the target moves and morphs into another shape.

It should be pointed out that, even if the shape model and the estimation procedure are robust and efficient, they cannot be accurate if there is little information to work with, as can happen when the sensor is far from the target. In order to address the third challenge, it is useful to take into account that in scenarios where measurements are taken from depth or RGB images, not only the target is being observed, but also objects around it. This means that we can obtain knowledge about where the target cannot be in the form of 'negative' measurements (blue dots in Figure 1.3c), which can help us to compensate when positive observations (red dots) are scarce. In order to exploit this additional source of information, we introduce **Negative Information Models**, capable of incorporating both positive and negative measurements from the scenario. Note that negative measurements represent actively observing an object that is not the target being tracked, and thus, it differs conceptually from the traditional idea of 'negative information', which means gaining knowledge from the fact that no measurement was received at all [80, 81, 82]. The proposed models are particularly useful in case of occlusions (such as the light gray region in Figure 1.3c), given that they make no assumptions in the case that fewer measurements are observed, unlike probabilistic models such as [26, 57, 83] which immediately assume that the target has shrunk. We show how models that exploit negative measurements perform similarly to state-of-the-art in optimal conditions, but outperform them in situations with outliers and occlusions.

Finally, as mentioned before, literature has traditionally focused on two-dimensional shape estimation, while work with three dimensions has usually been scarce [1] and dealt mostly with mere extensions of 2D models into 3D. While these approaches are mathematically sound, they fail to take into account issues that appear only when dealing with three-dimensional data. On the one hand, a much higher amount of information is required than in planar counterparts, meaning that trivial extensions from 2D may easily suffer from lack of robustness or overfitting. Shape and pose models also need to be adapted to avoid unobservable parameters, for example when trying to estimate the axial rotation of a cylinder. On the other hand, it is necessary to keep in mind the measurement quality provided by the sensors usually employed in 3D tracking scenarios, as they are often rife with outliers and artifacts. We propose a mechanism to extend the previously explored ideas into three dimensions while carefully taking these pitfalls into consideration, in the form of **Extrusion Models**. The key mechanism is to describe complex 3D shapes by interpreting them as extrusions, which can be seen as the process of shifting a flat shape in the xy-plane vertically in the z-axis, yielding a surface. For example, a cylinder can be obtained by extruding a circle. Furthermore, by scaling the shape as it is being shifted (as in Figure 1.3d), we can obtain even more detailed shapes, allowing for the description of real-life objects such as bottles, cans, or teapots. We explore different formulations and association models for extrusion models, and then evaluate in what measure they can overcome the low measurement quality and occlusions typical of 3D sensors.

1.3 Outline

In order to close this chapter, we will present a short outline of the remainder of this thesis.

- In Chapter 2, we discuss the topic of *Extended Object Tracking* in more detail, including mathematical formulations and technical concepts which will serve as the theoretical backbone for the following chapters.
- Then, in Chapter 3, we introduce *Partial Information Models* in order to address the issue of estimation bias caused by incorrect assumptions about the measurement sources. In this chapter, we also introduce our contribution Level-set Partial Information Models.
- Chapter 4 serves as a brief introduction into the topic of the extent problem in shape fitting, and introduces two innovations in the form of active models and *Active Random Hypersurface Models.*
- Chapter 5 deals with shape estimation for arbitrary non-convex shapes, and presents our contribution *Level-set Active Random Hypersurface Models.*
- Then, in Chapter 6 we discuss the incorporation of positive and negative measurements using *Negative Information Models*, and show the advantages of this contribution.
- After that, in Chapter 7, we talk about the topic of *Modeling Extrusions*, where we extend the previously proposed ideas into three dimensions and evaluate them.
- Finally, we close this thesis in Chapter 8 by presenting the *Conclusions.*

CHAPTER 2

Extended Object Tracking

This chapter presents a short introduction into the field of extended object tracking (EOT). It also presents a selected list of state-of-the-art publications and lays the theoretical foundation for the following chapters. First, we present a brief formulation of the problem being discussed. Then, we give an overview of object tracking and how traditional approaches deal with this topic. Finally, we extend these concepts to extended objects and derive measurement models describing the relationship between the shape parameters and how sensors observe them. In particular, we explain the ideas of *Spatial Distribution Models* (SDMs) and *Greedy Association Models* (GAMs), which are the starting points for the ideas and contributions presented later in this thesis.

2.1 Problem Formulation

The basic problem being considered is estimating the pose parameters, i.e., the position and orientation, of a moving target based on incoming measurements taken from it. The parameters to be estimated are contained in the state vector $\underline{x}_k$, where k denotes the discrete timestep. The received measurements take the form

$$\mathcal{Y}_k = \left\{\underline{y}_{k,1}, \ldots, \underline{y}_{k,n}\right\} ,$$

where $\underline{y}_{k,i} \in \mathbb{R}^d$ are points in Cartesian coordinates with $d = 2$ or $d = 3$.

In order to relate the received measurements to the state parameters, it is useful to develop a generative model that describes what measurements a sensor will observe as a function of a state $\underline{x}_k$. We assume that during sensor observation, the source point $\underline{z}_{k,i}$ is corrupted by an additive noise term $\underline{v}_{k,i}$, which yields the measurement $\underline{y}_{k,i}$, i.e.,

$$\underline{y}_{k,i} = \underline{z}_{k,i}(\underline{x}_k) + \underline{v}_{k,i} \ . \tag{2.1}$$

In this measurement equation, $\underline{z}_{k,i}(\underline{x}_k)$ is a sensor-specific function that selects a single source point based on the state $\underline{x}_k$, and the term $\underline{v}_{k,i}$ is a noise term whose probability distribution, for the sake of simplicity, is assumed to have the Gaussian pdf

$$\mathrm{p}(\underline{v}_{k,i}) = \mathcal{N}(\underline{v}_{k,i}; \underline{0}, \mathbf{C}^v_{k,i}) \ , \tag{2.2}$$

where the covariance matrix $\mathbf{C}^v_{k,i}$ is assumed to be known a priori. Note that we assume that $\underline{v}_{k,i}$ is independent of the state, i.e., $\mathrm{p}(\underline{v}_{k,i} \,|\, \underline{x}_k) = \mathrm{p}(\underline{v}_{k,i})$.

The relationship between state and measurement in (2.1) can be described by using the conditional probability distribution $\mathrm{p}(\underline{y}_{k,i} \,|\, \underline{x}_k)$. When multiple measurements arrive, the conditional pdf for the entire set can be described as

$$\mathrm{p}(\underline{y}_{k,1}, \ldots, \underline{y}_{k,n} \,|\, \underline{x}_k) = \prod_{i=1}^{n} \mathrm{p}(\underline{y}_{k,i} \,|\, \underline{x}_k) \ , \tag{2.3}$$

by assuming that the noise terms are independent from each other. In consequence, we only need to concern ourselves with probabilistic terms for individual measurements, as they can be combined easily by multiplying them. An extremely important property of the term $\mathrm{p}(\underline{y}_{k,i} \,|\, \underline{x}_k)$ is that, by plugging the received measurements into it, we obtain a function $f^L_k(\underline{x}_k)$ which can be interpreted as a likelihood function. In turn, this allows us to derive an estimator for any given generative model simply by probabilistically describing the relation between the measurements and the state. For convenience, in the following $\mathrm{p}(\underline{y}_{k,i} \,|\, \underline{x}_k)$ will be treated both as a conditional pdf in $\underline{y}_{k,i}$ and as a likelihood function in $\underline{x}_k$ depending on the situation. We will now drop the subindex i for legibility.

Once a likelihood function has been derived, we can estimate the state using techniques such as maximum likelihood estimators [84] or with recursive Bayesian estimators such as particle filters [85, 86, 87]. For estimators such as Linear Regression Kalman Filters (LRKFs) [88, 89, 90], briefly described in Appendix 9.4, the measurement function can be used directly without deriving the term $\mathrm{p}(\underline{y}_k \,|\, \underline{x}_k)$ explicitly. Note that this thesis is not concerned with deriving new filters, and will instead focus on developing models for extended targets, i.e., deriving likelihood functions and measurement equations for use with third-party estimators. Unless otherwise specified, the proposed modeling approaches do not impose any constraints on the estimator being used.

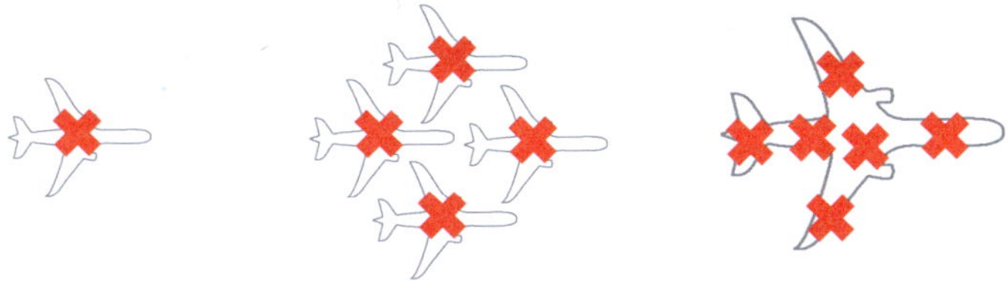

(a) Traditional tracking. **(b)** Group target. **(c)** Extended target.

Figure 2.1: Conceptual differences between traditional tracking (target is a single point), group target tracking (multiple targets are treated as a single object), and Extended Object Tracking (one target has multiple sources).

2.2 Dealing with Multiple Targets

Traditional tracking approaches (Figure 2.1a) assume low resolution sensors and a faraway target that generally yields only one measurement per scan [91], and thus, it becomes sensible to approximate the target shape as a single point without any spatial extent. In this case, $\underline{z}_k(\underline{x}_k)$ is well-defined, usually as the centroid of the target. By combining (2.1) and (2.2), we obtain the likelihood for point targets

$$\begin{aligned} \mathrm{p}(\underline{y}_k \,|\, \underline{x}_k) &= \int_{\mathbb{R}^d} \mathrm{p}(\underline{y}_k \,|\, \underline{x}_k, \underline{v}_k) \cdot \mathrm{p}(\underline{v}_k)\ \mathrm{d}\underline{v}_k \\ &= \int_{\mathbb{R}^d} \delta(\underline{y}_k - \underline{z}_k(\underline{x}_k) - \underline{v}_k) \cdot \mathrm{p}(\underline{v}_k)\ \mathrm{d}\underline{v}_k \\ &= \mathcal{N}(\underline{y}_k - \underline{z}_k(\underline{x}_k); \underline{0}, \mathbf{C}_k^v)\ , \end{aligned} \tag{2.4}$$

by using the sifting property of the Dirac-δ function. In particular, the special case $\underline{z}_k(\underline{x}_k) = \mathbf{H}_k \cdot \underline{x}_k$ leads to an estimator with a closed-form optimal solution, in the form of the well-known Kalman filter [4]. As the target is assumed to be moving, its motion also needs to be taken into account using approaches such as [92]. The specifics of motion models in object tracking are outside the focus of this thesis.

The single-source single-target model, however, becomes ineffective in scenarios where a scan receives measurements from different sources, in particular if they stem from different single-source targets moving close to each other. In this case, determining which target generated which measurement can become intractable [16]. The field of multiple target tracking (MTT) [58, 59] proposes many techniques to address these issues, which are mainly concerned with hypotheses of which measurement belongs to which target. Examples include Multiple Hypothesis Tracking (MHT) [60], Joint Probabilistic Data Association (JPDA) [61], Probabilistic Multiple Hypothesis Tracking (PMHT) [62, 63], and Random Finite Sets (RFS) [93]. In many scenarios, the targets do not move independently, but can be said to share some sort of common motion dynamics, which makes their states highly correlated (Figure 2.1b). In this case, instead of trying to manage individual tracks separately, it becomes more useful to track all the involved objects simultaneously as a single *group target* [64, 13, 16]. Still, the association problem, i.e., associating measurements to a source point, needs to be addressed.

We will now describe two basic ideas from the field of MTT, which will serve as the groundwork for the concepts presented in the following chapters. Assuming a list of possible targets $\mathcal{M}_k = \{m_1, \ldots, m_N\}$, two basic mechanisms to address the association problem stand out. First, we can assume that each target m_i has an independent probability $\mathrm{p}(m_i)$, known a priori, of generating a measurement. By marginalizing m_i out, we obtain

$$\mathrm{p}(\underline{y}_k \,|\, \underline{x}_k) = \sum_{i=1}^{N} \mathrm{p}(\underline{y}_k \,|\, \underline{x}_k, m_i) \cdot \mathrm{p}(m_i) \ , \tag{2.5}$$

where $\mathrm{p}(\underline{y}_k \,|\, \underline{x}_k, m_i)$ is the conditional probability of $\underline{y}_k$ if m_i generated it. In a way, this means that $\underline{y}_k$ is associated to all possible sources, using the source probabilities as weights [94, 95, 20, 96, 97]. The second mechanism consists of approximating $\mathrm{p}(m_i)$, usually unknown, as a function of the received measurement $\underline{y}_k$ itself, i.e.,

$$\mathrm{p}(m_i) \approx \mathrm{p}(m_i \,|\, \underline{y}_k) \ . \tag{2.6}$$

A common further simplification is to assume that $\mathrm{p}(m_i \,|\, \underline{y}_k) = 1$ for the closest m_i, and 0 for the rest, leading to a *greedy* association [94, 97]. Probabilistically speaking, this second approach may not appear to be mathematically sound, as we are using $\underline{y}_k$ itself to determine the a priori probability that it was generated, which, in an abuse of notation, could be written as $\mathrm{p}(\underline{y}_k \,|\, \underline{x}_k, \underline{y}_k)$. Nonetheless, this mechanism is time-efficient and easy to implement, and will produce accurate results as long as the approximation of m_i is relatively close to the true source.

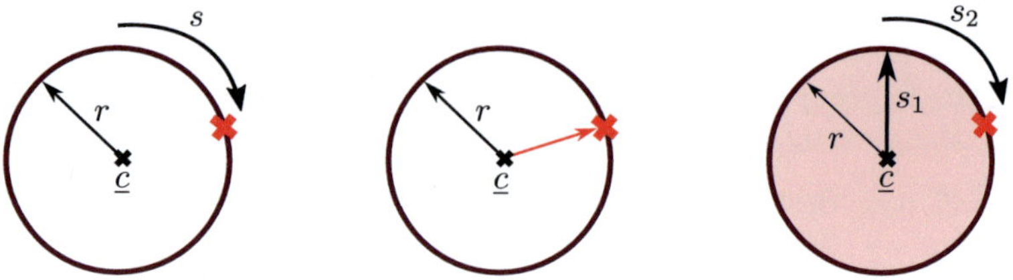

(a) Circle path, parametric. **(b)** Circle path, from distance. **(c)** Filled disk, parametric.

Figure 2.2: Describing a circle and a disk, either constructively (using a parameter to iterate through all points), or through a condition (e.g., a given distance) that only its points fulfill. The subindex k is omitted for legibility.

2.3 Extended Targets

While MTT deals with a finite, usually small number of possible single-source targets, the field of extended object tracking [12, 13, 98, 1], sometimes also known as extended target tracking (ETT), represents one target as a set of multiple source points, which are spatially structured (i.e., as *shapes*, see Figure 2.1c). Unlike point approximations, extended targets are assumed to have an *extension*, and almost always generate multiple measurements per scan. The number of potential sources is usually infinite, making hypothesis management impractical. The considered motion models also differ, as group targets can be assumed to fuse, split, or dissolve, while extended objects are usually only subject to rigid transformations. Nonetheless, many of the theoretical foundations of EOT can be constructed by drawing ideas from MTT, and conversely, EOT can find applications in MTT scenarios such as when tracking group targets [99] by approximating the entire group as a shape. A straightforward combination of MTT and EOT also arises when tracking multiple extended targets [65, 66, 67, 68].

Before we delve into the topic of EOT, we first need to introduce *shape models*, which give us information about the shape $\mathcal{S}_k^x$ related to a given state $\underline{x}_k$. In formal terms, a shape $\mathcal{S}_k^x$ is defined as a compact (i.e., closed and bounded) set in $\mathbb{R}^d$ that can be described using a finite parameter vector. The measure of the shape, i.e., its area or volume, is denoted as $\|\mathcal{S}_k^x\|$. It is generally assumed that the shape is a continuous set with infinitely many potential source points, but in some cases, such as when modeling specific sensors, it may be advantageous to assume that only a fraction of those sources may generate a measurement [158, 153, 100, 101]. As a remark, while some sensors can also provide direct measurements of the target extent [102, 103], this thesis only focuses on point measurements with Cartesian coordinates as explained in Section 2.1.

An important concept in this context is the *shape parametrization*, which allows us to iterate through all of the points in the shape. This, in turn, will allow for an easy way to determine all possible sources in the target. As an example, we will consider a unit circle and a unit disk in $\mathbb{R}^2$, with center $\underline{c}_k$ and radius 1. A circle is an example of a path (Figure 2.2a), i.e., a one-dimensional shape whose points can be traversed using a scalar s_k. It can be described in the form

$$\underline{\phi}_k(s_k) := \underline{c}_k + \begin{bmatrix}\cos(s_k)\\ \sin(s_k)\end{bmatrix} \ , \text{ for } s_k \in \big[0, 2\pi\big] \ . \tag{2.7}$$

This is also an example of a *parametrization by arc length*, i.e., the length of the arc between any pair of points $\underline{\phi}_k(s_{k,1})$ and $\underline{\phi}_k(s_{k,2})$ is exactly $|s_{k,2} - s_{k,1}|$. These parametrizations have the following two important properties that hold for every s_k,

$$\left\|\underline{\phi}_k'(s_k)\right\| = 1 \ , \tag{2.8}$$

$$\underline{\phi}_k'(s_k)^\top \underline{\phi}_k''(s_k) = 0 \ , \tag{2.9}$$

i.e., the derivative has always length 1, and the second derivative is always orthogonal to the first. Both properties will find applications in Chapter 3. The second considered shape is a disk, which is an example of a *filled* shape, i.e., a d-dimensional shape in $\mathbb{R}^d$ including its interior. In analogy to (2.7), the points of a disk can be traversed using the vector

$\underline{s}_k = \left[s_{k,1}, s_{k,2}\right]$ (Figure 2.2c) by using the parametrization

$$\underline{\phi}_k(\underline{s}_k) := \underline{c}_k + s_{k,1} \begin{bmatrix}\cos(s_{k,2})\\ \sin(s_{k,2})\end{bmatrix} \text{ , for } \underline{s}_k \in \left[0,1\right] \times \left[0, 2\pi\right] \text{ .} \quad (2.10)$$

Another useful concept to describe shapes is *implicit constraints*, i.e., a relation that only the points in the shape fulfill (Figure 2.2b). For example, a circle can be modeled using the equation

$$\underline{p}_k \in \mathcal{S}_k^x \leftrightarrow \left\|\underline{p}_k - \underline{c}_k\right\| - 1 = 0 \text{ ,} \quad (2.11)$$

for $\underline{p}_k \in \mathbb{R}^d$ and with $\| \cdot \|$ being the Euclidean norm. Analogously, the disk can also be described implicitly using the inequality constraint

$$\underline{p}_k \in \mathcal{S}_k^x \leftrightarrow \left\|\underline{p}_k - \underline{c}_k\right\| - 1 \leq 0 \text{ .}$$

We can generalize these ideas to arbitrary shapes by introducing *shape functions.*

Definition 2.1 (Shape Function). *The shape function of a surface $\mathcal{S}_k^x$ is any function $\underline{\varphi}_k : \mathbb{R}^d \to \mathbb{R}^n$ which fulfills*

$$\underline{p}_k \in \mathcal{S}_k^x \leftrightarrow \underline{\varphi}_k(\underline{p}_k) = \underline{0} \text{ .} \quad (2.12)$$

In literature, $\underline{\varphi}_k$ is called a distance function *if $n = 1$.*

Examples for shape functions include the algebraic or Euclidean distances to some sort of nearest source, common in the shape of curve fitting[104, 36, 37, 54, 105]. Note that a shape function can return any value, including scalars or multidimensional vectors.

For the sake of completeness, we will now define the Euclidean shape functions, the Mahalanobis shape functions, and the radial shape functions, which will be used throughout this thesis.

Definition 2.2 (Euclidean Shape Functions). *Given two points $\underline{p}_k \in \mathbb{R}^d$, $\underline{q}_k \in \mathbb{R}^d$, their Euclidean distance takes the form*

$$\begin{aligned} d^e(\underline{p}_k, \underline{q}_k) &:= \left\|\underline{p}_k - \underline{q}_k\right\| \\ &= \sqrt{(\underline{p}_k - \underline{q}_k)^\top (\underline{p}_k - \underline{q}_k)} \text{ .} \end{aligned}$$

We can apply this concept for shapes too. For example, the Euclidean projection of $\underline{p}_k \in \mathbb{R}^d$ *to the shape* $\mathcal{S}_k^x$ *follows as*

$$\underline{\pi}_k^e(\underline{p}_k) := \underset{\underline{p}_k^* \in \mathcal{S}_k^x}{\arg\min} \; (\underline{p}_k - \underline{p}_k^*)^\top (\underline{p}_k - \underline{p}_k^*) \; .$$

Based on this, we define the following three shape functions. First, the Euclidean difference becomes

$$\underline{\varphi}_k^{ed}(\underline{p}_k) := \underline{p}_k - \underline{\pi}_k^e(\underline{p}_k)$$

Second, we define the Euclidean distance as

$$\begin{aligned} \varphi_k^e(\underline{p}_k) &:= d^e(\underline{p}_k, \underline{\pi}_k(\underline{p}_k)) \\ &= \sqrt{(\underline{p}_k - \underline{\pi}_k(\underline{p}_k))^\top (\underline{p}_k - \underline{\pi}_k(\underline{p}_k))} \; . \end{aligned}$$

Finally, we define the signed *Euclidean distance as*

$$\varphi_k^{se}(\underline{p}_k) := \begin{cases} \varphi_k^e(\underline{p}_k) & \text{if } \underline{p}_k \text{ outside } \mathcal{S}_k^x \\ -\varphi_k^e(\underline{p}_k) & \text{otherwise} \; . \end{cases} \tag{2.13}$$

The Euclidean projection $\underline{\pi}_k^e$ *is usually denoted simply as the 'closest source'.*

Definition 2.3 (Mahalanobis Shape Functions). *The Mahalanobis distance [106] is an extension of the Euclidean distance that uses a covariance matrix* $\mathbf{\Sigma} \in \mathbb{R}^{d \times d}$ *as a weight. Given two points* $\underline{p}_k, \underline{q}_k \in \mathbb{R}^d$*, their Mahalanobis distance takes the form*

$$d^m(\underline{p}_k, \underline{q}_k) := \sqrt{(\underline{p}_k - \underline{q}_k)^\top \mathbf{\Sigma}^{-1} (\underline{p}_k - \underline{q}_k)} \; .$$

Note that the Euclidean distance is a special case of this term when $\mathbf{\Sigma} = \mathbf{I}$*. The extension of this concept to shapes follows similarly to Definition 2.2, and will be describe in the following for the sake of completeness. Thus, the Mahalanobis projection of* $\underline{p}_k \in \mathbb{R}^d$ *to* $\mathcal{S}_k^x$ *becomes*

$$\underline{\pi}_k^m(\underline{p}_k) := \underset{\underline{p}_k^* \in \mathcal{S}_k^x}{\arg\min} \; (\underline{p}_k - \underline{p}_k^*)^\top \mathbf{\Sigma}^{-1} (\underline{p}_k - \underline{p}_k^*) \; . \tag{2.14}$$

Then, the Mahalanobis difference is obtained from

$$\underline{\varphi}_k^d(\underline{p}_k) := \underline{p}_k - \underline{\pi}_k^m(\underline{p}_k) \ ,$$

while the Mahalanobis distance results from

$$\begin{aligned} \varphi_k^m(\underline{p}_k) &:= d^m(\underline{p}_k, \underline{\pi}_k(\underline{p}_k)) \\ &= \sqrt{(\underline{p}_k - \underline{\pi}_k(\underline{p}_k))^\top \mathbf{\Sigma}^{-1} (\underline{p}_k - \underline{\pi}_k(\underline{p}_k))} \ , \end{aligned} \tag{2.15}$$

and, finally, the signed Mahalanobis distance is simply

$$\varphi_k^{sm}(\underline{p}_k) := \begin{cases} \varphi_k^m(\underline{p}_k) & \textit{if } \underline{p}_k \textit{ outside } \mathcal{S}_k^x \\ -\varphi_k^m(\underline{p}_k) & \textit{otherwise .} \end{cases} \tag{2.16}$$

Definition 2.4 (Radial Parametrizations and Shape Functions)**.** *Let the shape $\mathcal{S}_k^x$ be star-convex, i.e., there exists a center point $\underline{c}_k$ so that, for any source point $\underline{z}_k \in \mathcal{S}_k^x$, the segment that connects $\underline{c}_k$ and $\underline{z}_k$ is completely contained in the shape. This allows us to derive a radial function $r_k(\theta_k)$ defined as the distance between $\underline{c}_k$ and the boundary at a given angle θ_k. In turn, this allows us to parametrize the shape based on its radial function, for example as*

$$\underline{\phi}_k(\theta_k) := \underline{c}_k + r_k(\theta_k) \cdot \begin{bmatrix} \cos(\theta_k) \\ \sin(\theta_k) \end{bmatrix} \ \textit{for } \theta_k \in [0, 2\pi] \ .$$

For a given point $\underline{p}_k$, let the function $\angle(\underline{p}_k)$ denote its direction in relation to the origin. We define the radial projection as

$$\underline{\pi}_k^r(\underline{p}_k) := \underline{\phi}_k(\angle(\underline{p}_k - \underline{c}_k)) \ ,$$

i.e., the point on the boundary located in the direction from $\underline{c}_k$ to $\underline{p}_k$. This projection can be plugged into (2.15) *or* (2.16) *to define radial Mahalanobis shape functions. We can also define the radial distance to the boundary as*

$$\begin{aligned} \varphi_k^r(\underline{p}_k) &:= \left\| \underline{p}_k - \underline{c}_k \right\| - r_k\left(\angle\left(\underline{p} - \underline{c}_k\right)\right) \\ &:= \left\| \underline{p}_k - \underline{c}_k \right\| - \left\| \underline{\pi}_k^r(\underline{p}_k) - \underline{c}_k \right\| \ . \end{aligned} \tag{2.17}$$

Note that this shape function fulfills the same sign criteria as (2.13) *and* (2.16)*, i.e., it is negative inside the shape and positive outside of it.*

In the following, we assume that the shape model is known a priori, i.e., we already have a parametrization $\underline{\phi}_k$ or a shape function φ_k of the target shape (or an approximation of it). Thus, when we speak of shape estimation, we refer to estimating the parameters of those functions, such as a center or a rotation, all of which are contained in the state vector $\underline{x}_k$. We will now aim to derive measurement equations and likelihood functions that probabilistically associate incoming measurements with the parameters to be estimated.

2.4 Spatial Distribution Models

When dealing with extended targets, unlike point targets, we need to take into account that measurements can potentially originate from any source point on the shape. In this context, the key idea of SDMs [20, 96] is to treat *all* points in $\mathbb{R}^d$ as potential sources $\underline{z}_k$ with probability $\mathrm{p}(\underline{z}_k \mid \underline{x}_k)$ of generating a measurement. Naturally, points outside the target would have a probability of zero and different points of the target may have varying probabilities depending on the sensor and the application.

Similar to (2.4), we now marginalize $\underline{z}_k$ in addition to $\underline{v}_k$, leading to

$$\begin{aligned}
\mathrm{p}(\underline{y}_k \mid \underline{x}_k) &= \int_{\mathbb{R}^d}\int_{\mathbb{R}^d} \mathrm{p}(\underline{y}_k \mid \underline{z}_k, \underline{v}_k, \underline{x}_k)\ \mathrm{p}(\underline{v}_k)\ \mathrm{p}(\underline{z}_k \mid \underline{x}_k)\ \mathrm{d}\underline{v}_k\ \mathrm{d}\underline{z}_k \qquad (2.18)\\
&= \int_{\mathbb{R}^d}\int_{\mathbb{R}^d} \delta(\underline{y}_k - \underline{z}_k - \underline{v}_k)\ \mathrm{p}(\underline{v}_k)\ \mathrm{p}(\underline{z}_k \mid \underline{x}_k)\ \mathrm{d}\underline{v}_k\ \mathrm{d}\underline{z}_k\\
&= \int_{\mathbb{R}^d} \mathcal{N}(\underline{y}_k - \underline{z}_k; \underline{0}, \mathbf{C}_k^v)\ \mathrm{p}(\underline{z}_k \mid \underline{x}_k)\,\mathrm{d}\underline{z}_k\ ,
\end{aligned}$$

essentially *convolving* the source distribution with the Gaussian pdf of the noise term, and yielding a result analogous to (2.5). This is a mathematically simple approach that yields accurate results in theory. In practice, however, using this formulation directly presents the following two challenges. First, it is often difficult to model $\mathrm{p}(\underline{z}_k \mid \underline{x}_k)$, as this distribution depends on a myriad of factors, such as sensor characteristics, occlusions, artifacts, how the target material physically responds to the sensor signal, and many others. In many cases, this distribution is unknown, and can be also assumed to change over time. Furthermore, a false approximation can lead to estimation bias or lack of robustness. There is also the problem that, even for simple shapes, (2.18) is usually either intractable or numerically unstable, especially given that the integral usually resolves to a difference of two almost equal terms. Even worse, it may be extremely difficult to obtaining the logarithm of the result, a representation preferred by robust implementations given that it can better represent values very close to 0.

In order to address these issues, a commonly used approach is to assume that sources are uniformly distributed on the shape $\mathcal{S}_k^x$ [20, 96, 147, 159]. This leads to

$$\mathrm{p}(\underline{z}_k \,|\, \underline{x}_k) = \frac{1}{\|\mathcal{S}_k^x\|} \cdot \mathbf{1}_{\mathcal{S}_k^x}(\underline{z}_k)$$

by using the indicator function of $\mathcal{S}_k^x$, defined as

$$\mathbf{1}_{\mathcal{S}_k^x}(\underline{z}_k) := \begin{cases} 1 & \text{if } \underline{z}_k \in \mathcal{S}_k^x \\ 0 & \text{otherwise} . \end{cases}$$

This allows (2.18) to be simplified as

$$\begin{aligned} \mathrm{p}(\underline{y}_k \,|\, \underline{x}_k) &= \int\limits_{\mathbb{R}^d} \mathcal{N}(\underline{y}_k - \underline{z}_k; \underline{0}, \mathbf{C}_k^v) \cdot \mathrm{p}(\underline{z}_k \,|\, \underline{x}_k) \, \mathrm{d}\underline{z}_k \\ &= \frac{1}{\|\mathcal{S}_k^x\|} \int\limits_{\mathcal{S}_k^x} \mathcal{N}(\underline{y}_k - \underline{z}_k; \underline{0}, \mathbf{C}_k^v) \, \mathrm{d}\underline{z}_k \, . \end{aligned} \tag{2.19}$$

This formulation allows SDMs to be interpreted as integrals over a region, which can be solved using change of variable techniques [107]. An illustrative example for a rectangle SDM, taken from [159], can be found in Section 9.2.1.

Nonetheless, in many cases, the change of variables may be difficult or a uniform distribution may be an inappropriate approximation. Another alternative is to define SDMs by modeling a probability for s_k directly, instead of over $\underline{z}_k$. For paths, this yields

$$\mathrm{p}(\underline{y}_k \,|\, \underline{x}_k) = \int_{\mathrm{S}_k} \mathcal{N}(\underline{y}_k - \underline{\phi}_k(s_k); \underline{0}, \mathbf{C}_k^v) \cdot \mathrm{p}(s_k \,|\, \underline{x}_k) \cdot \left\| \underline{\phi}_k'(s_k) \right\| \mathrm{d}s_k \ , \quad (2.20)$$

which for filled shapes translates to

$$\mathrm{p}(\underline{y}_k \,|\, \underline{x}_k) = \int_{\mathrm{S}_k} \mathcal{N}(\underline{y}_k - \underline{\phi}_k(\underline{s}_k); \underline{0}, \mathbf{C}_k^v) \cdot \mathrm{p}(\underline{s}_k \,|\, \underline{x}_k) \cdot \left| \det\left(\mathbf{J}_k^{\phi}(\underline{s}_k) \right) \right| \mathrm{d}\underline{s}_k \ , \quad (2.21)$$

where $| \cdot |$ denotes the absolute value, and S_k defines the set of possible values for s_k or $\underline{s}_k$. Note that, when considering paths with arc length parametrizations such as (2.7), the norm of the derivative vanishes due to (2.8). An illustrative example for a line segment SDM, taken from [160], can be found in Section 9.2.2.

An alternative derivation of SDMs can be obtained as a function of the measurement equations, similar to (2.1). This allows us to use straightforward and intuitive descriptions of a target shape, such as the parametrizations from (2.7) and (2.10), and incorporate them directly into an estimator. Generally speaking, we can say that the observed measurements are related to the state in the form of

$$\begin{aligned} \underline{y}_k &= \underline{\phi}_k(\underline{s}_k) + \underline{v}_k \\ &= \underline{h}(\underline{x}_k, \underline{v}_k, \underline{s}_k) \ , \end{aligned}$$

where $\underline{s}_k$ is interpreted as an additional "shape noise" term. Probabilistically speaking, this relation can be modeled as the conditional pdf

$$\mathrm{p}(\underline{y}_k \,|\, \underline{x}_k, \underline{v}_k, \underline{s}_k) = \delta(\underline{y}_k - \underline{\phi}_k(\underline{s}_k) - \underline{v}_k) \ . \quad (2.22)$$

Finally, by marginalizing $\underline{v}_k$ and s_k from this expression, we once again obtain (2.21).

Working with SDMs can be challenging when dealing with arbitrary shapes, even after applying the proposed approximations. On the one hand, as mentioned before, it can be difficult to obtain a numerically stable $\log(\,\cdot\,)$ form of the likelihoods. On the other hand, measurement equations may require adaptations in the used LRKFs, such as quadratic extensions [108, 147]. In order to alleviate these issues, a multitude of different techniques and approximations have appeared in literature, and in the following we describe some of them. Works like [159, 161, 147] have focused on accurate estimators of line segments and rectangles, as any compact shape can be approximated with arbitrary accuracy by combining them. Others approximate the source distribution of an elliptic shape by means of a Gaussian pdf with mean $\underline{x}_k^c \in \mathbb{R}^d$ and covariance matrix $\mathbf{X}_k \in \mathbb{R}^{d\times d}$, i.e., the state contains both $\underline{x}_k^c$ and $\mathbf{X}_k$. The resulting likelihood is

$$\begin{aligned} \mathrm{p}(\underline{y}_k \,|\, \underline{x}_k) &= \int\limits_{\mathbb{R}^d} \mathcal{N}(\underline{y}_k - \underline{z}_k; \underline{0}, \mathbf{C}_k^v) \cdot \mathcal{N}(\underline{z}_k; \underline{x}_k^c, \mathbf{X}_k)\, \mathrm{d}\underline{z}_k \\ &= \mathcal{N}(\underline{y}_k; \underline{x}_k^c, \mathbf{X}_k + \mathbf{C}_k^v)\ . \end{aligned} \tag{2.23}$$

In [16, 33], this idea is developed further by using the mean and covariance matrix of all received point measurements as a pseudo-measurement. This approach, based on the idea of *random matrices*, can also be extended to construct more complex shapes by combining multiple ellipses [31, 34, 109, 32]. An example implementation can be found in Section 9.5.1. Tracking multiple elliptic targets using random matrices has also been explored in [65, 66, 67]. While Gaussian elliptical approximations are fast and efficient, they omit important shape information. For example, a square would be reduced to a circle, and thus, its rotation could not be estimated.

Another probabilistic aspect related to SDMs is the number of expected measurements. Unlike traditional tracking, which generally produces one single measurement per scan, in EOT we can obtain information about the target based on the number of measurements, as it can be assumed that this amount is proportional to the target extent. Assuming that measurements are observed uniformly in the sensor field of view, the number of expected target measurements can be assumed to follow a binomial distribution, and as the number of measurements increase and target size in the sensor decreases, the binomial distribution converges towards a Poisson distribution. Models that incorporate a Poisson distribution for EOT include [20, 96, 68].

2.5 Greedy Association Models

An alternative approach to dealing with source probabilities is to minimize some sort of distance between the measurements and a corresponding point on the shape. This characterizes the field of *curve fitting*. In literature, explored approaches are generally based on least-squares minimization [110] of a distance metric, and focus particularly on conic [104, 36, 37, 54] or polygonal [105] approximations. In general, fitting is not concerned with dealing with dynamic models or probabilistic associations, preferring instead batch processing with ad-hoc scalar weights. However, techniques that implement fitting with a variation of Kalman filters, such as [111, 112, 40, 38], can be adapted to take these aspects into account. Also worth referencing are approaches that deal with estimating transformations for extended shapes [113, 114] but are not concerned with shape tracking, in particular the well-known Iterative Closest Point algorithm [44]. Furthermore, curve fitting is mostly concerned with paths which only generate measurements from their boundary, in contrast to SDMs, which can also handle filled shapes.

We observe that the theoretical background of distance minimization, in its multitude of applications, intersects with many aspects of probabilistic modeling. Because of this, we have worked to formalize these ideas and incorporate curve fitting into a probabilistic framework in the form of Greedy Association Models[150]. In contrast to the forward modeling of SDMs, the key idea of GAMs consists of treating $\underline{y}_k$ as if it was a priori knowledge, in a similar fashion as (2.6). In essence, we deal with measurement equations such as

$$\underline{0} = \underline{h}(\underline{x}_k, \underline{y}_k, \underline{v}_k) \ . \tag{2.24}$$

The main difference with (2.22) is that previously we only used the state $\underline{x}_k$ and noise terms in order to generate an expected measurement, to be compared against the observation $\underline{y}_k$ Here, we use $\underline{y}_k$ itself as part of the measurement equation in order to generate a *pseudo-measurement*, which we then relate to $\underline{0}$. As we will see, this has the effect of reducing the complexity of the resulting likelihood drastically.

Given a shape function, a simple approach to obtain a measurement equation in the form of (2.24) could be achieved by plugging the assumed source $\underline{z}_k = \underline{y}_k - \underline{v}_k$ into (2.12), yielding

$$\begin{aligned} \underline{0} &= \underline{\varphi}_k(\underline{y}_k - \underline{v}_k) \\ &:= \underline{h}(\underline{x}_k, \underline{y}_k, \underline{v}_k) \ . \end{aligned} \tag{2.25}$$

As in (2.22), we can derive a likelihood function using a Dirac-delta function in the form of

$$\mathrm{p}(\underline{y}_k \,|\, \underline{x}_k, \underline{v}_k) = \delta(\underline{0} - \underline{\varphi}_k(\underline{y}_k - \underline{v}_k)) \ ,$$

and marginalizing out $\underline{v}_k$. However, this mechanism leads to two problems. On the one hand, working with this pdf directly produces the same problems of intractability and lack of robustness present in SDMs. On the other hand, this approach indirectly causes the noise term to considered twice. This can be seen by plugging the Euclidean difference into (2.25), leading to

$$\underline{0} = \underline{y}_k - \underline{v}_k - \underline{\pi}_k(\underline{y}_k - \underline{v}_k) \ ,$$

i.e., the noise appears both in the distance and in the projection. GAMs deal with this problem in the following way [56, 150]. First, we simplify (2.25) by ignoring the noise term in the projection, i.e.,

$$\begin{aligned} \underline{0} &= \underline{y}_k - \underline{v}_k - \underline{\pi}_k(\underline{y}_k) \\ &:= \underline{h}(\underline{x}_k, \underline{y}_k, \underline{v}_k) \ . \end{aligned} \tag{2.26}$$

Second, we introduce the random variable

$$\underline{l}_k := \underline{h}(\underline{x}_k, \underline{y}_k, \underline{v}_k) \ .$$

obtained by propagating $\underline{v}_k$ through the measurement function. This yields the pdf

$$\begin{aligned}
\mathrm{p}(\underline{l}_k \,|\, \underline{x}_k) &= \int \mathrm{p}(\underline{l}_k \,|\, \underline{x}_k, \underline{y}_k, \underline{v}_k) \ \cdot \ \mathrm{p}(\underline{v}_k) \ \mathrm{d}\underline{v}_k \\
&= \int \delta(\underline{l}_k - \underline{h}(\underline{x}_k, \underline{y}_k, \underline{v}_k)) \ \cdot \ \mathrm{p}(\underline{v}_k) \ \mathrm{d}\underline{v}_k \\
&:= f_k^l(\underline{l}_k) \ .
\end{aligned}$$

Finally, we rewrite (2.26) probabilistically in function of $\underline{l}_k$ and $f_k^l(\underline{l}_k)$, leading to the term

$$\begin{aligned}
\mathrm{p}(\underline{y}_k \,|\, \underline{x}_k) &= \int \delta(\underline{l}_k - \underline{0}) \ \cdot \ \mathrm{p}(\underline{l}_k \,|\, \underline{x}_k) \ \mathrm{d}\underline{l}_k \\
&= f_k^l(\underline{0}) \ ,
\end{aligned}$$

which can, as previously done, be interpreted as a likelihood function by treating $\underline{x}_k$ as the free variable.

In general, $f_k^l(\underline{0})$ is still difficult to express when using non-linear shape functions. For the circle example, propagating $\underline{v}_k$ through an Euclidean distance yields a translated, scaled Rice distribution[115]. In practice, a closed-form solution of these expressions is generally either intractable or not available. Instead, an approximation using a Gaussian pdf with the same mean $\hat{\underline{l}}_k$ and covariance matrix $\mathbf{C}_k^l$, shown to yield accurate results in [148], can be used instead. This leads to

$$\mathrm{p}(\underline{y}_k \,|\, \underline{x}_k) \approx \mathcal{N}(\underline{0}; \hat{\underline{l}}_k, \mathbf{C}_k^l) \ . \tag{2.27}$$

Appendix 9.3 shows an algorithm to calculate these moments. Note that, being based on an exponential function, obtaining a $\log(\ \cdot\ )$ form of (2.27) becomes trivial.

Being an extension of curve fitting approaches, GAMs carry two important challenges from these techniques. On the one hand, the measurement equations (2.25) and (2.26) add the noise term on the measurement, instead of on a source on the shape, which in turns generates an *estimation bias*[150, 148]. This issue has been widely discussed in the field of curve fitting, and a more detailed treatment to deal with this issue is introduced in Chapter 3. On the other hand, GAMs and fitting have both a problem when the shapes related to multiple states share the same source points. In particular, this issue manifests itself egregiously in filled shapes. For example, if the true target is a disk, then all larger disks that contain the true target are also optimal, as the distances between the measurements and those disks will also be 0. Without additional probabilistic information on where the sources should come from, such as with SDMs, the estimator cannot differentiate between different states, and may end up diverging. This issue will be illustrated in more detail in Section 4.1.

2.6 Conclusions

In this chapter we presented a brief overview of the relationship between multiple target tracking and extended object tracking, which aim to address the problem of associating measurements with sources, and hence, relating measurements to the state. We saw two basic approaches to shape modeling and how they deal with the association problem. On the one hand, probabilistic methods such as Spatial Distribution Models simply associate each measurement to all possible sources, using a probability distribution to assign a weight to each hypothesis. On the other hand, greedy techniques such as Greedy Association Models, which aim to generalize curve fitting approaches using a Bayesian framework, assume that the source was the point in the shape that minimizes some sort of distance. Each model has their own strengths and weaknesses, as SDMs can deal with high noise levels but their likelihoods tend to be intractable and numerically unstable, while GAMs are easy to implement but suffer from estimation bias.

CHAPTER 3

Partial Information Models

In this chapter, we will introduce *Level-set Partial Information Models* (Level-set PIMs), which address the problem of estimation bias in GAMs when tracking targets approximated as paths, as mentioned in Section 2.5. This contribution, first proposed in [160], is an extension of previous work from Partial Information Models (PIMs), presented by Florian Faion and the author in [150, 148]. It will be shown how our contribution improves on PIMs by increasing their accuracy and resilience to occlusions even in scenarios with extremely high noise, where state-of-the-art approaches may fail and diverge. This chapter is structured as follows. First, we will present a short description of the issues present in curve fitting, and sketch the key idea for a solution. Then, we will introduce PIMs as a straightforward mechanism to address these challenges. After that, we will describe the details of our contribution, Level-set PIMs, which extend PIMs by employing level-sets to increase accuracy. Finally, we will present the evaluation results in order to validate the presented models.

3.1 Key Idea

The bias issue for GAMs is a direct consequence of the assumptions made in (2.25), in particular by naïvely applying the noise term on the measurement. This means that GAMs are concerned with how the shape function behaves around $\underline{y}_k$, while according to the measurement equation in (2.1), a more accurate formulation would consider the uncertainty around the true source instead [56, 148]. We can sketch a correction for this incorrect assumption by rewriting $\varphi_k(\underline{y}_k - \underline{v}_k)$ as

$$\begin{aligned} 0 &= h(\underline{x}_k, \underline{y}_k, \nu_k) \\ &= \varphi_k(\underline{y}_k) - \nu_k \ , \end{aligned} \tag{3.1}$$

i.e., we introduce a new noise term ν_k that takes correctly into account how the shape function $\varphi_k(\ \cdot\ )$ behaves around the true source . We denote ν_k as the *bias correction term.* The challenge for this chapter is, then, to find a formally appropriate formulation for ν_k.

Works in literature have proposed different ways to model this bias correction depending on the scenario. For example, for the circle from (2.11), and assuming isotropic noise $\mathbf{C}_k^v = \sigma_{v,k}^2 \cdot \mathbf{I}$, Okatani [43] proposes the approximation

$$\nu_k \sim \mathcal{N}\left(\frac{\sigma_{v,k}^2}{2r_k}, \sigma_{v,k}^2 \cdot \left(1 - \frac{\sigma_{v,k}^2}{4r_k^2}\right)^2\right) \ . \tag{3.2}$$

This approach can then be extended to other smooth shapes by approximating them locally as circles. Other works such as [36, 111, 79, 116, 38] have presented correction terms for general conics, while [144] presented a correction term for polygons, and [43] derived a bias correction for shapes where the local curvature is known.

In the following, we will describe a systematic framework called Partial Information Models [148, 56] to obtain bias correction terms for arbitrary shapes. The basic outline of PIMs is to use as correction term the random variable

$$\nu_k := \varphi_k(\underline{z}_k + \underline{v}_k) \ , \tag{3.3}$$

obtained by propagating $\underline{v}_k$ through $\varphi_k(\ \cdot\ )$. This formulation follows directly from (3.1), in that ν_k serves to compensate the effect of the actual values that $\varphi_k(\underline{y}_k)$ can take for a source point $\underline{z}_k$. However, this approach is not straightforward, as we do not know the real source from which

$\underline{y}_k$ stems. While we can use some sort of approximation $\underline{z}_k \approx \underline{\pi}_k(\underline{y}_k)$, errors in this approximation would also serve to introduce further sources of uncertainty, for which we would need even more correction terms. Instead, the main contribution of PIMs is the derivation of a carefully designed shape function $\varphi_k^*(\,\cdot\,)$ that is immune to the error in the source approximation, or at least is only minimally affected by it. By deriving a correction term ν_k based on this function, we can guarantee that the bias reduction is the best possible even if the approximation of the true source is not exact.

3.2 Deriving the Shape Function

An exhaustive and detailed treatment of PIMs can be found in [148, 56], but for the sake of thoroughness we will provide in this section a brief description. In principle, what we require is a transformation

$$\underline{y}_k = \underline{\Phi}_{\mathrm{k}}\left(s_k^y, l_k^y\right) \ , \tag{3.4}$$

with inverse function

$$\begin{aligned} \begin{bmatrix} s_k^y \\ l_k^y \end{bmatrix} &= \underline{\Phi}_k^{-1}(\underline{y}_k) \\ &= \begin{bmatrix} \underline{\phi}_k^{-1}(\underline{y}_k) \\ \varphi_k^*(\underline{y}_k) \end{bmatrix} \ , \end{aligned} \tag{3.5}$$

which represents a *reparametrization* of the measurement $\underline{y}_k$ into a new representation $\left[s_k^y, l_k^y\right]$, where s_k^y describes *where* in the shape the true source is, and l_k^y denotes *how distant* $\underline{y}_k$ is to the shape (Figure 3.1). The objective is that, when this term is later rewritten in the probabilistic model, the effect of s_k^y fades or becomes minimal, thus eliminating the effect of any error in the source approximation. In turn, this yields the following advantages. On the one hand, we only need to take into account the shape function value $l_k^y = \varphi_k^*(\underline{y}_k)$ which is usually easy to obtain. On the other hand, we can also avoid having to find a path parametrization $\underline{\phi}_k(s_k)$, a task which for many shapes is not straightforward.

From (3.3) and (3.5) we observe a conceptual link between l_k^y and ν_k, i.e., the measured l_k^y can be interpreted as a realization of the random variable ν_k. From this, it follows that $\mathrm{p}(l_k^y \,|\, \underline{x}_k) = \mathrm{p}(\nu_k \,|\, \underline{x}_k)$, and thus, once $\underline{\Phi}_k(\,\cdot\,)$ is obtained, we can obtain information about the distribution of ν_k simply by analyzing how l_k^y behaves. By plugging (2.1) into (3.5), we can describe the generative model of $\underline{y}_k$ in function of s_k^y and l_k^y, i.e.,

$$\begin{aligned}\left[s_k^y, l_k^y\right]^\top &= \underline{\Phi}_k^{-1}(\underline{y}_k) \\ &= \underline{\Phi}_k^{-1}(\underline{z}_k + \underline{v}_k) \ .\end{aligned} \tag{3.6}$$

By propagating $\underline{v}_k$ through this term, we obtain the pdf $\mathrm{p}(s_k^y, l_k^y \,|\, \underline{x}_k)$, which can be rewritten as

$$\mathrm{p}(s_k^y, l_k^y \,|\, \underline{x}_k) = \mathrm{p}(s_k^y \,|\, \underline{x}_k) \;\cdot\; \mathrm{p}(l_k^y \,|\, s_k^y, \underline{x}_k) \ .$$

In order to minimize the importance of the unknown true source, we need a reparametrization which causes the resulting s_k^y and l_k^y to be as independent from each other as possible. If that were the case, we could write

$$\mathrm{p}(l_k^y \,|\, \underline{x}_k) = \mathrm{p}(l_k^y \,|\, s_k^y, \underline{x}_k) \ . \tag{3.7}$$

This would mean that the probability of l_k^y behaves the same independently of the assumed source, and thus, we could simply say for any arbitrary $\underline{p}_k \in \mathcal{S}_k^x$ that

$$\nu_k = \varphi_k^*(\underline{p}_k + \underline{v}_k) \ ,$$

and we would be finished. Unfortunately, as [148] showed, this independence only holds for simple shapes such as lines or planes. It is generally impossible to apply these ideas to arbitrary shapes, as no general reparametrization exists that fulfills (3.7) for all s_k^y and l_k^y and any covariance matrix $\mathbf{C}_k^v$, except in very limited cases.

In order to solve this issue, [148] proposed for the reparametrization the following compromise. First, we need to find a source which closely approximates the true source of $\underline{y}_k$, for example, by finding the source $\underline{\pi}_k^*(\underline{y}_k)$ which most likely generated it according to the generative model, as explained in Section 3.3. Second, we use as shape function the signed Mahalanobis distance from (2.16), i.e., $\varphi_k^* = \varphi_k^{sm}$, using as weight $\mathbf{\Sigma} = \mathbf{C}_k^v$. Finally, by applying the approximation $\underline{z}_k \approx \underline{\pi}_k^*(\underline{y}_k)$ and plugging this into (3.6), we obtain as bias correction term the random variable

$$\nu_k \approx \underline{\varphi}_k^*(\underline{\pi}_k^*(\underline{y}_k) + \underline{v}_k) \ .$$

This leads to the bias-corrected measurement equation

$$\begin{aligned} 0 &= \varphi_k^*(\underline{y}_k) - \nu_k \\ &:= h(\underline{x}_k, \underline{y}_k, \nu_k) \ , \end{aligned} \tag{3.8}$$

Note that ν_k acts as a new scalar noise term, replacing the old term $\underline{v}_k$. By denoting the distribution of the correction term as $f_k^\nu(\nu_k) := \mathrm{p}(\nu_k \,|\, \underline{x}_k)$, we can obtain a likelihood function by interpreting (3.8) probabilistically, i.e.,

$$\mathrm{p}(\underline{y}_k \,|\, \underline{x}_k) \approx f_k^\nu(\varphi_k^*(\underline{y}_k)) \ . \tag{3.9}$$

and treating the state $\underline{x}_k$, which contains the parameters of $\varphi_k^*(\ \cdot\ )$, as the free variable. Note that this parametrization does not guarantee a complete independence between s_k^y and l_k^y all around the shape, as this is usually impossible. Instead, we can only say that both variables are independent in an infinitesimally small neighborhood around the true source. Thus, the quality of the bias reduction depends highly on the ability of $\underline{\pi}_k^*(\underline{y}_k)$ to approximate $\underline{z}_k$. Still, as [148] showed, the proposed approach still provides very accurate results.

3.3 Finding an Appropriate Source

As we need to analyze how the shape function behaves around the real source, we still have to deal with finding a meaningful approximation of $\underline{z}_k$. When dealing with this problem, literature usually assumes that the source is the 'closest point', i.e., a point which minimizes some sort of metric, such as the Euclidean distance[36, 104, 117]. For PIMs, it was proposed to use the *most likely* source by taking into account the measurement noise characteristics [148], i.e.,

$$\underline{\pi}_k^*(\underline{p}_k) := \arg\max_{\hat{\underline{p}}_k \in \mathcal{S}_k^x} \mathcal{N}(\underline{p}_k - \hat{\underline{p}}_k; \underline{0}, \mathbf{C}_k^v) \ .$$

for $\underline{p}_k \in \mathbb{R}^d$, by exploiting the definition of the additive noise term in (2.4). This is equivalent to the formulation

$$\underline{\pi}_k^*(\underline{p}_k) = \arg\min_{\hat{\underline{p}}_k \in \mathcal{S}_k^x} \left(\underline{p}_k - \hat{\underline{p}}_k\right)^\top (\mathbf{C}_k^v)^{-1} \left(\underline{p}_k - \hat{\underline{p}}_k\right) \ .$$

This is, in turn, the Mahalanobis projection from (2.14) with $\mathbf{\Sigma} = \mathbf{C}_k^v$. Note that, for non-isotropic measurement noise, a closed-form solution is generally not available for arbitrary shapes. In these situations we propose to approximate the path $\mathcal{S}_k^x$ as a polygon and use the closed-form solution presented in Appendix 9.2.4.

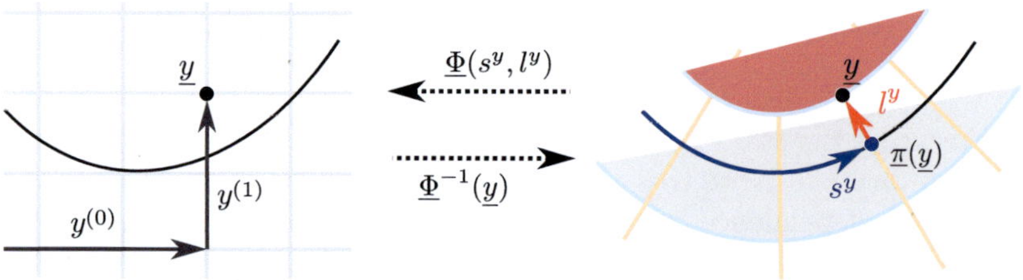

Figure 3.1: Change of coordinates. A measurement $\underline{y}_k = [y_k^{(0)}, y_k^{(1)}]$ is reparametrized as $[s_k^y, l_k^y]$. The coordinate s_k^y describes where on the shape the most likely source is, while l_k^y shows how 'distant' the measurement is. The subindex k is omitted for legibility.

3.4 Sample-based PIMs

Finding a closed-form solution for (3.9) is generally only possible for very simple shapes. For example, a circular path of radius r_k and isotropic measurement noise $\mathbf{C}_k^v = \sigma_{v,k}^2 \cdot \mathbf{I}$ yields [115]

$$\mathrm{p}(\nu_k \mid \underline{x}_k) = \mathrm{Rice}\left(\nu_k; r_k, \sigma_{v,k}\right) \ . \tag{3.10}$$

However, for the more general case, only approximations are tractable. [148] proposed a a sample-based PIM approximation which can be implemented as follows.

- First, we find the most likely source $\underline{\pi}_k^*(\underline{y}_k)$ as shown in Section 3.3.
- Second, assuming $\underline{z}_k \approx \underline{\pi}_k^*(\underline{y}_k)$, we propagate $\underline{v}_k$ through (3.3) using representative samples, and calculate the mean $\hat{\nu}_k$ and variance $\sigma^2_{\nu,k}$ of ν_k. An example approach to calculate these values is presented in Section 9.3.
- Finally, we use moment matching to say that $\nu_k \sim \mathcal{N}\left(\hat{\nu}_k, \sigma^2_{\nu,k}\right)$. In other words, we obtain the approximation

$$\mathrm{p}(\nu_k \,|\, \underline{x}_k) \approx \mathcal{N}\left(\nu_k; \hat{\nu}_k, \sigma^2_{\nu,k}\right) \ . \tag{3.11}$$

This is, in essence, the PIM analog of the Gaussian approximation for GAMs proposed in (2.27). Nonetheless, it may happen that the Gaussian approximation is too inaccurate for a given application, in particular as the noise level increases. Figure 3.2a shows an example with the circle shape, with the analytic solution and the Gaussian approximation for different $\sigma^2_{v,k}$. It becomes evident that, for higher noise, a Gaussian pdf ceases to be a good fit for $\mathrm{p}(\nu_k \,|\, \underline{x}_k)$. For these situations, a more accurate approach using level-sets is proposed in Section 3.5.

3.5 Level-set PIMs

In this section, we will describe an alternative formulation for $\mathrm{p}(\nu_k \,|\, \underline{x}_k)$ which allows for higher accuracy by using level-sets. This approach, proposed in [160], is one of the contributions of this thesis. We will also discuss a comparison between this new approach and the sample-based technique presented in Section 3.4.

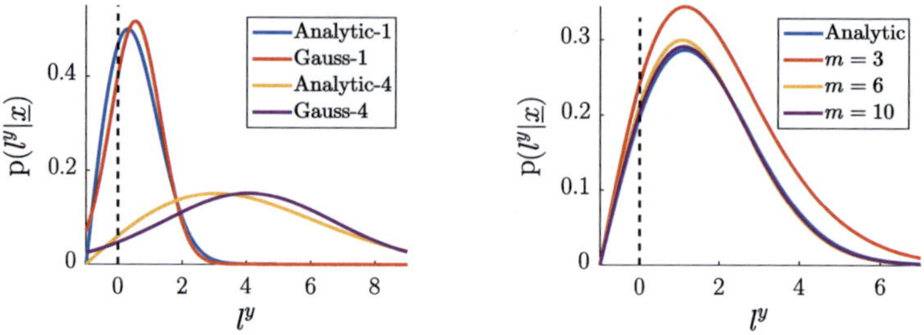

(a) Gaussian approximation $\sigma_{v,k} = 1$, $\sigma_{v,k} = 4$.

(b) Level-set with regular m-polygons, $\sigma_{v,k} = 2$.

Figure 3.2: Representations of the pdf $\mathrm{p}(l_k^y \,|\, \underline{x}_k)$ using sample-based Gaussian moment matching and polygonal level-set approximations with m vertices. The shape is a circle of radius 1, assuming isotropic noise $\mathbf{C}_k^v = \sigma_{v,k}^2 \cdot \mathbf{I}$. The ground truth is the analytic solution using the Rice distribution from (3.10). The subindex k is omitted for legibility.

The derivation is as follows. Let us assume that the measurement noise covariance matrix is isotropic, i.e., $\mathbf{C}_k^v = \sigma_{v,k}^2 \cdot \mathbf{I}$. In this case, the signed Mahalanobis distance becomes simply a state-independent multiple of the signed Euclidean distance. By ignoring the scaling factor we obtain

$$\varphi_k^*(\underline{p}_k) = \varphi_k^{sm}(\underline{p}_k) \text{ , with } \mathbf{\Sigma} = \mathbf{I} \text{ .}$$

Note that this change does not alter the closest source. Furthermore, we assume that there exists a differentiable arc length parametrization $\underline{\phi}_k(s_k)$ of the shape $\mathcal{S}_k^x$. This function is only used as an auxiliary term and does not need to be modeled explicitly. By rotating the tangent vector $\underline{\phi}_k'(s_k)$ by $\frac{\pi}{2}$, we obtain the normal vector

$$\underline{n}_k(s_k) := \underbrace{\begin{bmatrix} 0 & -1 \\ 1 & 0 \end{bmatrix}}_{\mathbf{R}_{\pi/2}} \underline{\phi}_k'(s_k) \text{ .} \tag{3.12}$$

It holds that $\mathbf{R}_{\pi/2}^\top \mathbf{R}_{\pi/2} = \mathbf{I}$. From (2.8) it follows for all s_k that $\|\underline{n}_k(s_k)\| = 1$. In addition, using (2.9) we observe that

$$\begin{aligned} \underline{n}_k'(s_k)^\top \underline{n}_k(s_k) &= \underline{\phi}_k''(s_k)^\top \cdot \mathbf{R}_{\pi/2}^\top \mathbf{R}_{\pi/2} \cdot \underline{\phi}_k'(s_k) \\ &= 0 \ , \end{aligned} \tag{3.13}$$

i.e., $\underline{n}_k(s_k)$ is always normal to its derivative. We can now write an explicit form of (3.4) as

$$\begin{aligned} \underline{\Phi}_\mathrm{k}\left(s_k^y, l_k^y\right) &:= \underline{z}_k + l_k^y \cdot \underline{n}_k(s_k^y) \\ &= \underline{\phi}_k(s_k^y) + l_k^y \cdot \underline{n}_k(s_k^y) \ . \end{aligned}$$

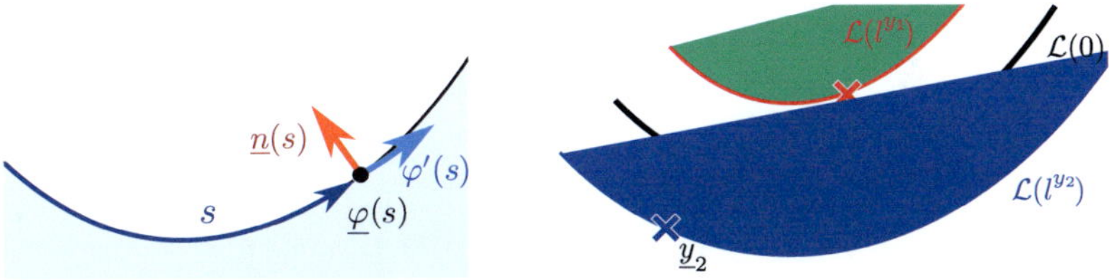

(a) Path parametrization and normal vector.

(b) Level-sets of a function $\varphi_k(\,\cdot\,)$ for l_k^{y1} and l_k^{y2}.

Figure 3.3: The left figure shows the parametrization functions for Level-set PIMs. The right figure shows how level-sets work. For the given curve (black), the level-set $\mathcal{L}_k(l_k^{y1})$ (green) contains $\underline{y}_{k,1}$ and all other points with the signed Euclidean distance l_k^{y1} to the shape. Similarly, $\mathcal{L}_k(l_k^{y2})$ (blue) contains all points with signed Euclidean distance l_k^{y2}. The subindex k is omitted for legibility.

A motivation for this formulation can be found in Figure 3.1 and Figure 3.3a. For clarification, s_k^y is the path parameter that corresponds to $\underline{y}_k$, while s_k is a generic argument. Based on this, the task now is to obtain $\mathrm{p}(l_k^y \,|\, \underline{x}_k)$ by marginalizing s_k^y out of $\mathrm{p}(s_k^y, l_k^y \,|\, \underline{x}_k)$. By applying a change of variables, we obtain

$$\begin{aligned} \mathrm{p}(s_k^y, l_k^y \,|\, \underline{x}_k) &= \mathrm{p}(\underline{y}_k \,|\, \underline{x}_k) \cdot \left|\det\left(\mathbf{J}_k^\Phi(s_k^y, l_k^y)\right)\right| \\ &= \mathcal{N}(\underline{y}_k - \underline{z}_k^m; \underline{0}, \mathbf{C}_k^v) \cdot \left|\det\left(\mathbf{J}_k^\Phi(s_k^y, l_k^y)\right)\right| \ , \end{aligned} \tag{3.14}$$

where $\underline{z}_k^m := \underline{\pi}_k^*(\underline{y}_k)$, and $|\cdot|$ is the absolute value. In order to simplify this term, we need the Jacobian matrix of $\underline{\Phi}_\text{k}\,(s_k^y, l_k^y)$, which takes the form

$$\begin{aligned}\mathbf{J}_k^\phi(s_k^y, l_k^y) &:= \left[\tfrac{\partial \underline{\Phi}_k}{\partial s_k^y}\,(s_k^y, l_k^y)\,,\ \ \tfrac{\partial \underline{\Phi}_k}{\partial l_k^y}\,(s_k^y, l_k^y)\right] \\ &= \left[\underline{\varphi}_k'(s_k^y) + l_k^y \cdot \underline{n}_k'(s_k^y),\ \ \underline{n}_k(s_k^y)\right] \ .\end{aligned}$$

The determinant of this matrix can be calculated easily by observing that both columns are orthogonal to each other as a consequence of (3.13) and (3.12), i.e.,

$$\left(\underline{\varphi}_k'(s_k^y) + l_k^y \cdot \underline{n}_k'(s_k^y)\right)^\top \cdot \underline{n}_k(s_k^y) = 0 \ ,$$

which, in turn, this means that the determinant is simply the product of the Euclidean norms of the columns,

$$\begin{aligned}\left|\det\left(\mathbf{J}_k^\Phi(s_k^y, l_k^y)\right)\right| &= \left\|\frac{\partial \underline{\Phi}_k}{\partial s_k^y}(s_k^y, l_k^y)\right\| \cdot \|\underline{n}_k(s_k^y)\| \\ &= \left\|\frac{\partial \underline{\Phi}_k}{\partial s_k^y}(s_k^y, l_k^y)\right\| \ .\end{aligned}$$

where the second factor vanishes as a consequence of (2.8). We now further simplify (3.14), in the form of

$$\begin{aligned}\mathrm{p}(s_k^y, l_k^y \,|\, \underline{x}_k) &= \mathcal{N}(\underline{y}_k - \underline{z}_k^m; \underline{0}, \mathbf{C}_k^v) \cdot \left|\det\left(\mathbf{J}_k^\Phi(s_k^y, l_k^y)\right)\right| \\ &= \mathcal{N}(\underline{\Phi}_k(s_k^y, l_k^y) - \underline{z}_k^m; \underline{0}, \mathbf{C}_k^v) \cdot \left|\det\left(\mathbf{J}_k^\Phi(s_k^y, l_k^y)\right)\right| \\ &= \mathcal{N}(\underline{\Phi}_k(s_k^y, l_k^y) - \underline{z}_k^m; \underline{0}, \mathbf{C}_k^v) \cdot \left\|\frac{\partial \underline{\Phi}_k}{\partial s_k^y}(s_k^y, l_k^y)\right\| \ .\end{aligned}$$

Finally, we marginalize s_k^y out of this expression, yielding

$$\mathrm{p}(l_k^y \,|\, \underline{x}_k) = \int_0^L \mathcal{N}(\underline{\Phi}_k(s_k, l_k^y) - \underline{z}_k^m; \underline{0}, \mathbf{C}_k^v) \left\|\frac{\partial \underline{\Phi}_k}{\partial s_k^y}(s_k, l_k^y)\right\| \mathrm{d}s_k \quad (3.15)$$

where $L := \|\mathcal{S}_k^x\|$. We observe that, by iterating through all s_k in $\underline{\phi}_k(s_k, l_k^y)$, this integral traverses all points that fulfill the condition $\varphi_k(\underline{p}_k) = l_k^y$, as seen in Figure 3.3b. In other words, this is an integral over a *level-set*.

Definition 3.1 (Level-set [118]). *A level-set $\mathcal{L}_k(l_k)$ of a shape function φ_k is the set of points*

$$\mathcal{L}_k(l_k) = \left\{ \underline{p}_k \in \mathbb{R}^d \,|\, \varphi_k(\underline{p}_k) = l_k \right\} .$$

We note that the final two terms of (3.15) are the derivative of $\underline{\phi}_k$ and $\mathrm{d}s_k$. This allows us, by applying a change of variables, to use any parametrization $\underline{\phi}_k^*(s_k^*)$ of the level-set $\mathcal{L}_k(l_k^y)$. In particular, we see that $\underline{\phi}_k^*$ does not need to be an arc parametrization. We obtain then

$$\mathrm{p}(l_k^y \,|\, \underline{x}_k) = \int_{s_{k,1}^*}^{s_{k,2}^*} \mathcal{N}(\underline{\phi}_k^*(s_k^*) - \underline{z}_k^m; \underline{0}, \mathbf{C}_k^v) \cdot \left\| \frac{\mathrm{d}\underline{\phi}_k^*}{\mathrm{d}s_k^*}(s_k^*) \right\| \mathrm{d}s_k \ , \qquad (3.16)$$

where $s_{k,1}^*$ and $s_{k,2}^*$ are the bounds of the path parametrization. Alternatively, we can say that $\mathrm{p}(l_k^y \,|\, \underline{x}_k)$ is simply the path integral of the pdf $\mathcal{N}(\underline{z}_k^m, \mathbf{C}_k^v)$ over the curve $\mathcal{L}_k(l_k^y)$. This term can also be used as the distribution of the bias correction term ν_k.

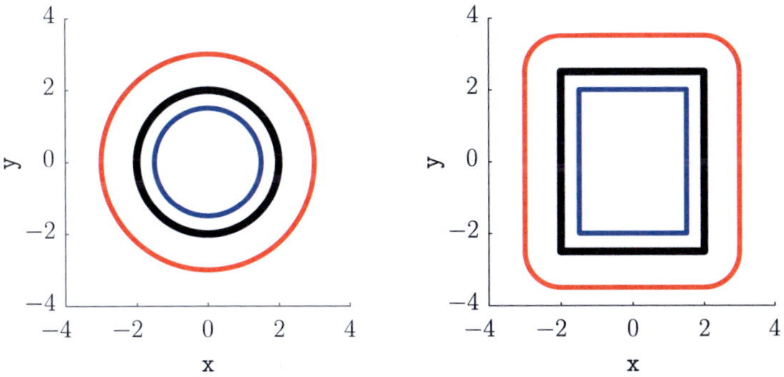

(a) Level-sets of a circle. **(b)** Level-sets of a rectangle.

Figure 3.4: Level-sets of a circle and a rectangle. In red, $\mathcal{L}_k(1)$ indicates all the points outside with a distance of 1. In blue, $\mathcal{L}_k(-0.5)$ contains all the points inside with a distance of 0.5.

The strengths and weaknesses of level-set PIMs stand out when compared to sample-based PIMs. On the one hand, for level-set PIMs it is necessary to construct a level-set for every measured $\underline{y}_k$. Techniques to construct level-sets can be found in [119], and Figure 3.4 shows examples with a circle and a rectangle. By approximating a level-set as a polygon, a closed-form solution for (3.16) can be calculated using the algorithm described in Section 9.2.5. Figure 3.2b shows how the level-set approach based on a polygonal approximation with m sides quickly converges to the analytic solution, almost reaching the true distribution with a simple hexagon. However, obtaining arbitrary level-sets for non-convex shapes is often extremely difficult, in particular for negative distances. This issue does not exist for sample-based PIMs which only require multiple evaluations in the shape function. Nonetheless, on the other hand, level-set PIMs provide a much more accurate representation of the true $\mathrm{p}(l_k^y \mid \underline{x}_k)$, even with a low-accuracy polygonal approximation. Thus, we see that level-set PIMs are extremely suitable in scenarios with very high noise. Section 3.6 explores the difference in estimation quality more deeply.

3.6 Evaluation of Sample-based PIMs and Level-Set PIMs

In this section we will estimate the shape parameters of a circle and a rectangle based on point measurements with different noise levels. Figure 3.5 shows an example setup. We will compare and contrast four approaches,

- *Naïve Least Squares* (LeastSq) as described in (2.27),
- *Okatani* correction shown in (3.2),
- *Sample-based PIMs* (PIM-Gauss) as illustrated in (3.11), and
- *Level-set PIMs* (PIM-LSet) as proposed in (3.16).

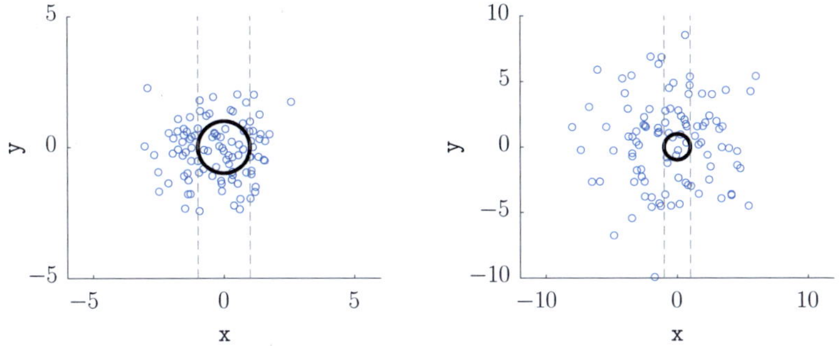

(a) Example measurements with $\sigma^2_{v,k} = 1$. **(b)** Example measurements with $\sigma^2_{v,k} = 9$.

Figure 3.5: Illustration of example measurements with the used noise levels. The vertical dotted lines serve as guides to visualize the circle size.

A good mechanism to visualize the magnitude of the estimation bias is by plotting the likelihood functions directly. Figure 3.6 shows the four approaches for different noise levels when estimating the radius x_k of a circle centered on the origin, with ground truth $x^g_k = 1$. The function values are obtained as the product of the likelihoods of 10^6 sample measurements as explained in (2.3). The vertical dotted lines denote the radius which yields the corresponding maximum likelihood, as calculated with the MATLAB function fminsearch. For very low noise, as seen in Figure 3.6a, all approaches behave similarly, with LeastSq showing already moderate bias. Only at higher noise in Figure 3.6c do we start seeing the differences between PIM-Gauss and PIM-LevelSet. Okatani starts to become unreliable, as it is incapable of modeling shapes where the radius of curvature is much lower than the noise level. By Figure 3.6d the bias in LeastSq becomes so high that the shape becomes virtually unrecognizable, while both PIMs remain very close to the ground truth.

Figure 3.7 shows the results of a similar evaluation using the same scenario, where the state to be estimated consisted of the center position and the radius. We analyze two cases, one without occlusion and another where parts of the circular arc are not visible. For the scenarios without occlusion, all approaches had no trouble estimating the center. However, the issue of bias is clearly present, so that by Figure 3.7d only the PIMs are close to the ground truth. Then, occlusions were enabled, first by hiding half (Figure 3.7e) and then by hiding three fourths (Figure 3.7f) of the shape. In this case, all approaches show a consistent position bias in the direction opposite to the occlusion. The bias is once more notable, and even the PIMs have some trouble finding the center. Still, the PIMs were again the best performers, with PIM-LSet on the lead.

Finally, in order to illustrate the applicability of PIMs for something other than circles, Figure 3.8 shows the results of estimating the shape of a rectangle with different noise levels. The state to be estimated consisted of the center, the height, and the width, while the ground truth was located on the origin with height 4 and width 2. This scenario is different from the circle, as the curvature is undefined on the corners, and thus, Okatani could not be used. Furthermore, the most likely source for most of the points also coincides with the corners, far from the true sources, rendering bias reduction approaches less effective. Nonetheless, both PIM approaches still produced relatively good results, even if the bias is moderate, but still less than LeastSq. In the left row there are no occlusions, but in the right row the top right quarter is hidden. As with the circle scenario, this occlusion produced a bias in the opposite direction of the hidden parts. However, as with the other experiments, PIM-LSet still outperformed PIM-Gauss, which in turn was still much better than the LeastSq approach.

3.7 Conclusions

In this section we presented an approach to reduce bias when estimating paths, called Level-set Partial Information Models. This contribution was based on Partial Information Models, which aimed to compensate for the failings of GAMs by centering the uncertainty on an appropriate approximation of the true source, instead of on the measurement itself. The key idea was to reparametrize a measurement into two components, one which described where the source was, and another which denoted its distance to the shape. This allows for the derivation of a 'partial likelihood' by ignoring the component related to the source, and focusing only the distribution of distances. Our extension, Level-set PIMs, built upon this idea by reinterpreting the distance distribution as an integral over a level-set. The applicability of our contribution was then compared with Sample-based PIMs from previous work. The evaluation showed that both forms of PIMs were capable of highly reducing the estimation bias even in the presence of very high noise. While Level-set PIMs were more accurate, however, they were less performant and its implementation was more complex than sample-based PIMs.

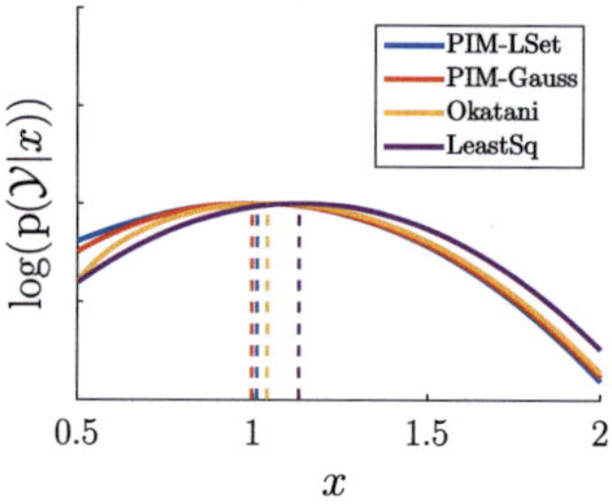

(a) Likelihood function for $\sigma^2_{v,k} = 0.25$.

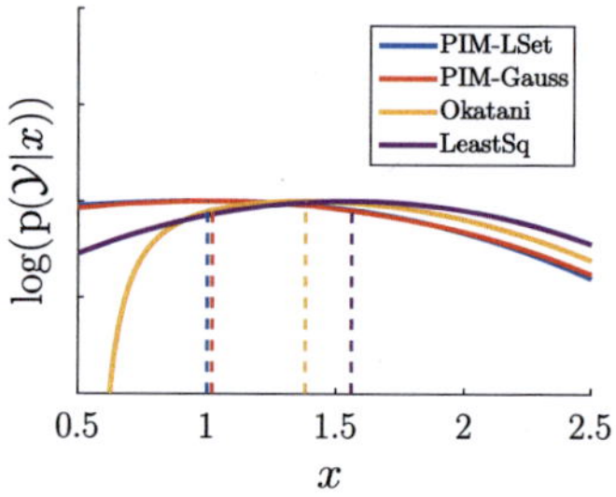

(b) Likelihood function for $\sigma^2_{v,k} = 1$.

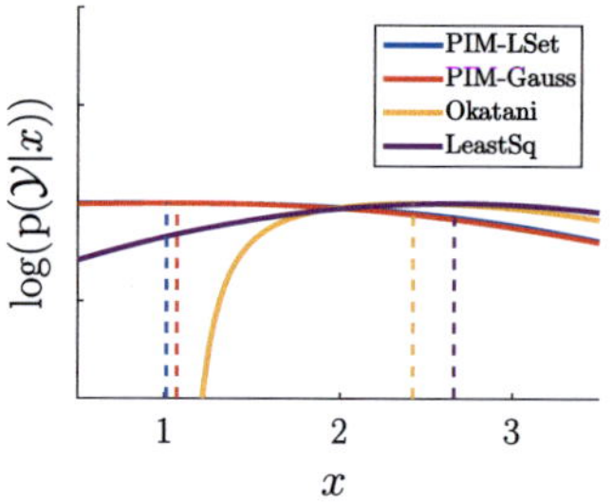

(c) Likelihood function for $\sigma^2_{v,k} = 4$.

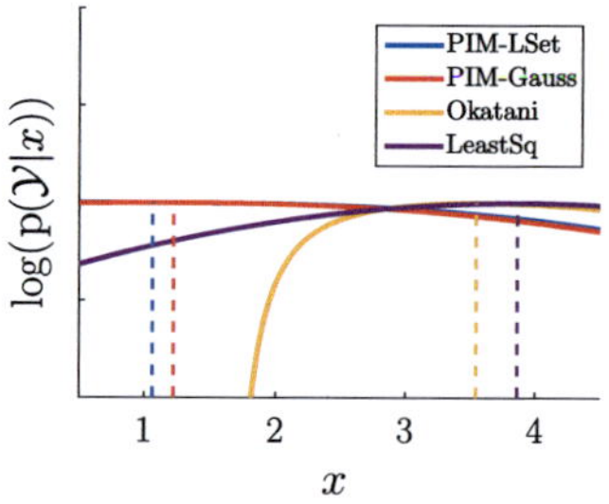

(d) Likelihood function for $\sigma^2_{v,k} = 9$.

Figure 3.6: Log-likelihood functions for different noise levels. The vertical dotted line denotes the radius that yields the maximum value. Ground truth is $x^g_k = 1$. The logarithm is used to make sure all curves can be compared appropriately, and the results have been translated vertically so that their maximum values coincide. The subindex k is omitted for legibility.

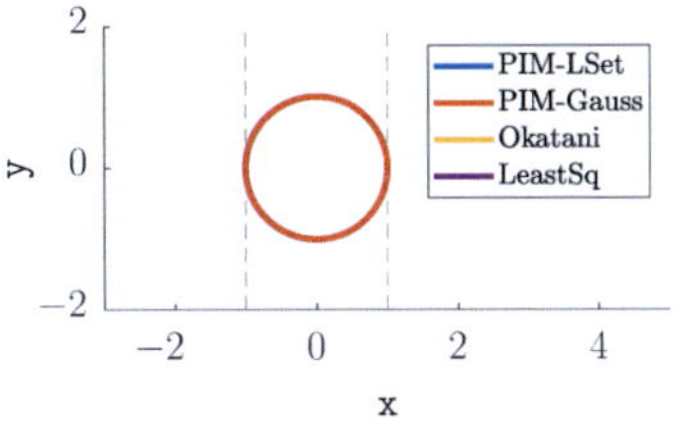

(a) Results for $\sigma_{v,k}^2 = 0.01$.

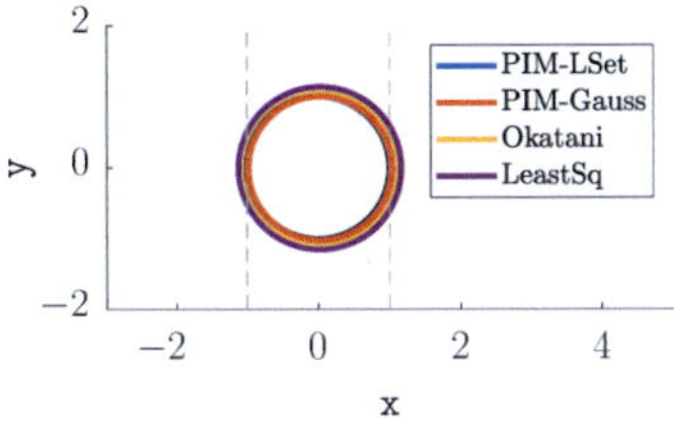

(b) Results for $\sigma_{v,k}^2 = 0.25$.

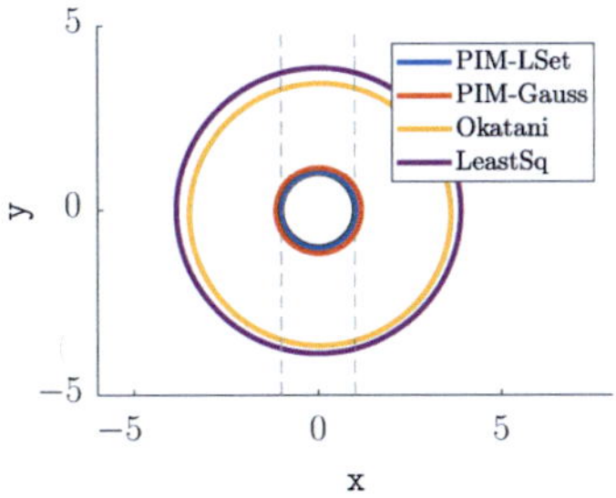

(c) Results for $\sigma_{v,k}^2 = 9$.

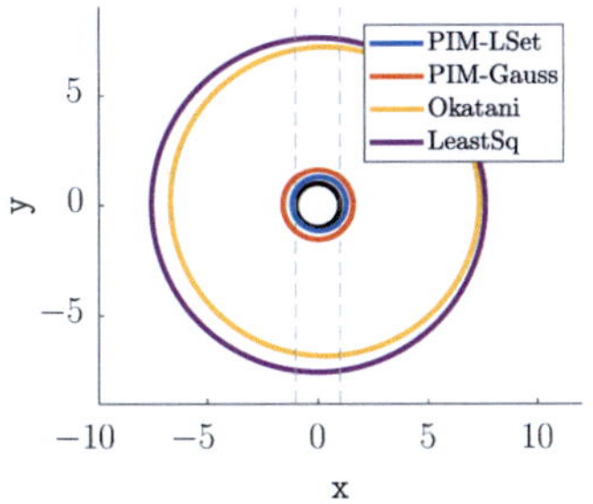

(d) Results for $\sigma_{v,k}^2 = 36$.

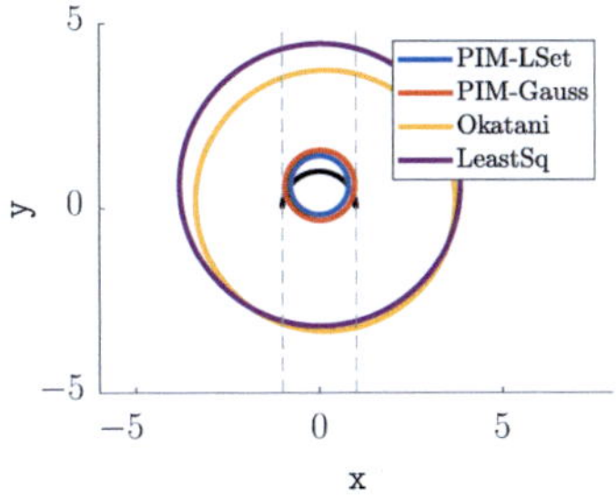

(e) Results for $\sigma_{v,k}^2 = 9$, half occluded.

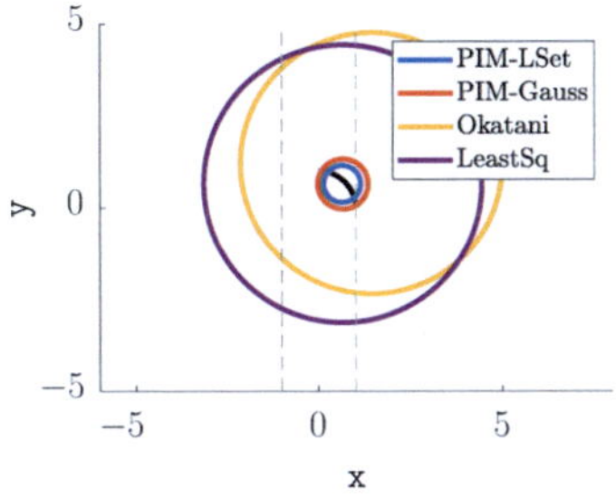

(f) Results for $\sigma_{v,k}^2 = 9$, three fourths occluded.

Figure 3.7: Results for circle evaluation with different noise levels and occlusions.

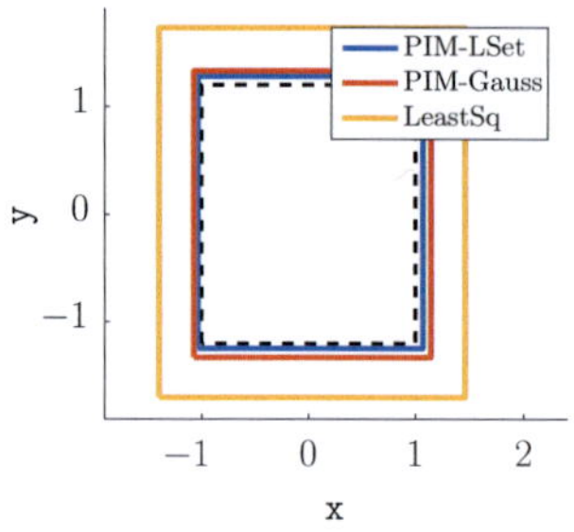

(a) Results for $\sigma^2_{v,k} = 1$.

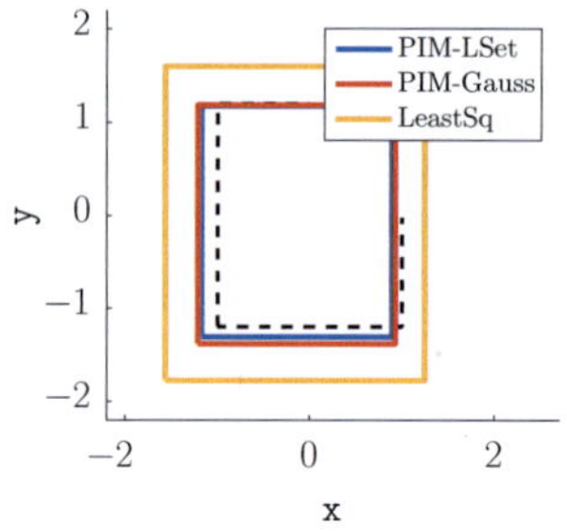

(b) Results for $\sigma^2_{v,k} = 1$, occlusion.

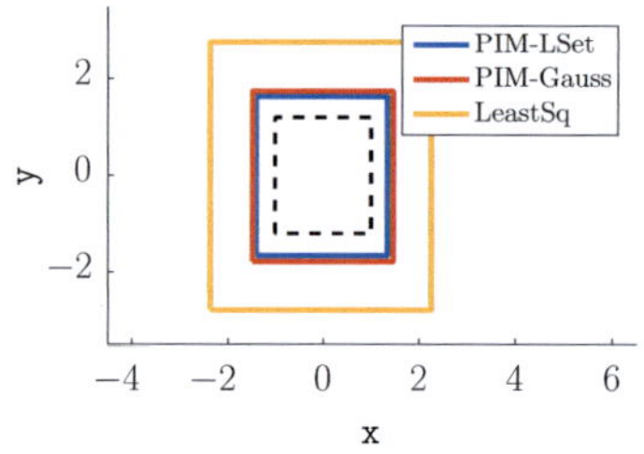

(c) Results for $\sigma^2_{v,k} = 4$.

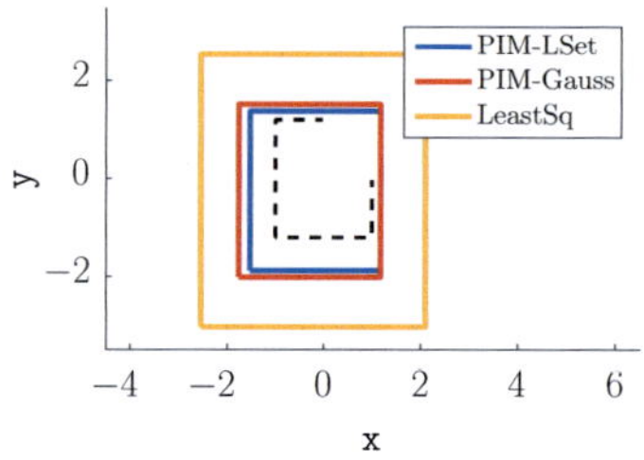

(d) Results for $\sigma^2_{v,k} = 4$, occlusion.

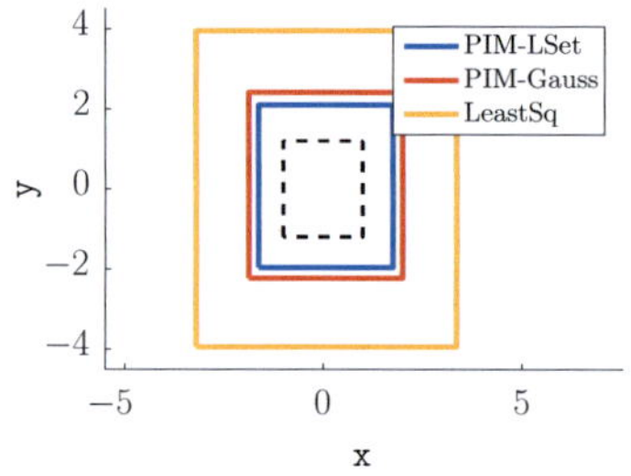

(e) Results for $\sigma^2_{v,k} = 9$.

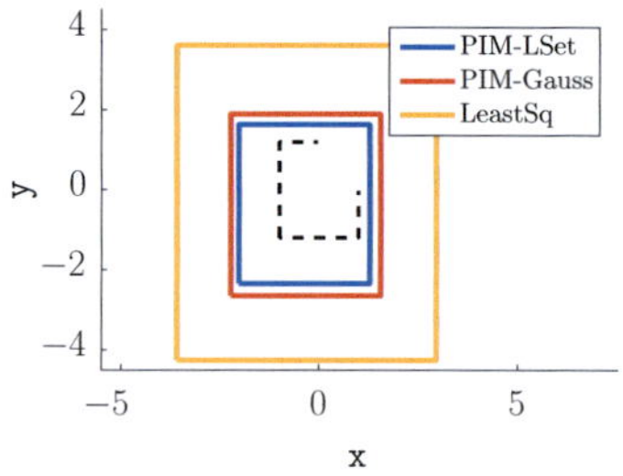

(f) Results for $\sigma^2_{v,k} = 9$, occlusion.

Figure 3.8: Results for rectangle evaluation with different noise levels and occlusion.

CHAPTER 4

Active Random Hypersurface Models

In this chapter, we will briefly describe the theoretical background for the *extent problem* (first mentioned in Section 2.5), which occurs when estimating filled shapes using GAMs [148, 160]. We observe that, while SDMs do not suffer from this issue, we want to avoid their use, as they are generally difficult to evaluate and become numerically unstable for complex shapes. Instead, we will explore different approaches that extend GAM ideas for filled shapes while retaining their simplicity and efficiency, and then compare the strengths and weaknesses of these ideas. This chapter is intended as a discussion of state-of-the-art models, and serves as a stepping stone for the contributions introduced in the next chapters. It also introduces two of our innovations, namely i) *active models* and ii) *Active Random Hypersurface Models* (ARHMs).

The structure is as follows. First, we provide a mathematical formulation for the extent problem, and show why it makes the estimation of filled shapes difficult. Then, we introduce the concept of *Random Hypersurface Models* (RHMs), which solve the extent problem by describing parts of the shape as simple SDMs and the remainder as GAMs. We also present a regularization approach based on ideas from active contours, called active models, which address the extent problem by applying some sort of corrective geometrical force on the shape. Finally, we show how the strengths of both ideas can be combined in the form of Active Random Hypersurface Models. For each presented model, we also show a brief evaluation in order to validate the presented ideas.

4.1 The Extent Problem

The extent problem can easily be illustrated with the following experiment. We consider a rectangle with width x_k, modeled as

$$\mathcal{S}_k^x = \left\{ \begin{bmatrix} x_k \cdot s_{k,1} \\ s_{k,2} \end{bmatrix} ; s_{k,1} \in \left[-1, 1\right], s_{k,2} \in \left[-1, 1\right] \right\} ,$$

i.e., a *filled* rectangle centered on the origin that extends in the $\mathbf{x}$-coordinate in the range of $\left[-x_k, x_k\right]$, and which in the $\mathbf{y}$-coordinate spans the fixed interval $\left[-1, 1\right]$ (see Figure 4.1a). This shape is filled, i.e., measurements also stem from the shape interior. Then, assuming a ground truth width of $x_k^g = 2$, we generate 10^5 measurements uniformly from the rectangle and perturb them with additive zero-mean Gaussian noise with covariance matrix $\mathbf{C}_k^v = \sigma_{v,k}^2 \cdot \mathbf{I}$, with four different noise levels $\sigma_{v,k} = 0.01, 0.1, 0.5$, and 1. Then, we calculate the batch likelihoods for all measurements combined, using SDMs with a uniform source distribution (Section 2.4), and GAMs (Section 2.5) using the Euclidean difference. Note that the GAM shape function takes into account the nearest source on the entire shape, including the interior. The result of the likelihoods for all measurements are shown in Figure 4.1.

On the one hand, from Figure 4.1b it becomes clear that SDMs have no problem finding the ground truth, as the maximum is located there even for high noise levels. Alternatively, for numerical stability and ease of calculation, we could try to approximate the rectangle shape as a coarse Gaussian pdf as in (2.23). This simplified SDM approach, even if it ignores important shape information, can still estimate the target extent (Figure 4.1c). GAMs, on the other hand (Figure 4.1d), have a maximum that is slightly different than the ground truth of 2 as a consequence of estimation bias. But far more importantly, after reaching their maximum value, the likelihood functions become flat (i.e., constant).

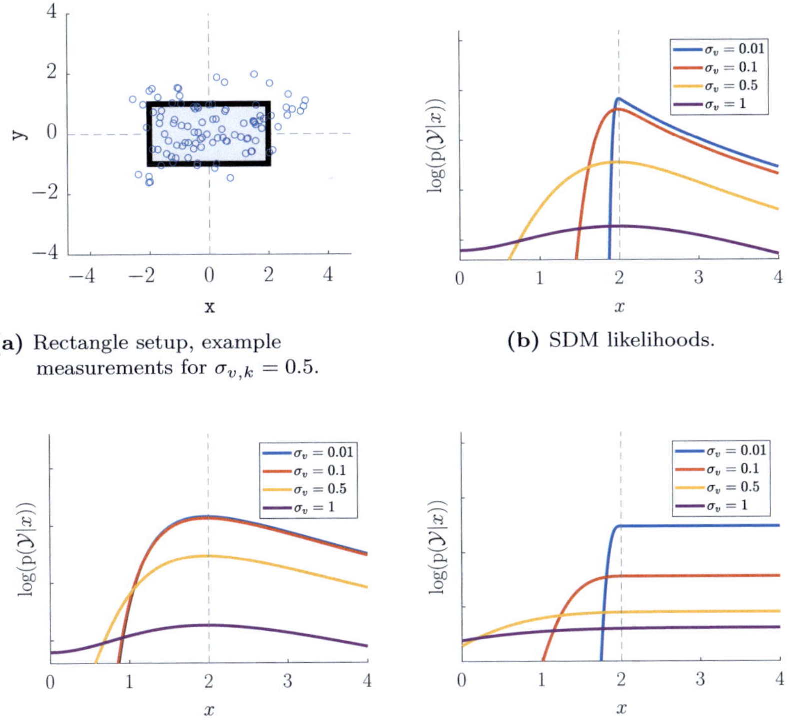

(a) Rectangle setup, example measurements for $\sigma_{v,k} = 0.5$.

(b) SDM likelihoods.

(c) Gauss-SDM likelihoods.

(d) GAM likelihoods.

Figure 4.1: Likelihood functions for the rectangle using different types of SDMs and GAMs. The vertical dashed line denotes the ground truth. The logarithm is used in the lower row for legibility, in order to make sure all curves can be compared appropriately.

This happens because GAMs only consider the distance to the nearest source, and thus, once the rectangle becomes large enough, it will contain every possible measurement. At this point, by definition, the shape function will always be 0, making this rectangle, and every other rectangle larger than it, optimal. This is the essence of the extent problem, which arises any time that multiple (large) shapes can contain the ground truth shape. Note that this issue cannot be solved with PIMs (Chapter 3), as they also work with some sort of nearest source.

This raises the need for an approach that combines the simplicity and numerical stability of GAMs with the accuracy of SDMs, while addressing the issue of the extent problem. The following two sections introduce models that deal with this challenge.

4.2 Random Hypersurface Models

RHMs [83] aim to develop a generative model by describing arbitrary shapes as being constructed from simpler shapes. This mechanism allows for some parts of the shape to be described using GAMs and others as SDMs, combining the strengths of both approaches. Thus, for the filled rectangle example, we can say that only the width needs to be modeled as an SDMs, while the rest can be represented using simple GAMs.

A short theoretical derivation follows. We proceed to define the concept of *random shapes*, related to the ideas of random sets [120] and set-theoretic EOT models[121].

Definition 4.1 (Random Shape[1]). *A random shape is a set of shapes* $\{\mathcal{S}_k^x(t_k) \,|\, t_k \in T_k\}$ *parametrized by the random variable* t_k*, so that each shape has a probability* $\mathrm{p}(t_k \,|\, \underline{x}_k)$ *of being randomly drawn. The term* t_k *is denoted as the transformation parameter, and a realization* $\mathcal{S}_k^x(t_k)$ *of the random shape is called a slice.*

Figure 4.2 shows slice examples for different shapes. In Figure 4.2a, the example rectangle was constructed by translating a vertical line (gray) horizontally. The other shapes include slices for a disk in Figure 4.2b, a filled square in Figure 4.2c, and a non-convex shape in Figure 4.2d.

[1] For arbitrary higher-dimensional spaces, a more specific name for shapes would be 'hypersurfaces'. Hence the name of Random Hypersurfaces.

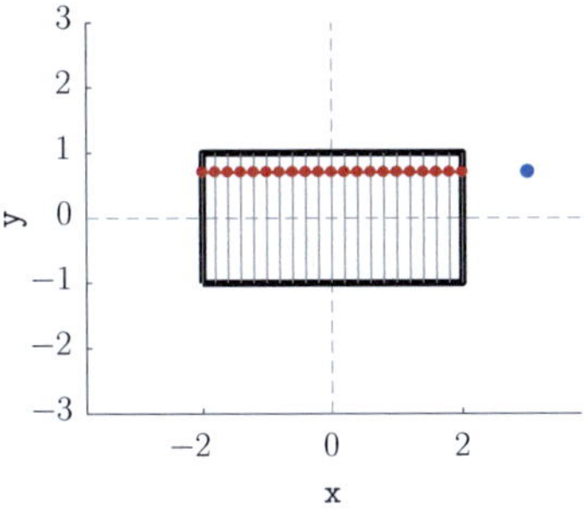

(a) Slices for a filled rectangle with constant height.

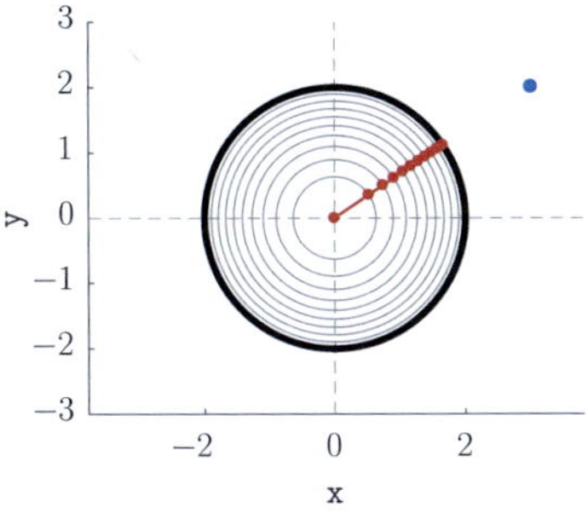

(b) Slices for a filled circle (a disk).

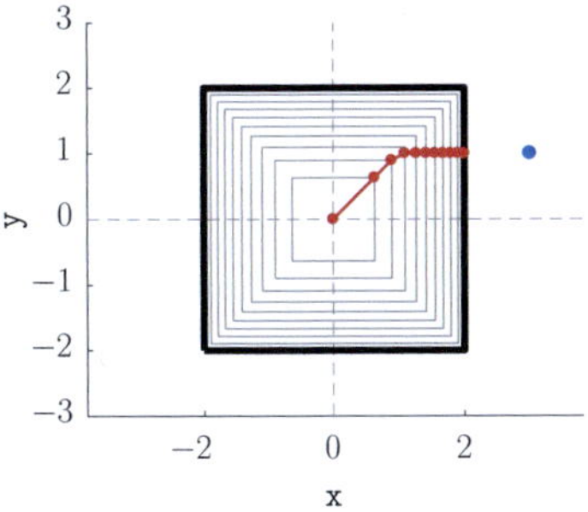

(c) Slices for a filled square.

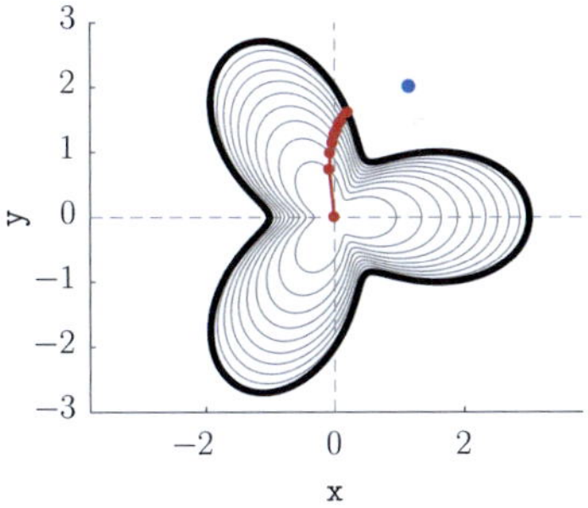

(d) Slices for a filled non-convex shape.

Figure 4.2: Example slices and Euclidean projections for different shapes. The blue dot is an example measurement, the red dots are the Euclidean projections for each slice.

We can now define a generative model for RHMs. In the first step, we draw a realization of the transformation parameter t_k, from which we obtain the shape $\mathcal{S}_k^x(t_k)$. From this shape, a source point $\underline{z}_k$ is drawn by the sensor, which in turn is corrupted by the additive zero-mean Gaussian noise term $\underline{v}_k$. As in (2.1), this yields the observed measurement $\underline{y}_k$. This model can be used to derive both a measurement equation and a likelihood function. On the one hand, it is assumed that each shape $\mathcal{S}_k^x(t_k)$ has an association model, for example a GAM or PIM, with measurement equation

$$\underline{h}(\underline{x}_k, \underline{y}_k, \underline{v}_k, t_k) = \underline{0} \ .$$

We can then simply use this same expression as a measurement equation for the entire shape, by treating t_k as an additional noise term. On the other hand, we can also say that the association model for each slice can be described with a conditional pdf $\mathrm{p}(\underline{y}_k \,|\, \underline{x}_k, t_k)$. By marginalizing out t_k, we obtain

$$\mathrm{p}(\underline{y}_k \,|\, \underline{x}_k) = \int_{\mathrm{T}_k} \mathrm{p}(\underline{y}_k \,|\, \underline{x}_k, t_k) \ \cdot \ \mathrm{p}(t_k \,|\, \underline{x}_k) \, \mathrm{d}t_k \ ,$$

which we can interpret as a likelihood function as we did with SDMs and GAMs. Thus, this likelihood can describe a two-dimensional filled shape using a one-dimensional integral, which can be contrasted to the more complex two-dimensional integrals in SDMs from Section 2.4. Of course, RHMs can also be extended to three-dimensions. For example, a filled 3D shape can be described by applying two transformations $\underline{t}_k \in \mathbb{R}^2$ on a planar shape.

As an example, we will now show how to derive an RHM for a filled star-convex shape in 2D. Assuming $\mathcal{S}_k^x$ is the shape boundary, and that the shape is centered on the origin, i.e., $\underline{c}_k = \underline{0}$, an easy way to describe the interior is by using homogeneous scaling as the transformation mechanism. This yields the slices

$$\mathcal{S}_k^x(t_k) = t_k \ \cdot \ \mathcal{S}_k^x \ ,$$

which can be visualized in Figure 4.2b, Figure 4.2c, and Figure 4.2d. It can be seen that, for $t_k = 1$, we obtain the boundary itself, while for $t_k = 0$ this yields the origin. The selection of the shape function is also important. While Euclidean shape functions can be used, they require the calculation of the Euclidean projection for each slice, and it can be seen from Figure 4.2 that they are not straightforward to calculate and may lie in unintuitive positions. However, when using radial shape functions, it holds for each point that all of its projections lie on the same line, i.e., for each $\underline{p}_k \in \mathbb{R}^d$ the projection to the slice t_k is simply

$$\underline{\pi}_k^r(\underline{p}_k, t_k) = t_k \cdot \underline{\pi}_k^r(\underline{p}_k) \, .$$

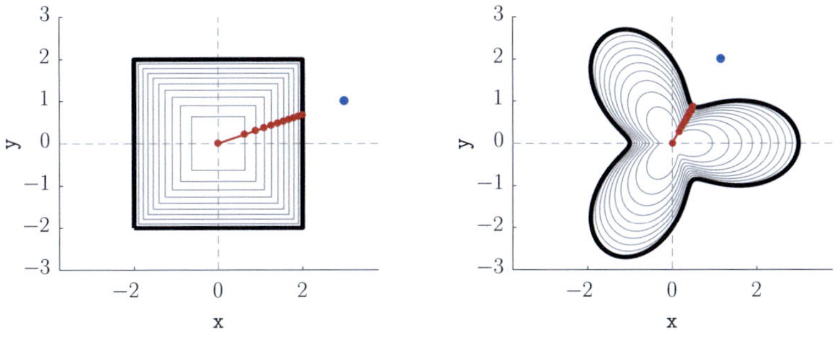

(a) Slices for a filled square.

(b) Slices for a non-convex shape.

Figure 4.3: Example slices and radial projections for different shapes. The blue dot is an example measurement, the red dots are the radial projections for each slice. Note that all projections lie in a straight line from the center.

This can be visualized in Figure 4.3a and Figure 4.3b. This allows us to obtain a GAM-like measurement equation by using the radial shape functions from (2.17), i.e.,

$$\begin{aligned} \underline{h}(\underline{x}_k, \underline{y}_k, \underline{v}_k, t_k) &= \left\| \underline{y}_k - \underline{v}_k - \underline{\pi}_k^r(\underline{y}_k, t_k) \right\| \\ &= \left\| \underline{y}_k - \underline{v}_k \right\| - \left\| \underline{\pi}_k^r(\underline{y}_k, t_k) \right\| \\ &= \left\| \underline{y}_k - \underline{v}_k \right\| - t_k \cdot \left\| \underline{\pi}_k^r(\underline{y}_k) \right\| \, . \end{aligned}$$

Thus, t_k appears as a multiplicative noise term, and the term containing $\underline{v}_k$ is independent from the slice. This means that the projection function only needs to be calculated once and extensions using PIMs [56] only need to consider the boundary and not the interior. Note that, similar to SDMs, the distribution of t_k should approximately correspond to how the sensor observes the target. [122] shows an easy way to calculate the distribution of this term for star-convex RHMs when sources are uniformly distributed. This generally allows for a derivation of the RHM likelihood in closed form [108, 153] and even an analytic solution for the update step of LRKFs[122, 27, 56]. For all of these reasons, RHMs with radial shape functions and scaling transformations have proven to be popular, as seen for example in [27, 122, 153, 162, 29, 28].

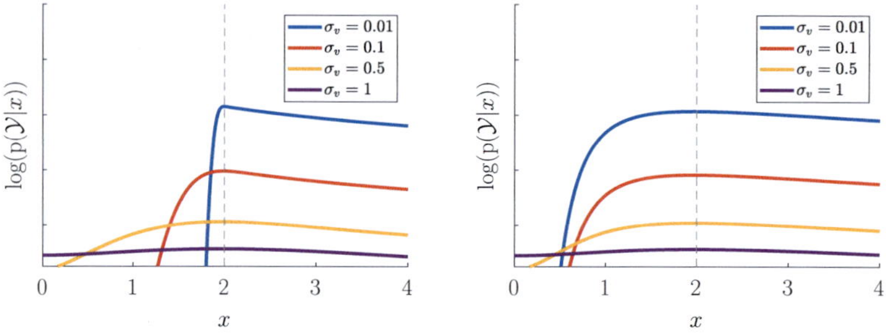

(a) RHM likelihoods for rectangle. **(b)** RHM-Gauss likelihoods for rectangle.

Figure 4.4: Likelihood functions for the rectangle using different types of RHMs. The vertical dashed line denotes the ground truth.

Beyond that, RHMs have been used in literature to described a variety of shapes, for example line segments [147]. In [122], an RHM approach was presented to track filled ellipses, which was evaluated in [123] against the Random Matrices technique from [33]. Filled star-convex RHMs were modeled in [27] and an explicit likelihood for this was presented in [153]. Works like [29, 28] also model the interior as a scaling transformation of the boundary, even if they do not refer to themselves as RHMs. The transformation can also include translations of the base shape in the z-axis, in order to describe cylinders [57] and more general extrusions [158].

4.3 Active Models

Another approach to deal with the extent problem is to use ideas from the field of active contours [124] and snakes [76, 125]. Informally, a snake is a closed path on which two competing geometrical forces are applied (Figure 4.5a). One force attempts to minimize the *internal* energy, which can be visualized by interpreting the snake (red) as a set of springs with each point in the curve constantly pulling its neighbors (red arrows). The resulting effect is to reduce the curvature by making the shape flatter and smoother. The other force aims to minimize the *external* energy by pushing the snake away (grey arrows) from the image (light grey). The end result is that the snake path closely follows the shape boundary. This section aims to transfer these ideas to the field of EOT, which is not a straightforward task, as snakes are meant to work with *dense* measurement sets, such as pixel grid images, where a large amount of measurements are available simultaneously. In contrast, for this thesis we are also concerned with relatively few point measurements, which may arrive at different time steps. This makes finding a balance between shrinking and pushing difficult, as the snake may easily fall through sparsely observed regions, and thus, in the absence of external energy, the path will inevitably collapse into a single point.

A more appropriate approach is, instead, to take the concepts from active contours and apply them to the state parameter space. For recursive Bayesian estimators, this idea can be implemented as a 'shape dynamic model', which we denote as *active models* [154, 156]. The concept of energies is reinterpreted as follows. The reduction of internal energy is modeled as a prediction step which applies some sort of operation on the state, such as making the corresponding shape smaller or applying a force in a given direction. This effect is counteracted by the measurement update step, which pushes the shape towards its correct form and acts as the external energy. We denote the application of an active model to the state as the *regularization step.* Note that active models do not exclude other dynamic models, such as motion models, which can also be used as additional prediction steps. Furthermore, we want to emphasize that regularization is an operation on the state $\underline{x}_k$. This means that, for recursive estimators, the entire state pdf needs to be transformed, not just the mean or a representative value.

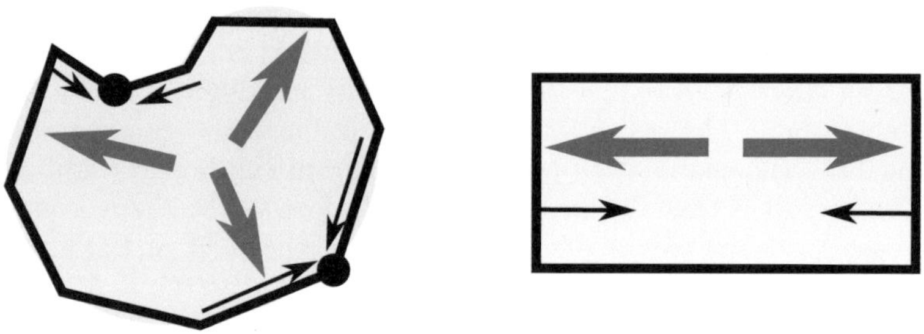

(a) Snake applied on an image. (b) Active forces on a rectangle.

Figure 4.5: An illustration of active models. We use an active force (red) as part of a shape dynamic model, which pulls the shape towards a smaller, smoother form. The update step acts as a counterforce (dark gray) which pushes the estimate back towards the true shape (light gray).

For illustration, we will now implement an active model for the example rectangle in Figure 4.1a and we will show how it solves the extent problem for GAMs. The active model can be described with

$$x^p_{k+1} = (1 - \mathsf{c}_k) \cdot x^e_k ,$$

where $0 \leq \mathsf{c}_k \ll 1$ is a coefficient that ensures that the predicted rectangle width x^p_{k+1} shrinks a bit from the estimated width x^e_k at each time step (Figure 4.5b). Thus, the regularization step takes the form of a linear operation, allowing for the state pdf to be easily propagated. In order to better demonstrate the results, we implemented an evaluation using a Progressive Gaussian Filter[87]. The state is Gaussian distributed and initialized with variance $\sigma^2_{x,0} = 0.01$, with three different means $\hat{x}_0 = 2, 5, \text{and } 8$. Furthermore, the measurement noise covariance matrix is $\mathbf{C}_k^v = 0.1 \cdot \mathbf{I}$, and the regularization coefficient is $\mathsf{c}_k = 0.015$. There is a single measurement for each timestep. Figure 4.6a shows the results averaged over 100 runs. We can see that, effectively, the ground truth was approximately found after 80 measurements for all initial states.

The advantage of this approach is that it does not require knowledge of any probability distribution, and thus, does not suffer from numerical instability or low robustness in cases of high uncertainty or occlusions. Furthermore, a regularization approach tends to be helpful in case of bad initialization, as it pushes the estimate away from a potential local minimum. However, this mechanism raises several challenges. First, the state will not converge to the ground truth as long as regularization is applied, as it is constantly being pulled and pushed in different directions. This can be seen in Figure 4.6a, where the final value is always slightly below 2, even for the green line which was initialized with the correct value. Second, it is difficult to obtain an appropriate value for the regularization coefficient c_k, as its relationship to the shape characteristics, measurement uncertainty, and process noise is not intuitive. This issue is made more difficult by the fact that all of these factors may change over time. Furthermore, in practice the specific mechanism for regularization and the selection of the coefficients are generally ad-hoc, and thus, cannot be generalized and may need to be reconfigured for each scenario.

In literature, the idea of 'pulling' and 'shrinking' a shape is, as mentioned before, a staple in active contours[124]. In the context of shape representation using Gaussian processes, it serves a similar function as the 'forgetting factor' in [29], which makes the shape flatter. The idea of a shrinking coefficient has also been used in motion models, for example in the Singer acceleration model [126]. Finally, in contrast to approaches that 'forget' shape information either by increasing the state uncertainty or artificially reducing the number of observed measurements, such as in [16, 33], the idea presented here is meant to be interpreted as an intuitive geometrical function applied on the state.

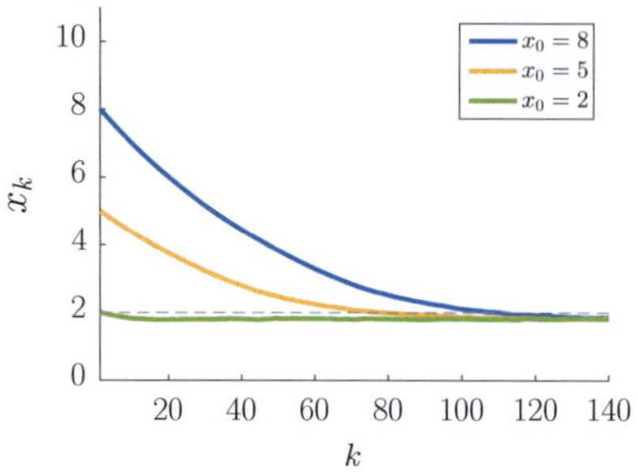

(a) Length using GAM with an active model, $c_k = 0.015$.

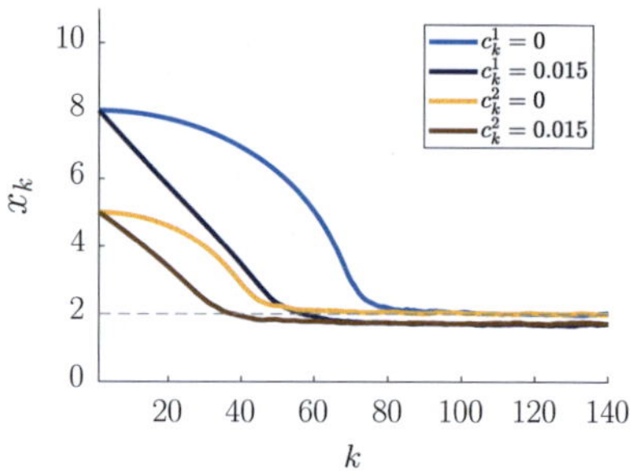

(b) Length using RHMs with and without active models.

Figure 4.6: Length estimates at a given timestep, using a single measurement per update, for GAMs and ARHMs. While RHMs can estimate the length on their own, the additional application of active models reduce the time until convergence. Horizontal dotted line denotes ground truth of 2.

4.4 Active Random Hypersurface Models

We define an ARHM as a random hypersurface model which also employs an active model. In Section 4.2 we noted how RHMs solved the extent problem, and in Section 4.3 we described many ways in which active models may raise challenges which have to be addressed. This raises the question of why would it be beneficial to combine both models. The problem is that the scenarios previously considered only take into account theoretical aspects and do not contemplate challenges present in real-life environments such as bad initializations, outliers, incorrect models for sensors and motions, or occlusions. These practical issues reduce robustness and can easily cause the estimator to become stuck in a local minimum or even diverge, in particular for the more complex shape models presented in the following chapters. This serves as a motivation to analyze the potential benefits of using active models, for example right after initialization or in a low information situation.

We will now present an example scenario where it helps to combine RHMs with active models, using the same rectangle setup as in Section 4.3. The main idea is to emulate a bad initialization far from the ground truth, i.e., with initial state means $\hat{x}_0 = 5$ and 8, and variance $\sigma^2_{x,0} = 0.001$, which is 100 times more certain than in Figure 4.6a. The results are presented in Figure 4.6b. The light blue and yellow lines denote RHMs without an active model (i.e., $\mathsf{c}_k = 0$), and can be compared with the blue and yellow lines from Figure 4.6a which employed GAMs. The slowness in convergence at the beginning is evident, due to the very low uncertainty of the initial state. However, it is also interesting to note that RHMs still converged faster than GAMs with active models, which can be explained by the transformation parameter using the correct distribution, which is unfortunately often not known in real-life scenarios. Then, we proceeded to enable active models with $\mathsf{c}_k = 0.015$, which in effect multiplied the width by 0.985 after each measurement. In this case, we see that convergence is much faster (dark blue and yellow lines), reducing the number of required timesteps by about 25%. We also observe, as we explained in Section 4.3, that a permanent active model does not permit the estimator to converge to the true value, as it is constantly pushing it towards a given direction. However, this artifact did not cause much damage, as the final value is barely below the ground truth, ensuring that RHMs will rapidly recover after regularization is deactivated.

4.5 Conclusions

In this brief chapter we explored the extent problem, which appears when estimating filled shapes using GAMs. This issue arises whenever multiple states produce the same sources, and thus, an estimator cannot differentiate between multiple states if they all contain the ground truth. This artifact will, in turn, usually cause the estimator to diverge. We presented two main approaches to deal with this issue. On the one hand, RHMs treat complex shapes as the transformations of simple shapes, in effect dividing the representation of the target shape in two parts, one to be described with GAMs, and the other to be modeled as an SDM. This allows for the implementation of efficient and robust estimators, as the probabilistic component only affects the transformation parameter. On the other hand, active models draw ideas from active contours and snakes, and apply a geometric force on the shape as part of a regularization step. The implementation is generally simple, usually as a linear transformation, and can be applied independently from the update step and other prediction steps. While both of these ideas address the extent problem on their own, we also saw the advantage of combining them in the form of ARHMs. We also showed simple synthetic evaluations in order to validate the presented ideas. The following chapters will present more practical applications where ARHMs are used as key components.

CHAPTER 5

Level-set ARHMs

While the previous chapters explored the theoretical background of extended object tracking, we will now present an implementation of these ideas that can be used in practical scenarios. To achieve this, we introduce *Level-set Active Random Hypersurface Models* (Level-set ARHMs), a novel technique for shape and pose estimation that can deal with arbitrary targets, improving on state-of-the-art approaches, which usually deal exclusively with convex or star-convex shapes. Being an implementation of ARHMs, it builds upon the concepts presented in Chapter 4, and can be used both for filled shapes or path boundaries. The content presented here is based on work published by the author in [154, 156], and its ideas were further explored in [155]. This chapter is structured as follows. First, we present a short discussion of the problem we are trying to solve and explain the gaps in state-of-the-art literature that our contribution is addressing. Then, we introduce our novel technique for tracking arbitrary non-convex shapes, which builds upon the ideas of RHMs and implements the transformation mechanism using level-sets. We will also discuss the advantages and the pitfalls of this formulation, in particular with relation to robustness and accuracy. Finally, we refine these ideas by combining them with active models, which leads to Level-set ARHMs.

5.1 Motivation

The field of EOT is generally concerned with sparse measurements and low measurement quality, leading to a focus on *parametric* representations, which approximate a target as simple shapes with a small amount of parameters. This stands in contrast to approaches in computer vision, which employ techniques such as occupancy grids [11] or voxel trees [127], where the number of parameters is variable and usually several orders of magnitude higher. However, these increased requirements have the advantage of being able to describe and reconstruct target shapes in arbitrary detail. As sensors become capable of capturing more information about the target, it becomes necessary to bring some of this flexibility in shape representation to the field of EOT, raising the need for a probabilistic model capable of describing arbitrary, non-convex shapes, while retaining the simplicity and ease of implementation of traditional EOT estimators.

(a) Ellipse. **(b)** Z-shape. **(c)** M-shape. **(d)** H-shape.

Figure 5.1: Example shapes, which include convex, star-convex, and non-convex shapes.

Figure 5.1 shows examples of the shapes that we will consider in this chapter. EOT has traditionally focused on convex shapes, such as the ellipse in Figure 5.1a, which are easy to parametrize and estimate [104, 122, 123]. For more complex shapes, a popular mechanism to describe detailed forms is by using radial functions, explained in Definition 2.4. This allows for a shape parametrization in the form of

$$\underline{\phi}_k(\theta_k) = \underline{c}_k + r_k(\theta_k) \cdot \begin{bmatrix}\cos(\theta_k)\\ \sin(\theta_k)\end{bmatrix} \text{, for } \theta_k \in [0, 2\pi] \ ,$$

with center point $\underline{c}_k$ and radial function $r_k(\theta_k)$. While there are many possible representations for r_k in literature, such as Bézier curves in [41], functions that are periodic in 2π tend to be preferred, as they guarantee that the boundary remains continuous everywhere. The following three types of radial functions stand out.

- *Piecewise linear functions* define the boundary at a set support angles $\theta_k^1, \cdots, \theta_k^n$, and approximate the remaining parts as a closed polygonal chain joining the contiguous vertices $\underline{\phi}_k(\theta_k^i)$ and $\underline{\phi}_k(\theta_k^{i+1})$. An application can be found in [40].
- *Fourier series* use boundaries that are the result of a sum of translated and scaled trigonometric functions. This naturally ensures that the boundary is both periodic and smooth. Implementation details can be found in Appendix 9.5.2 and works that use this parametrization include [27, 162, 153, 28].
- *Radial Gaussian processes* employ, as the name suggests, a radial function based on ideas from Gaussian processes (GP). The periodicity of the boundary can be guaranteed by using a periodic covariance function, such as a $\sin(\,\cdot\,)$ function [29]. An example implementation can be found in Appendix 9.5.3.

However, these representations are only appropriate for star-convex shapes, as for arbitrary shapes, such as the Z-shape in Figure 5.1b, there is no guarantee that all points on the boundary can be traversed by a radial function. Figure 5.2 shows estimates of a real-life cardboard Z-shape captured with a Kinect sensor, using Random Matrices (Figure 5.2a), a GP RHM (Figure 5.2b), and a Fourier RHM (Figure 5.2c). It can be seen that these shapes overestimate the extent in most directions, and thus, they will yield inappropriate results in scenarios where accurate rotations or translations are needed. Given that this sort of shapes appear often in practical scenarios, such as the contour of an airplane or the silhouette of a person, we observe that there is a need in state-of the art for more flexible shape estimation techniques.

The objective of this chapter is to implement an ARHM to estimate arbitrary filled shapes, independent of whether they are convex or not (as in Figure 5.2d). However, the major challenge is that we cannot use radial functions, which, as we saw in Section 4.3, had the major advantage of allowing for an extremely straightforward implementation of RHMs. Therefore, if we are going to develop an alternative parametrization for arbitrary shapes, it is indispensable to first propose a corresponding transformation mechanism that is just as easy to implement, without imposing any requirement of star-convexity. The next section explores a solution to this challenge.

5.2 RHMs with Level-sets

In this section, we aim to derive a transformation mechanism for arbitrary shapes that retains the same simplicity as the RHMs with radial functions from Section 4.3. This will in turn lead to a measurement equation that is easy to evaluate, from which a robust likelihood function can be obtained. In order to achieve this, we propose as transformation mechanism the use of level-sets (see Definition 3.1) of the signed Euclidean distance $\varphi_k^{se}(\,\cdot\,)$ (see Definition 2.3). As a reminder, the signed Euclidean distance of a point $\underline{p}_k \in \mathbb{R}^d$ is the distance to the nearest point in the shape $\mathcal{S}_k^x$, but if $\underline{p}_k$ is inside the shape, we set the sign to negative. Furthermore, a level-set $\mathcal{L}_k(l_k)$ is the set of all the points where the shape function returns the value l_k (see Figure 5.3). Given that the target shape is compact, i.e., closed and bounded, we know that when we evaluate the points of $\mathcal{S}_k^x$ in the shape function, there exists somewhere a minimum value of

$$\varphi_k^{min} := \min_{\underline{p}_k \in \mathcal{S}_k^x} \varphi_k^{se}(\underline{p}_k) \; .$$

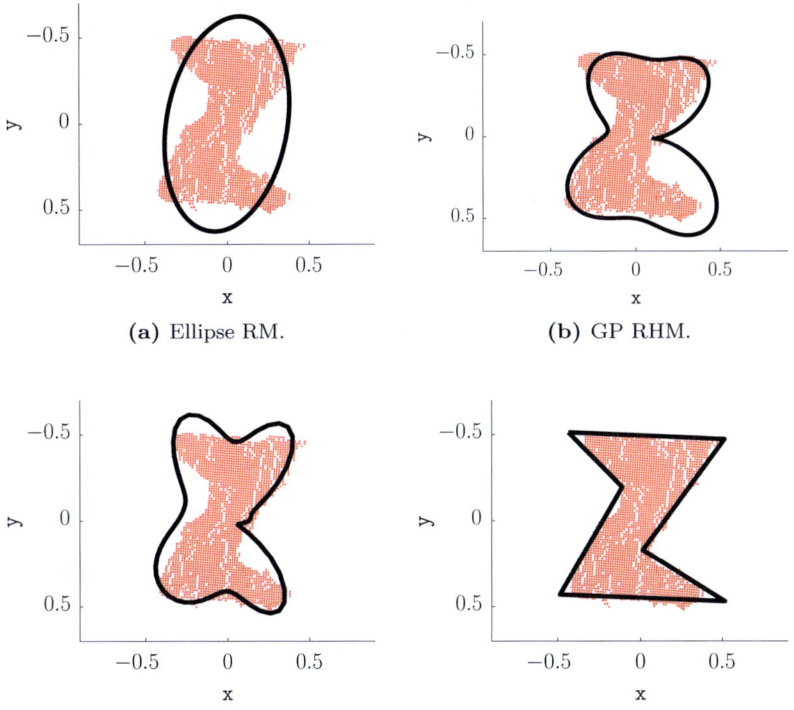

(a) Ellipse RM.

(b) GP RHM.

(c) Fourier RHM.

(d) Level-set ARHM.

Figure 5.2: A real Z-shape target made of cardboard as observed with a Kinect depth camera (red points). Note the irregular edges and outliers. Approximations using state-of-the-art techniques and our proposed shape model are illustrated in black.

This value can be interpreted as the (negative) height of the peaks in Figure 5.3. We can now define the slice shape corresponding to a given t_k using level-sets, in the form of

$$\begin{aligned}\mathcal{S}_k^x(t_k) &= \mathcal{L}_k(t_k \cdot \varphi_k^{min}) \\ &= \left\{\underline{p}_k \in \mathbb{R}^d \,|\, \varphi_k^{se}(\underline{p}_k) = t_k \cdot \varphi_k^{min}\right\} .\end{aligned}$$

In order to visualize these slices, we can employ a technique used with level-sets that consists of shifting a horizontal plane vertically and seeing where it intersects the shape function. An example level-set (and the shifted plane) can be seen in red in Figure 5.3. The resulting slices for the Z-shape and the M-shape can be seen in Figure 5.4. This slice mechanism is related in some ways to the one presented previously in Section 4.2 for star-convex shapes, but there is a critical difference. Previously, $t_k = 0$ represented a scale of 0, i.e., the center point, and $t_k = 1$ yielded the boundary itself. However, here the situation is flipped. Thus, on the one hand, $t_k = 0$ returns the level-set where the shape function is 0, which by definition is the boundary itself. On the other hand, $t_k = 1$ represents the points where the shape function is minimal, which as Figure 5.3 shows are the innermost points. Nonetheless, we observe that we can still describe the entire shape interior by using the range $t_k \in \big[0, 1\big]$. For convenience, in the following we will use $\mathrm{T}_k := \big[0, 1\big]$.

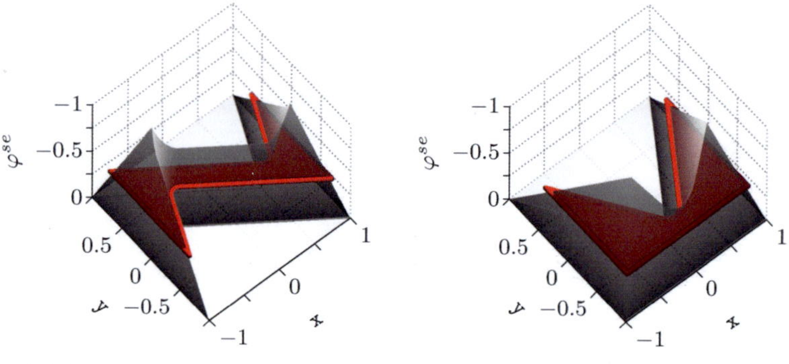

(a) Shape function of Z-shape. **(b)** Shape function of M-shape.

Figure 5.3: Example plot of the signed Euclidean distances for the interior of a Z-shape and an M-shape. The level-set $\mathcal{L}_k(-0.3)$ is highlighted in red. The peaks correspond to the points that yield φ_k^{min}.

In order to obtain a measurement equation, we first need to discuss an appropriate shape function that is easy to extend to any individual slice. As we are working with level-sets, the most straightforward approach is to use signed Euclidean distances. However, using this mechanism raises two issues. On the one hand, we would need to construct each level-set explicitly, which is usually not straightforward as was mentioned in Section 3.5. On the other hand, the projections do not necessarily lie on the same line, as we saw in Figure 4.2c back in Chapter 4. This is undesirable, as the collinearity allows for a strong simplification of the measurement equation.

In order to address this problem, we will use the following approximations. In essence, we will start with a simple GAM with the form

$$0 = \varphi_k^{se}(\underline{y}_k - \underline{v}_k, t_k) \; . \tag{5.1}$$

For this derivation, we will at first ignore the sign of the shape function. As we are working with Euclidean distances to the shape, it follows for any $\underline{p}_k \in \mathbb{R}^d$ that the shape function is equal to its distance to the projection $\underline{\pi}_k(\underline{p}_k, t_k)$, i.e.,

$$\begin{aligned} \varphi_k(\underline{p}_k, t_k) &= \left\| \underline{p}_k - \underline{\pi}_k(\underline{p}_k, t_k) \right\| \\ &= \left\| \underline{p}_k - \underline{\pi}_k(\underline{p}_k) + \underline{\pi}_k(\underline{p}_k) - \underline{\pi}_k(\underline{p}_k, t_k) \right\| \; , \end{aligned}$$

where $\underline{\pi}_k(\underline{p}_k)$ represents the projection to the boundary, added and subtracted in the second line as an auxiliary term. We will now introduce the strong approximation that $\underline{p}_k$ and its projections $\underline{\pi}_k(\underline{p}_k)$ and $\underline{\pi}_k(\underline{p}_k, t_k)$ are collinear. This is a useful assumption, as it allows us to say that

$$\varphi_k(\underline{p}_k, t_k) \approx \left\| \underline{p}_k - \underline{\pi}_k(\underline{p}_k) \right\| + \left\| \underline{\pi}_k(\underline{p}_k) - \underline{\pi}_k(\underline{p}_k, t_k) \right\| \; .$$

Then, we observe that this expression can be simplified even further. On the one hand, the left term is simply the shape function of the boundary, i.e., $\varphi_k(\underline{p}_k)$. On the other hand, the right term is the distance between $\underline{\pi}_k(\underline{p}_k, t_k)$ and the boundary, which can be easily obtained from the fact that this point lies on the level-set $\mathcal{L}_k(t_k \cdot \varphi_k^{min})$. Using the definition of a level-set, it follows that

$$\varphi_k(\underline{p}_k, t_k) \approx \varphi_k(\underline{p}_k) + t_k \cdot \varphi_k^{min} .$$

While these terms hold for Euclidean distances, we can easily extend these same ideas for signed Euclidean distances too. This allows us to plug these results into (5.1), and obtain the simplified measurement equation

$$\begin{aligned} 0 &= \varphi_k^{se}(\underline{y}_k - \underline{v}_k, t_k) \\ &\approx \varphi_k^{se}(\underline{y}_k - \underline{v}_k) + t_k \cdot \varphi_k^{min} \\ &= h(\underline{x}_k, \underline{y}_k, \underline{v}_k, t_k) . \end{aligned} \tag{5.2}$$

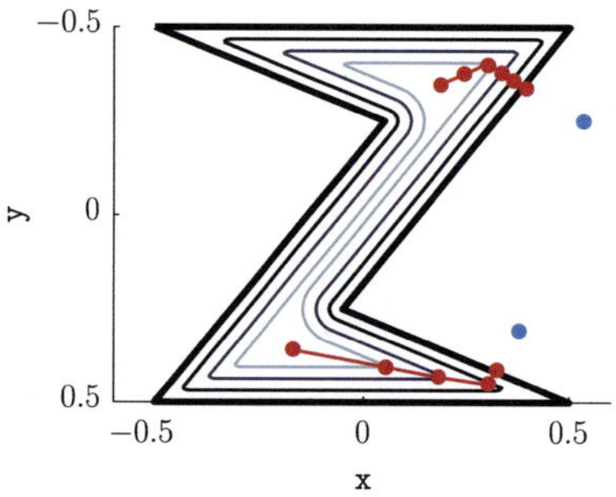

(a) Example slices of Z-shape.

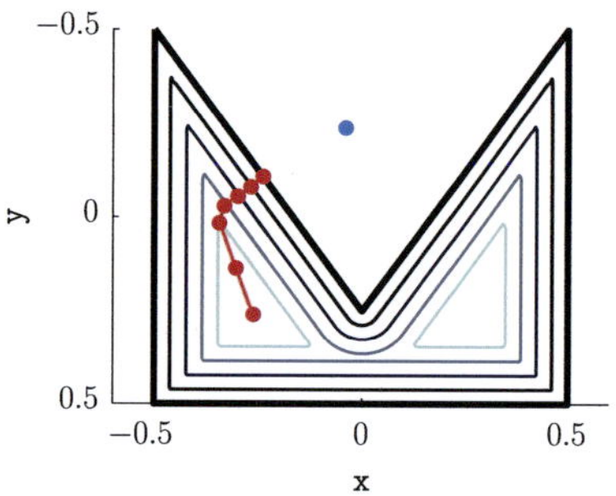

(b) Example slices of M-shape.

Figure 5.4: Example slices for the interior of a Z-shape and an M-shape, constructed using level-sets. This can be contrasted with the slices using scaling from Figure 4.2, and note that level-sets do not necessarily shrink to a single point. In particular, they can consist of unconnected paths, as can be seen in light gray for the M-shape. In blue, example measurements. In red, the slice projections.

We can make three observations. First, note that this measurement equation only requires us to evaluate the measurement on the shape function once, as the term t_k appears outside of it. Second, we can apply the same refinement on (5.2) as we did with GAMs in (2.26), in order to avoid applying the noise term $\underline{v}_k$ twice [156]. Third, we see that this formulation allows for a PIM bias correction term that is independent of the slice [56, 156]. However, in practice, we cannot say that this approximated model holds completely, as the three considered points are often not collinear. This can be clearly seen in Figure 5.4, which shows example measurements (in blue) and their slice projections (in red). It becomes evident that the projections are only collinear to the measurement in the outer parts of the shape. Nonetheless, as the evaluation will show, even with these compromises the proposed estimators still produce accurate results.

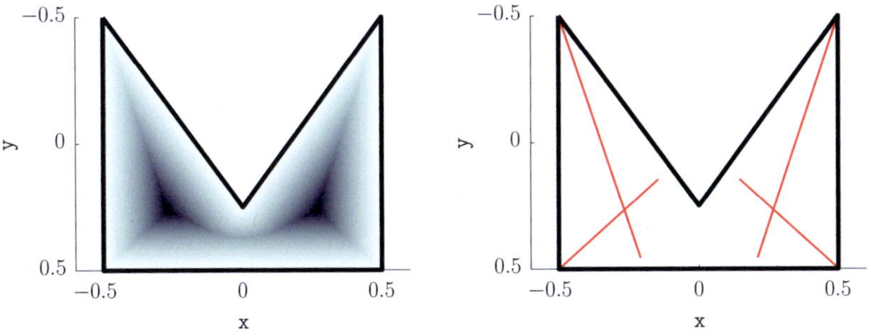

(a) Shape function, darker means lower. **(b)** Angle bisectors.

Figure 5.5: Illustration of how the intersection of angle bisectors can be used to find the minimum of the shape function. Shape function plotted only for the interior.

5.3 Shape Representation

We are now interested in finding a flexible representation capable of describing a variety of shapes such as those in Figure 5.1. As a key requirement, this shape model must allow for a fast calculation of the term φ_k^{min}. To achieve this, we propose to use an n-polygonal chain, i.e., a closed polygon of n vertices. The state takes the form

$$\underline{x}_k = \left[\underline{b}_{k,1}^\top, \cdots, \underline{b}_{k,n}^\top\right]^\top , \tag{5.3}$$

i.e., a list of vertices $\underline{b}_{k,i} \in \mathbb{R}^2$ stacked vertically. A polygonal representation has the advantage of allowing for an easy calculation of the projection, which is equivalent to the most likely source as described in Appendix 9.2.4. This algorithm works in $\mathcal{O}(n)$. Finally, a polygon also allows for an easy calculation of φ_k^{min}. This can be seen by observing Figure 5.5a, where it is clear that the shape function descends the fastest along the bisectors, i.e., the lines at the middle angle between two edges. Thus, by plotting the bisectors inside the shape (Figure 5.5b), we can see that the point that yields φ_k^{min} is always one of the intersections. While this requires $\mathcal{O}(n^2)$ steps, the vertices whose bisectors generate the minimum generally remain the same and can be cached, so that in practice this calculation can be done in constant time.

5.4 Transformation Parameter

In order to use the derived measurement equations, it is first necessary to find a proper distribution for the transformation parameter t_k. As in SDMs, this is an important aspect, as an incorrect assumption can lead to estimation bias or lack of robustness. Assuming no other information is known, it is a reasonable assumption to say that measurement sources are uniformly distributed on the shape, as was done in Section 2.4. Based on this, we can simply model all possible sources as a random variable $\underline{z}_k$ uniformly distributed in $\mathcal{S}_k^x$. Then, by propagating it through

$$t_k = \frac{\varphi_k^{se}(\underline{z}_k)}{\varphi_k^{min}} , \tag{5.4}$$

we can obtain a distribution for t_k. However, this approach requires knowing the ground truth shape, and even then, an exact solution is unfortunately intractable for most shapes. Instead, we will explore an alternative mechanism. We take as starting point the distribution proposed by [122] for circular shapes, i.e.,

$$p(t_k) = 2 \cdot (1 - t_k) \ . \tag{5.5}$$

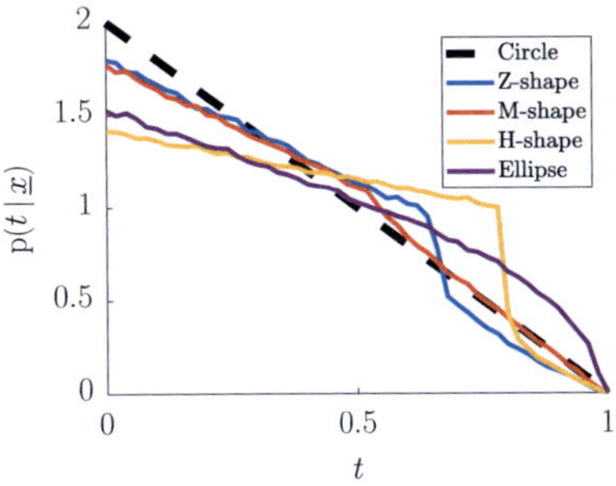

(a) Empiric distributions.

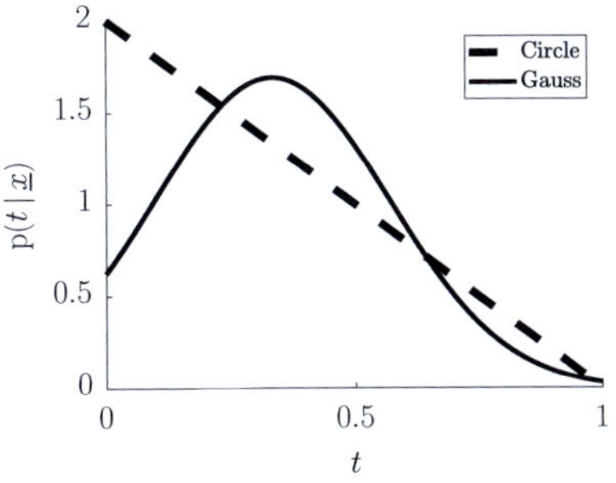

(b) Gaussian approximation.

Figure 5.6: Empiric distribution of the transformation parameter for a Z-shape, H-shape, M-shape, and an ellipse based on a uniform source distribution, together with a Gaussian approximation. The distribution for a circle (dotted black line) is taken as reference. The subindex k is omitted for legibility.

This distribution can be seen in Figure 5.6a as the black dotted line. We will now calculate the empiric distribution of t_k for the shapes in Figure 5.1, by drawing 10^6 sources uniformly from the corresponding shapes and propagating them through (5.4). It can be seen that, while they take different forms, all of them approximately follow the same distribution as the circle. However, for the narrower shapes such as the ellipse or the H-shape, it skews slightly towards a uniform distribution, i.e., $p(t_k) = 1$. Nonetheless, we can conclude that, in general, (5.5) is a safe approximation for most shapes.

Note that, in many cases, the triangle distribution from (5.5) cannot be used directly, for example when employing estimators based on LRKFs, as they assume Gaussian distributions. In order to address this, we can approximate t_k as also being Gaussian distributed (Figure 5.6b). By moment matching, this takes the form of

$$p(t_k) \approx \mathcal{N}\left(t_k; \frac{1}{3}, \frac{1}{18}\right) . \tag{5.6}$$

5.5 Active Models

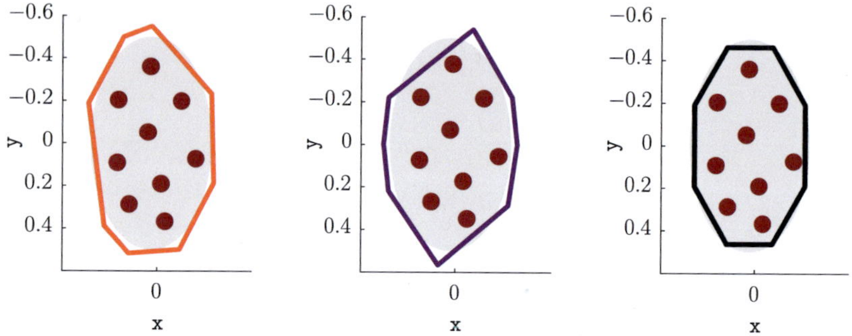

(a) Estimate A. **(b)** Estimate B. **(c)** With active model.

Figure 5.7: Example showing how the ambiguous polygonal representation of a shape raises the need for regularization. Ellipse ground truth in gray. If there are few sources (red), then both the orange and the purple polygons cover all sources. If the process noise is high, the state can 'glide' between different representations, causing instability. Active models, however, yield a more regular and robust representation.

In Section 5.3, we modeled the state as consisting on the individual vertex positions stacked together. While this allows for an extremely flexible representation, in this section we want to discuss an egregious side effect of this approach. As a reminder, when we discussed GAMs with filled shapes in Section 2.5, we concluded that we should avoid situations where multiple states produce shapes with the same sources, as this invariably leads to ambiguities and other problems during estimation. Unfortunately, this artifact can also appear with RHMs under certain circumstances, as illustrated in Figure 5.7. In this scenario, we try to approximate the ellipse (gray) by using a polygon with six sides, but we observe that both the Estimate A (Figure 5.7a) and the Estimate B (Figure 5.7b) cover more or less the same area. If the number of measurements (red) is particularly low, then for the estimator both shapes are approximately equivalent. More egregiously, the vertices can slide around the ellipse and still cover most sources, which in turn produces a destabilizing ambiguity similar to that of filled shapes, especially when the process noise is high. In the worst case scenario, the edges will cross or collapse into a point, leading to a situation from which the estimator cannot recover. Of course, a potential solution would be to introduce shape-specific constraints on the vertex positions based on a priori knowledge, or switch to a more appropriate representation without this ambiguity. However, this goes against the basic idea of this thesis, which is that the proposed shape and association models should be usable with any shape complexity and level of uncertainty, as there is no guarantee of any a priori knowledge.

In essence, we observe that this artifact is similar to the extent problem, which we addressed in Section 4.3 using ideas from active contours. We can apply the same concepts here by introducing a shape dynamic model where each vertex slowly pulls its neighbors towards itself. Using a regularization coefficient $0 \leq \mathsf{c}_k \ll 1$, we apply the following operation for each vertex $1 \leq j \leq n$,

$$\begin{aligned} \underline{b}^r_{j,k} &= \underline{b}_{k,j} + \mathsf{c}_k \cdot \left(\underline{b}_{k,j-1} - \underline{b}_{k,j}\right) + \mathsf{c}_k \cdot \left(\underline{b}_{k,j+1} - \underline{b}_{k,j}\right) \\ &= \mathsf{c}_k \cdot \underline{b}_{k,j-1} + (1 - 2\mathsf{c}_k) \cdot \underline{b}_{k,j} + \mathsf{c}_k \cdot \underline{b}_{k,j+1} \ , \end{aligned}$$

where $j-1$ and $j+1$ wrap around the interval $\left[1, n\right]$, and $\underline{b}^r_{k,j}$ is the regularized vertex position. It can be seen that this operation is linear in relation to each vertex $\underline{b}_{k,j}$, and in consequence, in $\underline{x}_k$ too. This means that we can aggregate the vertex operations into a matrix

$$\underline{x}^r_k = \mathbf{A}^{reg}_k(\mathsf{c}_k) \cdot \underline{x}_k \ , \tag{5.7}$$

where $\underline{x}^r_k$ is the regularized state. This allows for regularization to be implemented easily in any kind of estimator as part of a prediction step, as was done in Section 4.3. The end effect of this operation is to make the shape flatter and smoother, which has the side effect of making the edge lengths more uniform. Figure 5.7c shows the ellipse estimate after enabling the active model. We observe that this solution is more regular and robust, as the regularization keeps the vertices from gliding around the ellipse. We denote RHMs with level-sets and active models as *Level-set ARHMs*.

Note that using Level-set ARHMs do not completely eliminate ambiguities, as there are still multiple states representing similar shapes. However, by applying active models we can ensure that the modes in the likelihood are relatively far apart, thus allowing estimators such as LRKFs to simply stick to the closest mode, gaining a sufficient amount of stability. Furthermore, it is also useful to remember that this approach brings the same caveats as described in Section 4.3, such as the lack of convergence as long as the active model is in use. We will now present an evaluation to show how much of an effect these issues have in practice.

5.6 Evaluation

In this section we will present an evaluation of Level-set ARHMs. Two scenarios will be explored, which estimate a static target and a dynamic target using synthetic data. The shape being considered is a Z-shape, illustrated for example in Figure 5.4a. The recursive estimator we used was a S^2KF [88] with 13 state samples, with the measurement equation from (5.2). A sketch of how the estimator works is presented in Appendix 9.4. It is assumed that measurement sources are uniformly distributed on the shape, and thus, the transformation parameter was set as in (5.5). For simplicity, the estimator used the Gaussian approximation presented in (5.6).

An important aspect to take into consideration is the type of evaluation metric being used. As the estimated shapes are usually approximations of an unknown target that does not necessarily follow the assumed models, comparing the state parameters directly is generally not meaningful. Instead, approaches in EOT generally quantify the estimation error in function of mismatched extents or areas. However, for this specific application, commonly used metrics such as Intersection Over Union (IOU) can be misleading, as a small movement of a vertex on a sharp corner can cause the mismatched area to increase dramatically, even if the estimated shape is still visually very close. Instead, we introduce the following measure for the area error,

$$E(k) = \frac{\text{area}\left(\mathcal{S}_k^x \Delta \mathcal{S}_G\right)}{\text{area}\left(\mathcal{S}_G\right)} ,$$

where $\mathcal{S}_k^x$ is the estimated shape and $\mathcal{S}_G$ is the ground truth shape. The operator Δ is the symmetric difference, i.e., $\mathcal{S}_k^x \, \Delta \, \mathcal{S}_G$ returns the set of points which are either only in $\mathcal{S}_k^x$, or only in $\mathcal{S}_G$, but not both. The result of this operation is non-negative, but unlike the IOU, it is not bounded. Thus, for example, $E(k) = 0$ indicates a perfect match, and other values indicate how large the mismatched area is in proportion to the ground truth. Similarly, a value of $E(k) = 2$ says that the incorrect regions, i.e., those who belong to either the ground truth or to the estimate but not to both simultaneously, are twice as large as the real target.

The setup is as follows. At each timestep k, one single measurement source is drawn uniformly from the ground truth target and corrupted with zero-mean Gaussian noise. Three levels of measurement noise are considered,

- low noise with $\mathbf{C}_k^v = 10^{-4} \cdot \mathbf{I}$,
- medium noise with $\mathbf{C}_k^v = 10^{-3} \cdot \mathbf{I}$, and
- high noise with $\mathbf{C}_k^v = 10^{-2} \cdot \mathbf{I}$.

The ground truth shape is a Z-shape that fits in a square of 1 unit width, in the same fashion as in Figure 5.4a. For the polygonal representation, the number of vertices is assumed to be known a priori to be 6. As usual with LRKFs, the state is assumed to be Gaussian distributed. The shape parameters of the state mean $\underline{\hat{x}}_0$ are initialized as an hexagon with apothem $\frac{1}{2}$, as can be seen in Figure 5.8a. Other state parameters, such as the velocities, are set to 0. The state covariance matrix is initialized as $\mathbf{P}_0 = 10^{-2} \cdot \mathbf{I}$.

5.6.1 Static Scenario

For the static scenario, we measure how the proposed Level-set ARHMs can estimate a non-moving Z-shape. The state has the form presented in (5.3). At each timestep, the estimation procedure consists of an update step incorporating the generated measurement $\underline{y}_k$ and a prediction step determined by the system equation

$$\underline{x}_{k+1} = \mathbf{A}_k^{reg}(\mathsf{c}_k) \cdot \underline{x}_k + \underline{w}_k \ ,$$

using the regularization matrix from (5.7) with $\mathsf{c}_k = 10^{-4}$ and with a Gaussian distributed, zero-mean process noise term $\underline{w}_k$ with covariance matrix $\mathbf{Q}_k = 10^{-5} \cdot \mathbf{I}$. Figure 5.11a shows the area error results averaged over 20 runs, while Figure 5.8 illustrates a representative run with intermediate results as the shape is being estimated. Note that the figure shows multiple measurements only as illustration, given that just a single measurement was used per timestep.

From Figure 5.11a it can be seen that the estimator has converged at about 1100 measurements. However, the area error never reached 0, as a consequence of three factors. First, the regularization approach was not disabled for the sake of evaluating its effects. Of course, it is highly recommended to do so once it is known that the state is close to converging. Second, the assumed distribution of t_k does not match the true pdf perfectly, as was shown in Figure 5.6a. Finally, the fact that we used a simple GAM, instead of a more complex PIM, means that the results are slightly biased. However, as can be seen for the low noise scenario, the final results are very close (Figure 5.8f), with $E = 0.09$. Alternatively, Figure 5.12a shows the final estimate for medium noise with $E = 0.14$, and Figure 5.12b for high noise with $E = 0.40$.

We also applied this evaluation setup on an M-shape and an H-shape. Figure 5.12 shows the results after 2000 measurements, using polygons with 5 and 14 sides respectively. As before, multiple measurements are shown for illustration, as the estimator incorporated only one per timestep. The area errors for the M-shape were $E = 0.09$ for medium noise, and $E = 0.23$ for high noise. For the more complex H-shape, the area errors were $E = 0.095$ for medium noise, and $E = 0.18$ for high noise.

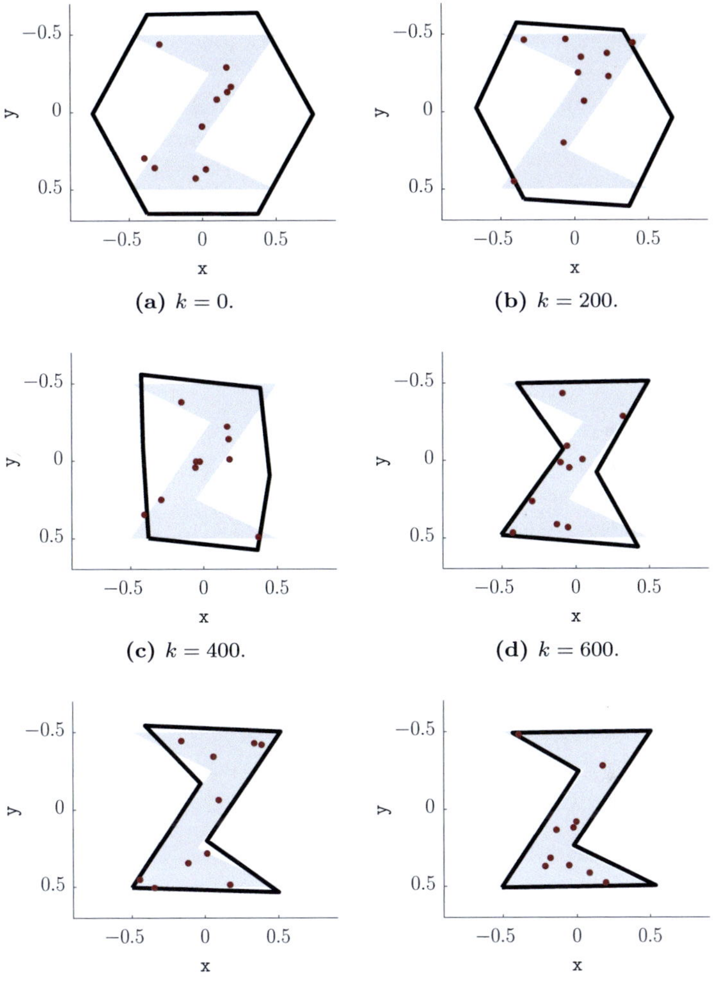

(a) $k = 0$.

(b) $k = 200$.

(c) $k = 400$.

(d) $k = 600$.

(e) $k = 800$.

(f) $k = 1000$.

Figure 5.8: Representative low noise run at different timesteps k for the static evaluation. Ground truth in light gray, estimate in black, example measurements in dark red.

One aspect that might stand out is the fact that this evaluation used 2000 measurements, which is unusually high especially compared with fitting approaches. However, it should be taken into account that the shapes are *filled*, and thus, most of the measurements did not contribute much information. An illustration of this was presented in Figure 4.4a. Thus, when the shape is small and most measurements are outside, the slope of the likelihood function is very steep. However, when most measurements are inside, the likelihood is relatively flat, meaning that the estimate benefits little from those measurements. Requiring this amount of measurements is also not unreasonable, given that sensors can yield thousands of measurements per capture as shown in Figure 5.2.

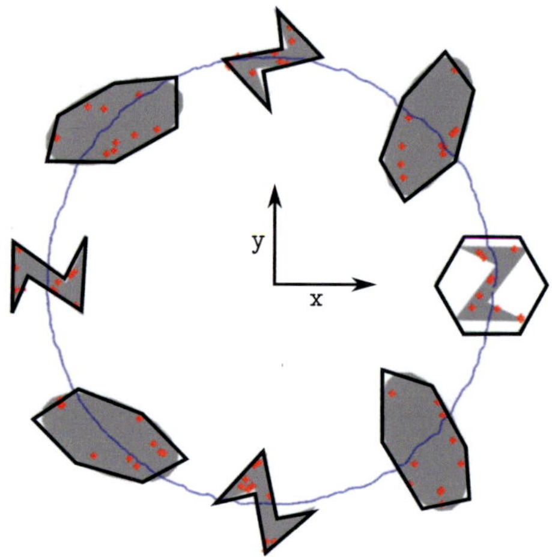

Figure 5.9: Setup and representative results of the dynamic experiment. Ground truth in gray, estimate in black, example measurements in red. The starting position is to the right at 0 degrees. Path of estimated center point is shown in blue.

5.6.2 Dynamic Scenario

For this experiment, we wanted to evaluate how Level-set ARHMs work in a dynamic scenario, where the target was not only moving but changing its shape as well. The experiment setup is illustrated in Figure 5.9. For the motion, the target rotated clockwise in a circular path describing a radius of 6 units, starting at $\left[6, 0\right]^\top$. In each timestep, the target moved along a circular arc at a speed of 3000 timesteps for every 90° degrees. Simultaneously, it was also spinning around its midpoint at an angular velocity of one turn at every 3600 timesteps. Furthermore, it was also morphing its shape as shown in Figure 5.10, back and forth from a Z-shape (Figure 5.10a) to an ellipse (Figure 5.10d), where each cycle took 3000 timesteps.

In order to take into account this motion, we extended the state to include a constant velocity model,

$$\underline{x}_k = \left[\underline{b}_{k,1}^\top, \cdots, \underline{b}_{k,6}^\top, \dot{\underline{b}}_k^\top\right]^\top ,$$

where $\dot{\underline{b}}_k \in \mathbb{R}^2$ represents the velocity of all vertices. At each timestep, the estimation consisted of an update step, which corrected the estimate by incorporating one single measurement $\underline{y}_k$, and a prediction step described by the system equation

$$\underline{x}_{k+1} = \mathbf{F}_k \cdot \mathbf{A}_k^{reg}(\mathsf{c}_k) \cdot \underline{x}_k + \underline{w}_k ,$$

where $\mathbf{A}_k^{reg}$ applied the regularization step from (5.7) with $\mathsf{c}_k = 5 \cdot 10^{-4}$. The system matrix $\mathbf{F}_k$ served to implement the constant velocity model by adding the velocity parameter $\dot{\underline{b}}_k$ to every vertex position. More specifically, the operation for each vertex had the form

$$\underline{b}_{k+1,j}^p = \underline{b}_{k,j}^r + \Delta T_k \cdot \dot{\underline{b}}_k ,$$

where $\underline{b}_{k,j}^r$ was the corresponding vertex after regularization, and ΔT_k was the elapsed time. Finally, the term $\underline{w}_k$ represented a zero-mean Gaussian distributed process noise term with covariance matrix $\mathbf{Q}_k = 10^{-4} \cdot \mathbf{I}$. Note that there was no explicit dynamic model for the rotation or the shape morphing.

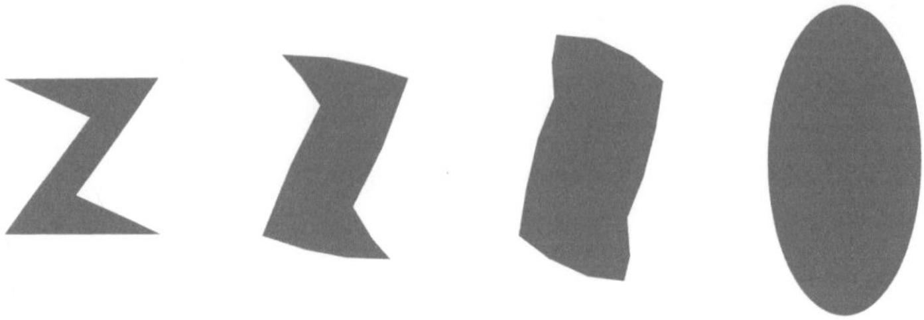

(a) $\alpha = 0^o$. **(b)** $\alpha = 15^o$. **(c)** $\alpha = 30^o$. **(d)** $\alpha = 45^o$.

Figure 5.10: Morphing stages, ranging from Z-shape to ellipse.

A representative result of the dynamic evaluation is seen in Figure 5.9, depicting the target shape and the estimates. The area errors averaged over 30 runs are shown in Figure 5.11b. One striking aspect is that the morphing stages are evident. On the one hand, the ellipses at $\left[45^o, 135^o, \dots\right]$ have a convex shape, and thus, the level-set ARHM had no problem describing it. In consequence, the area error is minimal at these points. On the other hand, the Z-shape at $\left[90^o, 180^o, \dots\right]$ was more complex, as it was difficult for the estimated polygon to bend inwards to describe the non-convex regions. The area error can be seen to be maximal for these positions. It can also be seen, by comparing the area errors between cycles, that the area error tends to increase, but stabilizes after two or three cycles. Note, however, that the errors are not much higher than the static scenario, even considering that the rotation and morphing were not explicitly modeled. The path of the center point, defined as the mean of the vertex positions, can also be seen in blue in Figure 5.9. Even at high noise levels, it never deviated more than 0.2 units, and for low noise levels, it always remained within 0.1 units. Once more, it stands out that a high number of measurements are required for estimation, explained by the fact that the shapes are filled.

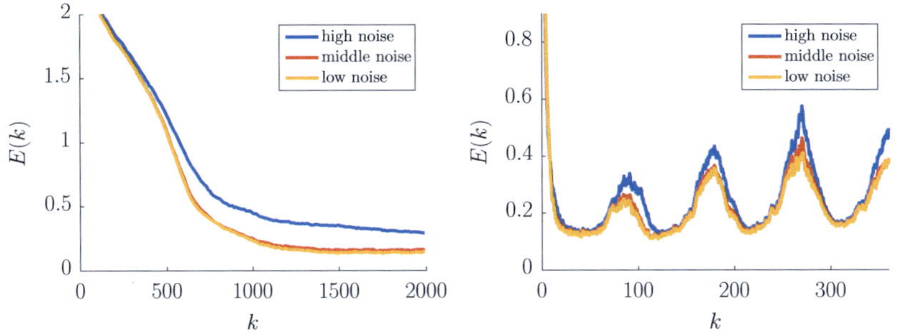

(a) Area error of static scenario. **(b)** Area error of dynamic scenario.

Figure 5.11: Area errors of the static and the dynamic scenarios.

5.7 Conclusions

In this chapter, we introduced a new shape modeling approach, called Level-set ARHMs, which allows for tracking targets with arbitrary non-convex filled shapes that cannot be described using a radial function. The key idea was to describe the shape interior by using level-sets as the RHM transformation mechanism. This allowed for a straightforward derivation of a measurement equation and a likelihood function. For representation we chose a polygonal chain, for which a distance function can easily be implemented. This flexible approach, however, results in an ambiguous state representation, where different parametrizations could cover the same sources. In order to correct this issue, we introduced an active model that slowly pulls each vertex towards its neighbors, ensuring that the side lengths are more regular and the shape becomes smoother. The evaluation shows that a static Z-shape target could be accurately estimated even when using a single measurement per time step. Furthermore, a rotating, morphing shape could also be precisely tracked as it moved, even when the shape changes were not explicitly modeled.

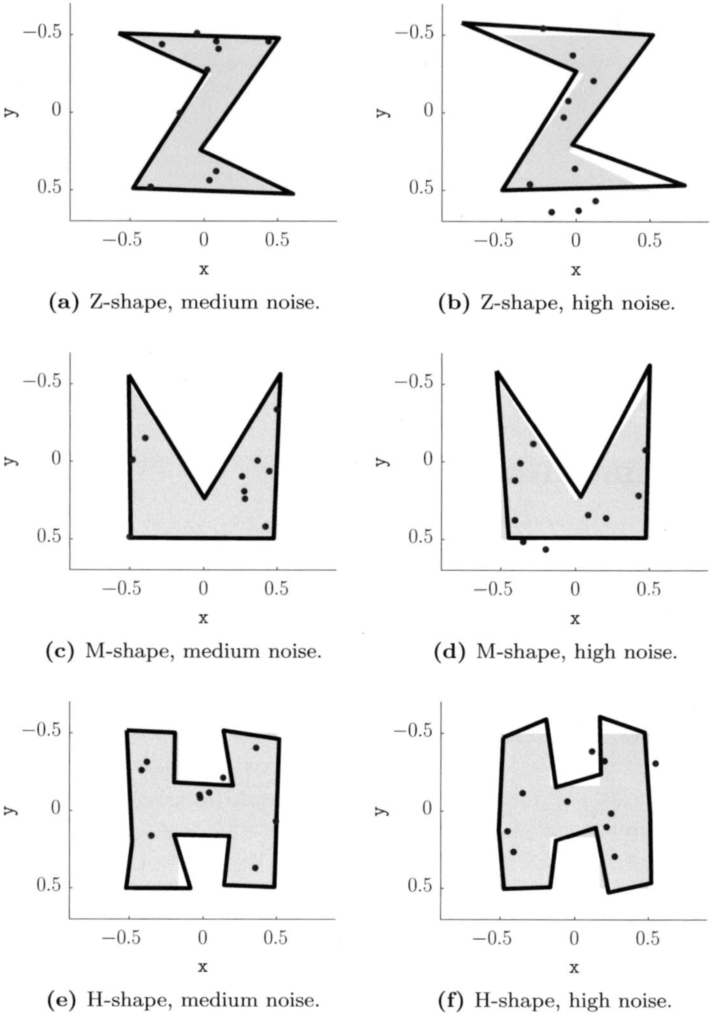

(a) Z-shape, medium noise.

(b) Z-shape, high noise.

(c) M-shape, medium noise.

(d) M-shape, high noise.

(e) H-shape, medium noise.

(f) H-shape, high noise.

Figure 5.12: Representative run at $k = 2000$ for middle and high noise scenarios. Ground truth shape in light gray, estimate in black, example measurements in red.

CHAPTER 6

Negative Information Models

This chapter introduces *Negative Information Models* (NIM), a probabilistic association model that can incorporate negative measurements carrying information about where the target *cannot* be, in addition to traditional positive measurements, which tell us where the target is located. This is, to our knowledge, the first approach in literature that estimates the pose of a target by explicitly incorporating point measurements that do not belong to it. The contributions described in this section were proposed by the author in [159, 161, 162]. This chapter is structured as follows. First, we describe a motivation of the benefits of incorporating negative measurements in addition to positive observations. Then, we develop a mathematical formulation for both types of measurements, and discuss an implementation for SDMs. Later, we extend these ideas to PIMs, and show the advantages of doing so. We conclude the chapter with an evaluation of the proposed ideas.

6.1 Motivation

For this chapter, let us consider a scenario such as Figure 6.1, where a room is being observed with a Microsoft Kinect depth camera. The idea of depth cameras is to capture an image where the intensity of each pixel represents the distance at that point between the camera and the observed scene (Figure 6.1a). This allows for the reconstruction of entire scenes in three dimensions and also raises new possibilities for target tracking, as they provide numerous and relatively accurate 3D measurements instead of reconstructing the depth from sparse two-dimensional features. In this case, the objective is to track the person in the middle of the room. However, in order to estimate the target we first need to classify which points in the captured image belong to it. This process is called *segmentation*, and can be implemented using information such as color or spatial data. The result of this process is shown in Figure 6.1b, and can be seen to yield three kinds of measurements,

- *positive* measurements, assumed to belong to the target (red),
- *negative* measurements, known **not** to stem from the target (blue), and
- *indefinite* measurements, which represent missing or incomplete information (white gaps).

In this case, negative measurements belong to the floor or to a wall behind the target, but in any case, we can be sure that the target is not there. Note that we differentiate between negative measurements, which were generated from a different source, and indefinite measurements, of which we know nothing. This does not mean that the target is not at that position, simply that we cannot decide one way or the other.

At this point, traditional tracking approaches generally discard negative measurements and exploit only positive measurements. However, knowing where the target cannot be also brings valuable information about the target state, which becomes particularly helpful in two circumstances. On the one hand, if the shape estimate is too large, a negative measurement can quickly bring the estimate back to its correct size. This can be used to solve the extent problem of GAMs and PIMs, without requiring any assumption about the source distribution or the introduction of active models. On the other hand, if a motion model causes the estimate to overshoot due to missing information, negative measurements can be used to correct the position. Both issues are extremely critical in scenarios with occlusions, where positive information about the target can be scarce or of low quality. Because of this, it makes sense to develop a mechanism that can incorporate both positive and negative measurements into the estimation procedure. This chapter proposes an approach to achieve that.

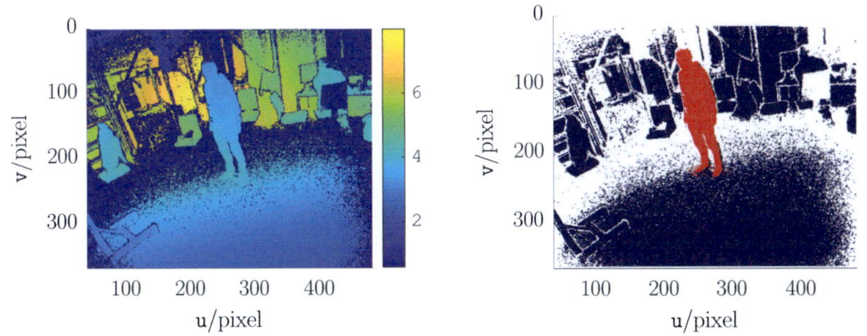

(a) Depth image, color encodes depth in meters.

(b) Segmented image.

Figure 6.1: Measurements from the target, obtained from a Kinect depth camera. In the right picture, pixels in red belong to the target, pixels in blue are known *not* to stem to the target, and white pixels (encoded with a depth value of 0) denote regions without information.

The concept of using negative measurements is related to negative information, generally defined as the event of not receiving a measurement of the target, i.e., missing a detection [128, 129]. Works treating this aspect for EOT include [128, 129, 81], with some also focusing on localization [82] and multiple object tracking [80, 130]. Note that, in this thesis, we define negative measurements as the result of actively measuring something that does not belong to the target. The explored techniques are also related to estimation and modeling with silhouettes [73, 131, 74]. However, these works deal with interval ranges and regions, while this thesis is only concerned with point measurements.

6.2 Negative Information Models

In order to incorporate both positive and negative measurements, first we need to extend the generative model in order to take into account both types of information. We assume that observed measurements consist of two components: a *position* and a *type*, and are the result of the following process. First, a source position $\underline{z}_k$ is drawn from an arbitrary part of the sensor field of view (FOV), denoted as the set $\mathcal{F}_k \subset \mathbb{R}^d$, in most cases for $d = 2$. Then, the source type $z_k^{\mathcal{T}}$ is determined as either $\odot^+$ or $\odot^-$ according to

$$z_k^{\mathcal{T}} = \text{inside}\,(\underline{x}_k, \underline{z}_k) := \begin{cases} \odot^+ & \text{if } \underline{z}_k \in \mathcal{S}_k^x \\ \odot^- & \text{if } \underline{z}_k \notin \mathcal{S}_k^x \end{cases} .$$

Finally, the position is corrupted with an additive zero-mean Gaussian noise term $\underline{v}_k$, leading to the measured position $\underline{y}_k$. The type can also be corrupted with a noise $v_k^{\mathcal{T}}$ causing it to flip to the opposite type, yielding the measured type $y_k^{\mathcal{T}}$. It is important to note that, in contrast to traditional generative models, we assume here that source positions are drawn from the entire FOV, not just the target.

Assuming that there is no corruption on the measurement type, we can describe this process using the measurement equation

$$\begin{bmatrix} \underline{y}_k \\ y_k^{\mathcal{T}} \end{bmatrix} = \begin{bmatrix} \underline{z}_k + \underline{v}_k \\ z_k^{\mathcal{T}} \end{bmatrix} . \tag{6.1}$$

In probabilistic terms, we can rewrite this as the likelihood

$$\mathrm{p}(\underline{y}_k, y_k^{\mathcal{T}} \,|\, \underline{x}_k) = \mathrm{p}(y_k^{\mathcal{T}} \,|\, \underline{x}_k) \cdot \mathrm{p}(\underline{y}_k \,|\, \underline{x}_k, y_k^{\mathcal{T}}). \tag{6.2}$$

In the following, we will assume that measurement positions are drawn uniformly from the FOV. This assumption is reasonable, given that, except in cases of artifacts or similar issues, a sensor usually receives some sort of data from its entire measured range (e.g., pixels, cells, or angles). With this in mind, let us consider first the case in (6.2) when it holds that $y_k^{\mathcal{T}} = \odot^+$. On the one hand, we see that the probability of receiving a positive measurement is proportional to the size of the target as seen by the sensor, which can be described as a function of the FOV as

$$\mathrm{p}(\odot^{+} \,|\, \underline{x}_k) = \frac{\|\mathcal{S}_k^x\|}{\|\mathcal{F}_k\|} \ . \tag{6.3}$$

On the other hand, we can simply reinterpret $\mathrm{p}(\underline{y}_k \,|\, \underline{x}_k, \odot^{+})$ as the probability of observing a position $\underline{y}_k$ for a scenario that only yields positive measurements. This is equivalent to the traditional SDMs from Section 2.4. This allows us to reuse (2.19), which yields

$$\mathrm{p}(\underline{y}_k \,|\, \underline{x}_k, \odot^{+}) = \frac{1}{\|\mathcal{S}_k^x\|} \underbrace{\int_{\mathcal{S}_k^x} \mathcal{N}(\underline{y}_k - \underline{p}_k; \underline{0}, \mathbf{C}_k^v) \ \mathrm{d}\underline{p}_k}_{:= P_k(\underline{y}_k)} \ , \tag{6.4}$$

where we introduce the auxiliary term $P_k(\underline{y}_k)$ for convenience. Plugging (6.3) and (6.4) into (6.2) we obtain

$$\begin{aligned} \mathrm{p}(\underline{y}_k, \odot^{+} \,|\, \underline{x}_k) &= \frac{\|\mathcal{S}_k^x\|}{\|\mathcal{F}_k\|} \cdot \frac{1}{\|\mathcal{S}_k^x\|} \cdot P_k(\underline{y}_k) \\ &= \frac{1}{\|\mathcal{F}_k\|} \cdot P_k(\underline{y}_k) \ . \end{aligned}$$

In order to obtain the terms for $\odot^{-}$, we can use the following identity

$$\mathrm{p}(\underline{y}_k \,|\, \underline{x}_k) = \mathrm{p}(\underline{y}_k, \odot^{+} \,|\, \underline{x}_k) + \mathrm{p}(\underline{y}_k, \odot^{-} \,|\, \underline{x}_k) \ ,$$

which follows directly from marginalizing $y_k^{\mathcal{T}}$ out of $\mathrm{p}(\underline{y}_k, y_k^{\mathcal{T}} \,|\, \underline{x}_k)$. By exploiting the previous assumption that measurement positions are drawn uniformly from the sensor, we obtain

$$\mathrm{p}(\underline{y}_k \,|\, \underline{x}_k) = \frac{1}{\|\mathcal{F}_k\|} \ .$$

This leads to

$$\begin{aligned} \mathrm{p}(\underline{y}_k, \odot^{-} \,|\, \underline{x}_k) &= \mathrm{p}(\underline{y}_k \,|\, \underline{x}_k) - \mathrm{p}(\underline{y}_k, \odot^{+} \,|\, \underline{x}_k) \\ &= \frac{1}{\|\mathcal{F}_k\|} \cdot \Big(1 - P_k(\underline{y}_k)\Big) \ . \end{aligned}$$

Finally, we can simplify the resulting terms and group them together, yielding

$$\mathrm{p}(\underline{y}_k, y_k^{\mathcal{T}} \mid \underline{x}_k) = \frac{1}{\|\mathcal{F}_k\|} \cdot \begin{cases} 0 & \text{if } \underline{y}_k \notin \mathcal{F}_k \\ P_k(\underline{y}_k) & \text{if } y_k^{\mathcal{T}} = \odot^{+} \\ 1 - P_k(\underline{y}_k) & \text{if } y_k^{\mathcal{T}} = \odot^{-} \end{cases} \tag{6.5}$$

which can be used directly as a likelihood function. As in (2.3), this expression can be extended to incorporate multiple measurements simply by multiplying their individual likelihoods. Furthermore, as the measure of $\mathcal{F}_k$ acts as a state-independent constant coefficient in the likelihood, it can generally be ignored during estimation. In consequence, the FOV does not need to be explicitly modeled in most cases. In the following, we denote approaches that incorporate both positive and negative measurements as Negative Information Models (NIMs) [159].

6.3 Discussion

NIMs, as proposed in Section 6.2, are conceptually very similar to SDMs, and in this section we want to show a preliminary evaluation to compare both ideas. The findings will, in turn, allow us to discuss the strengths and weaknesses of our NIM formulation, which serve as a motivation for the extensions presented later in this chapter. For this, we implemented an experiment where the filled rectangle in Figure 6.2a was to be tracked, in the same way as the motivational example in Section 4.1. The center was locked on the origin, the height of the rectangle was constant and known a priori, while its width on both sides was denoted by the scalar state x_k. We generated 10^5 measurements according to the generative model described in Section 6.2, using three noise covariance matrices $\mathbf{C}_k^v$ taken from $\{0.2 \cdot \mathbf{I}, 0.3 \cdot \mathbf{I}, 0.5 \cdot \mathbf{I}\}$. For reference, the field of view was $\mathcal{F}_k = [-4, 4] \times [-1.5, 1.5]$. The likelihood was evaluated based on a rectangle SDM implemented according to Section 9.2.1. Figure 6.2d shows the result of combining the corresponding likelihoods in batch.

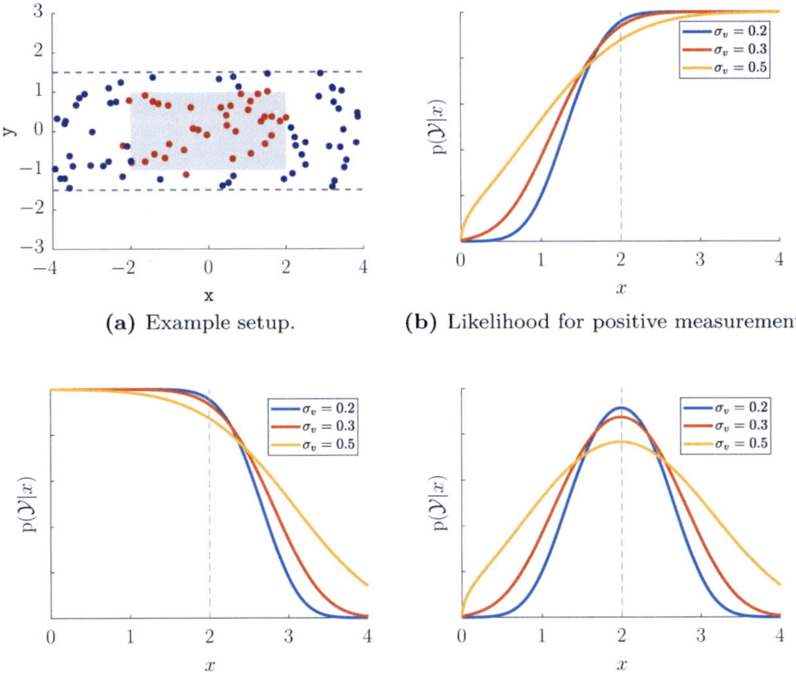

(a) Example setup.

(b) Likelihood for positive measurements.

(c) Likelihood for negative measurements.

(d) Combined likelihood.

Figure 6.2: Results of the NIM likelihood function for 10^5 samples. Example positive measurements in red, negative in blue, ground truth is $x_k^g = 2$.

When comparing the NIM likelihood in (6.5) with the SDM likelihood from (2.19), we see that the key difference is that SDMs use the measure of the shape as normalization factor, while NIMs use the size of the FOV. The consequence of this becomes clear in the likelihood function when considering only positive measurements (Figure 6.2b), where we see that the width can become arbitrarily large in a similar fashion as GAMs, as there is no mechanism that penalizes oversized estimates. When considering only negative measurements, the problem is the exact opposite, as the state can become arbitrarily small (Figure 6.2c). Only after combining both measurement types (Figure 6.2d) we can find the correct estimate. For reference, the SDM likelihood for an equivalent scenario was illustrated in Figure 4.1b. This serves to show an important contrast between both models. While SDMs only exploit positive measurements, NIMs can incorporate both positive and negative observations, but they also *require* both types to be available for correct estimation.

In this context, it makes sense to also explore how much the result changes when the proportion of positive and negative measurements changes. Figure 6.3a shows a modified setup (Setup A) where half of the positive measurements are occluded. From Figure 6.3b we can observe that the likelihood function is not substantially different, and the maximum likelihood is still on $x_k^g = 2$. Thus, we can conclude that NIMs can work with a skewed proportion of positive and negative measurements, and an 'extent problem' artifact only appears if the unbalance is extremely high.

Taking this line of discussion further, we want to explore the issue of how different occlusions can affect the estimate of NIMs. As a reminder, a challenge when working with SDMs is that they require an appropriate source distribution $\mathrm{p}(\underline{z}_k \mid \underline{x}_k)$, which is usually difficult to model as it depends on multiple factors such as occlusions, artifacts, and sensor characteristics. NIMs present a similar challenge, as we implicitly assume that sources are uniformly distributed on the target. Thus, we extended our evaluation to explore how both models behave when different parts of the target are occluded. Figure 6.3 and Figure 6.4 show the results. In Setup B (Figure 6.3c), all points in $\mathbf{x} \in [-1.5, 1.5]$ were removed. As SDMs and NIMs expect sources to be uniformly distributed in the target, it is not surprising that the SDM was biased in Figure 6.3d. However, NIMs remained unbiased and unaffected, as any oversized estimate was *quickly* corrected by the negative measurements, as evidenced by the steep gradient on the right side of the likelihood.

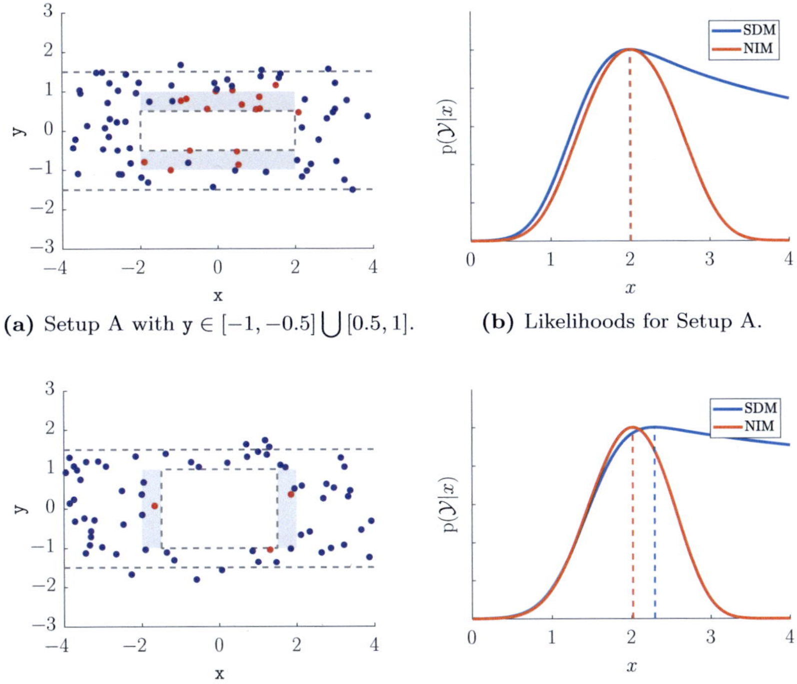

(a) Setup A with $\mathbf{y} \in [-1, -0.5] \bigcup [0.5, 1]$.

(b) Likelihoods for Setup A.

(c) Setup B with $\mathbf{x} \in [-2, -1.5] \bigcup [1.5, 2]$.

(d) Likelihoods for Setup B.

Figure 6.3: Comparison of NIM and SDM likelihood functions with 10^5 samples, showing Setups A and B. Different occlusions (white boxes with gray borders) remove the corresponding sources from view. Positive measurements in red, negative measurements in blue, ground truth is $x_k^g = 2$. On the right, the dotted lines represent the value that yields the maximum likelihood.

An even more challenging situation is presented in Setup C (Figure 6.4a), where all sources in $\left[-1.5, -0.5\right]$ and $\left[0.5, 1.5\right]$ were removed. On the one hand, SDMs, which only employ positive measurements, had no option but to assume that the target had a width of 0.5 (Figure 6.4b). NIMs, on the other hand, could differentiate between positive, negative, and missing measurements. Thus, detecting that there is a gap between 0.5 and 1.5, the likelihood became maximal but constant in that region, showing that any of these values are equally likely. This is extremely critical in Bayesian recursive estimators, as any previously correct estimate will remain unaffected in the case of occlusions, unlike SDMs which will immediately begin to shrink. This proves the robustness of NIMs against general occlusions.

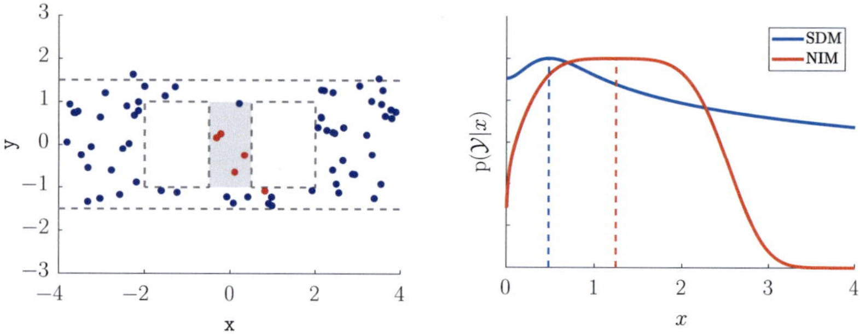

(a) Setup C with $\mathbf{x} \in [-0.5, 0.5]$.

(b) Likelihoods for Setup C.

Figure 6.4: Comparison of NIM and SDM for Setup C with the same conditions as Figure 6.3.

There is one missing issue left undiscussed, which affects both SDMs and NIMs. As also mentioned in Section 2.4, it can be very difficult to evaluate (6.5) for arbitrary targets, especially in $\log(\,\cdot\,)$ form as required by numerically stable implementations. And even for situations where such an expression is (relatively) tractable or robust for positive measurements, such as Section 9.2.1 for rectangles, there is no guarantee this also holds for negative observations in arbitrary shapes. For instance, this issue was already present in scenarios like Figure 6.2 and Figure 6.3, where the calculated likelihood is incorrectly calculated as 0 if the state is too far from the ground truth, making it impossible to obtain its logarithm. In practice, this means that a NIM-based estimator cannot work if the initial state is moderately incorrect, which strongly limits its usability. This raises the need to use the same key ideas from Section 6.2, but extend them for use with the more robust PIMs instead.

6.4 Extensions for PIMs

While SDMs can describe targets either as filled shapes or paths, until now PIMs have only been applied for shape boundaries, due to the extent problem explained in Section 4.1. However, the fact that negative measurements can be used to correct oversized estimates can be used to compensate for this weakness. This would allow for the simplicity and robustness of these models to be used with filled shapes, as an alternative to RHMs. In order to achieve this, we can extend the projection and shape functions we previously used for boundaries. However, they need to take into account that measurements now have a corresponding type, and that the shapes are now filled.

Informally, we are looking for an extended projection function $\underline{\pi}_k^n(\underline{p}_k, p_k^\tau)$ which fulfills that

- if $p_k^\tau = \odot^+$, we are looking for the nearest point to $\underline{p}_k$ inside $\mathcal{S}_k^x$, and
- if $p_k^\tau = \odot^-$, we require the nearest point to $\underline{p}_k$ outside $\mathcal{S}_k^x$.

With this in mind, we can extend any given boundary projection $\underline{\pi}_k$, such as those given in Section 2.5, by using

$$\underline{\pi}_k^n(\underline{p}_k, p_k^\tau) := \begin{cases} \underline{p}_k & \text{if } p_k^\tau = \text{inside}\left(\underline{x}_k, \underline{p}_k\right) \\ \underline{\pi}_k(\underline{p}_k) & \text{otherwise.} \end{cases}$$

In analogy, an extended shape function $\varphi_k^n(\underline{p}_k, p_k^\tau)$ must fulfill that

- if $p_k^\tau = \odot^+$, we consider the distance between $\underline{p}_k$ and the nearest point within the shape, and
- if $p_k^\tau = \odot^-$, we request the distance to the shape exterior.

In a similar fashion, we can extend any shape function φ_k by using

$$\varphi_k^n(\underline{p}_k, p_k^\tau) := \begin{cases} 0 & \text{if } p_k^\tau = \text{inside}\left(\underline{x}_k, \underline{p}_k\right) \\ \varphi_k(\underline{p}_k) & \text{otherwise.} \end{cases}$$

Based on these ideas, we can now derive a PIM for NIMs based on the ideas presented in Chapter 3. Given a measurement $\underline{y}_k$ of type y_k^τ, we can rewrite (6.1) into

$$\begin{bmatrix} 0 \\ y_k^\tau \end{bmatrix} = \begin{bmatrix} \varphi_k^n(\underline{y}_k, y_k^\tau) - \nu_k \\ \nu_k^\tau \end{bmatrix} , \tag{6.6}$$

where ν_k is the PIM correction term obtained by propagating $\underline{v}_k$ through

$$\nu_k := \varphi_k^n\left(\underline{\pi}_k^n(\underline{y}_k) + \underline{v}_k, y_k^\tau\right) , \tag{6.7}$$

and similarly, ν_k^τ is a new random variable derived by propagating $\underline{v}_k$ through

$$\nu_k^\tau := \text{inside}\left(\underline{x}_k, \underline{\pi}_k^n(\underline{y}_k) + \underline{v}_k\right) . \tag{6.8}$$

We assume that ν_k has the continuous distribution $f_k^\nu(\nu_k)$, and ν_k^τ has the discrete distribution $f_k^\tau(\nu_k^\tau)$. Finally, in the same way as PIMs, we can rewrite (6.6) probabilistically as

$$\begin{aligned} \mathrm{p}(\underline{y}_k, y_k^\tau \,|\, \underline{x}_k) &= \mathrm{p}(y_k^\tau \,|\, \underline{x}_k) \cdot \mathrm{p}(\underline{y}_k \,|\, \underline{x}_k, y_k^\tau) \\ &= f_k^\tau(y_k^\tau) \cdot f_k^\nu(\varphi_k^n(\underline{y}_k, y_k^\tau)) . \end{aligned} \tag{6.9}$$

We denote this model as NIM-PIM [162]. The distributions of (6.7) and (6.8) can be implemented by propagating $\underline{v}_k$ in a similar way as explained in Appendix 9.3. In particular, when using a Gaussian approximation proposed in Section 3.4, it also becomes straightforward to obtain the NIM-PIM likelihood function in $\log(\,\cdot\,)$ form, solving the issues of numerical stability raised by the previous approach.

$y_k^{\mathcal{T}}$ \ $z_k^{\mathcal{T}}$	$\odot^+$	$\odot^-$
$\odot^+$	$\mathrm{p}_{\mathrm{TP},k}$	$\mathrm{p}_{\mathrm{FP},k}$
$\odot^-$	$\mathrm{p}_{\mathrm{FN},k}$	$\mathrm{p}_{\mathrm{TN},k}$

Table 6.1: List of terms used to describe $\mathrm{p}(y_k^{\mathcal{T}} \mid z_k^{\mathcal{T}})$. A positive source can be detected either as positive (true positive), or as negative (false negative). A negative source can be observed as positive (false positive) or negative (true negative).

6.5 Modeling Clutter

In the previous sections, we modeled the measurement type as being undisturbed by noise. However, issues such as errors in segmentation, sensor artifacts, and other factors can cause the source type to switch during observation, leading to so-called *clutter* measurements. We model this process as being independent of the state and the position, and thus, we can describe the perturbation by means of the probability distribution $\mathrm{p}(y_k^{\mathcal{T}} \mid p_k^{\mathcal{T}})$. This term can be described using the four parameters described in Table 6.1, which fulfill the condition that they need to be non-negative and

$$\begin{aligned}
\mathrm{p}_{\mathrm{TP},k} + \mathrm{p}_{\mathrm{FN},k} &= 1 \ , \\
\mathrm{p}_{\mathrm{FP},k} + \mathrm{p}_{\mathrm{TN},k} &= 1 \ .
\end{aligned}$$

Incorporating these terms is straightforward, and can be implemented with the following steps. As with (2.18), we can extend the likelihoods (6.5) and (6.9) by marginalizing $z_k^{\mathcal{T}}$ out, i.e.,

$$\mathrm{p}(\underline{y}_k, y_k^{\mathcal{T}} \mid \underline{x}_k) = \sum_{p_k^{\mathcal{T}} \in \{\odot^+, \odot^-\}} \mathrm{p}(y_k^{\mathcal{T}} \mid p_k^{\mathcal{T}}) \cdot \mathrm{p}(\underline{y}_k, p_k^{\mathcal{T}} \mid \underline{x}_k) \ .$$

Then, as there are only four terms, we can unroll this sum and rewrite it as

$$\mathrm{p}(\underline{y}_k, \odot^+ \,|\, \underline{x}_k) = \mathrm{p}_{\mathrm{TP},k} \cdot \mathrm{p}(\underline{y}_k, \odot^+ \,|\, \underline{x}_k) + \mathrm{p}_{\mathrm{FP},k} \cdot \mathrm{p}(\underline{y}_k, \odot^- \,|\, \underline{x}_k) \text{ , and}$$

$$\mathrm{p}(\underline{y}_k, \odot^- \,|\, \underline{x}_k) = \mathrm{p}_{\mathrm{FN},k} \cdot \mathrm{p}(\underline{y}_k, \odot^+ \,|\, \underline{x}_k) + \mathrm{p}_{\mathrm{TN},k} \cdot \mathrm{p}(\underline{y}_k, \odot^- \,|\, \underline{x}_k) \text{ .}$$

6.6 Evaluation

In this section, we will evaluate the proposed NIM-PIM approach, and contrast it with other state-of-the-art techniques. Two scenarios were considered. In the first, the shape of a static target was estimated with varying degrees of occlusion. In the second, a moving target was tracked while in the presence of clutter. For the sake of brevity, as NIM-PIMs will be referred simply as 'PIMs'. The results of these experiments were as follows.

6.6.1 Static Target with Occlusions

For this experiment, we wanted to evaluate how NIMs work for shape estimation. As a reminder, NIMs are association models, in the same way as RHMs or PIMs, and do not prescribe any specific shape model. Thus, NIMs can be used with any arbitrary shape parametrization, such as Fourier series, representations based on Gaussian processes (GP), or polygons (see Section 5.1). With this in mind, we will track the star shape in Figure 6.5 using two association models, NIMs and RHMs. In order to represent this shape, we will employ star-convex approximations in the form of Fourier series and GPs. Furthermore, we will contrast how these association and shape models behave in the presence of occlusions.

The evaluation consisted of the following procedure. First, we generated $1.5 \cdot 10^5$ source positions from the field of view $\mathcal{F}_k = [-0.5, 0.5] \times [-0.5, 0.5]$. Then, we determined the position type and corrupted the position according to the generative model explained in Section 6.2. The covariance matrix of the noise term was $\mathbf{C}_k^v = 10^{-3} \cdot \mathbf{I}$, and we disabled the corruption of the noise type, i.e., $\mathrm{p}_{\mathrm{FN},k} = \mathrm{p}_{\mathrm{FP},k} = 0$. Using these measurements, we calculated the likelihood functions for the combinations of the two shape and the two association models, yielding four results: Fourier with RHMs, Fourier with NIMs, GP with RHMs, and GP with NIMs. Example implementations for the Fourier and GP shape functions can be found in Appendix 9.5.2 and Appendix 9.5.3. For the RHMs, the transformation parameter was assumed to be

$$\mathrm{p}(t_k) \approx \mathcal{N}\left(t_k; \frac{2}{3}, \frac{1}{18}\right) , \tag{6.10}$$

which approximates through moment matching the triangle distribution proposed in [122]. The state $\underline{x}_k$ consisted of

$$\underline{x}_k = \left[\underline{c}_k^\top, \alpha_k, (\underline{x}_k^s)^\top\right]^\top ,$$

where $\underline{c}_k$ was the center position, α_k the rotation, and $\underline{x}_k^s$ the shape parameters. For the Fourier series, $\underline{x}_k^s$ consisted of 9 coefficients as required by a 4th degree Fourier series, while the GP employed 8 coefficients which sampled the circle in regular intervals of $\pi/4$. For this evaluation, we are interested in the 'best possible' results for each approach, and thus, we processed all measurements simultaneously and calculated the state that yielded the maximum likelihood (ML). To achieve this, we employed as optimizer the MATLAB function fminsearch with default parameters. The starting value $\underline{x}_0$ corresponded to a circle of radius 0.5, with the remaining values set to 0.

Figure 6.5 shows the results, from which we can observe two points. On the one hand, even though neither Fourier nor GP could reproduce the star shape exactly, NIMs showed consistently a 'tighter' fit than RHMs for both shape models. This can be explained from the fact that negative measurements provided more information about the shape in narrow corners than could be obtained from positive observations alone. On the other hand, we can see that the responses for occlusions depend on both the shape models and the association models. As a reminder, NIMs exploited both positive and negative measurements, while RHMs used only positive observations but made an assumption on how they were distributed. This assumption, of course, becomes incorrect when the occlusion is enabled. As neither NIM variant needs information about the source distribution, they were highly tolerant against the occlusion. RHMs, however, failed to approximate the shape appropriately, providing different types of errors for Fourier and GP representations. This difference can be explained by taking into account the following. On the one hand, in Fourier shape functions (Figure 6.5b), all coefficients have influences on all parts of the shape, and thus, an occlusion in one region causes a change in the entire estimate. Thus, the RHM failed to approximate the shape not only in the occluded region, but on the opposite side as well. On the other hand, for GP representations (Figure 6.5d), each coefficient is related to a specific angle, and thus, only the right-hand side was affected.

6.6.2 Dealing with Clutter

The next experiment consisted on evaluating how NIMs work for estimating targets in the presence of clutter, divided in two parts: one with a static target, and another where the target was moving. The shape to be tracked was the airplane shown in Figure 6.6, with size 100×100 units^2. The setup was similar to the one presented in Section 6.6.1. At each timestep, 200 source positions were generated from a field of view $\mathcal{F}_k = [-50, 50] \times [-50, 50]$ centered on the target. The measurement position was corrupted with additive Gaussian noise with covariance matrix $\mathbf{C}_k^v = 4 \cdot \mathbf{I}$. In relation to the measurement type, two scenarios were considered, one without clutter, i.e., $\mathrm{p}_{\mathrm{FN},k} = \mathrm{p}_{\mathrm{FP},k} = 0$, and another with clutter where $\mathrm{p}_{\mathrm{FN},k} = \mathrm{p}_{\mathrm{FP},k} = 0.1$.

The state $\underline{x}_k$ had the form

$$\underline{x}_k = \left[\underline{c}_k^\top, \alpha_k, \dot{c}_k, \dot{\alpha}_k, \left(\underline{x}_k^s\right)^\top\right]^\top ,$$

where $\underline{c}_k$ was the center position, α_k the rotation, and $\dot{\alpha}_k$ the angular velocity. It was assumed that the target was moving with constant velocity, with speed $\dot{c}_k$ and direction α_k. The component $\underline{x}_k^s$ represented the shape parameters of a 7th degree Fourier series, encompassing 15 parameters.

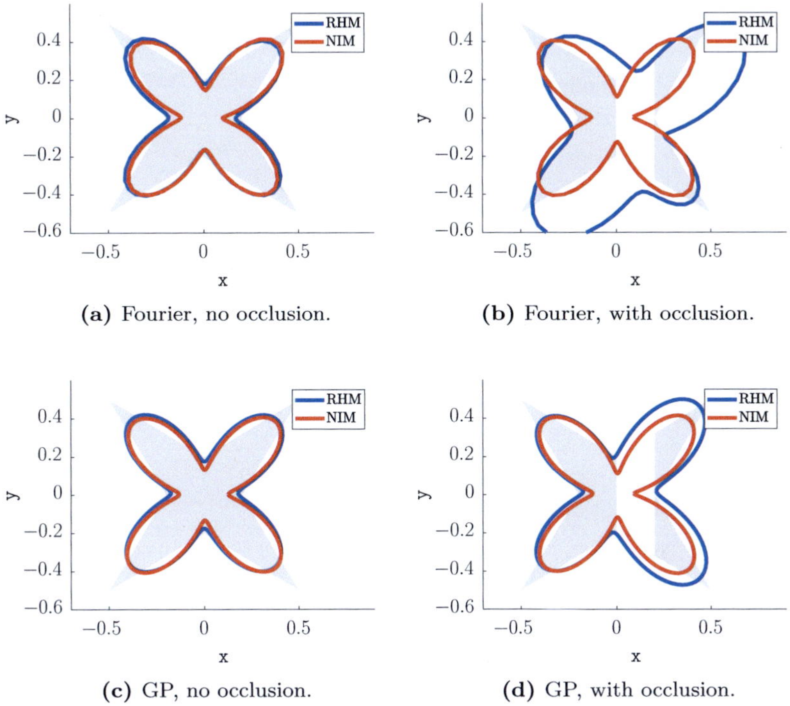

(a) Fourier, no occlusion.

(b) Fourier, with occlusion.

(c) GP, no occlusion.

(d) GP, with occlusion.

Figure 6.5: Comparison between RHM and NIM for different radial functions and occlusions. Target in light gray, Fourier star-convex approximations in red and blue.

At each timestep, we applied a prediction step based on the system equation

$$\underline{x}_{k+1} = \mathbf{F}_k \cdot \underline{x}_k + \underline{w}_k \ ,$$

where $\mathbf{F}_k$ served to apply the velocities scaled by the elapsed time, and $\underline{w}_k$ was a Gaussian zero-mean process noise term with covariance matrix $\mathbf{Q}_k = \text{diag}(1, 1, 10^{-4}, 1, \underline{1}_{15})$. For estimation, an S^{2}KF was used with 304 state samples. Two association models were compared, NIM and RHM. For the latter, the transformation parameter was approximated as shown in (6.10). For the scenario with clutter, a gating approach was employed as explained in Algorithm 9, allowing 99% of valid measurements. This implies a gating parameter of $\gamma_k = \text{chi2inv}\,(0.99, 1) \approx 6.6349$.

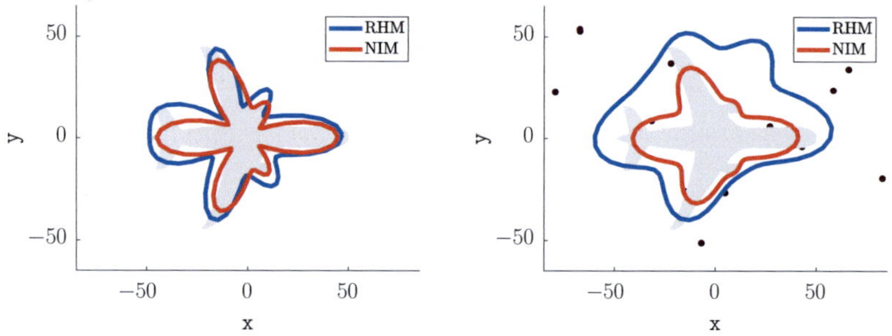

(a) No clutter. **(b)** With clutter.

Figure 6.6: Experiment with a static target. For the scenario with clutter, example clutter measurements are shown in dark red.

In order to validate the setup, the first part of the experiment considered a static target, i.e., we applied the constraint that $\dot{c}_k = \dot{\alpha}_k = 0$. Figure 6.6 shows the result, averaged over 50 runs. It can be seen that, while both models are capable of reasonably approximating the target, the NIM estimate tends to be *tighter*, i.e., closer to the target (Figure 6.6a). This is consistent with the observation made in Section 6.6.1, where we saw that negative measurements allow for a more accurate description of sharp corners. However, when clutter is enabled (Figure 6.6b), the assumption of the source distribution for the RHM fails to be appropriate, even considering that gating removes most of the false positives. Still, the NIM estimate is nonetheless capable of obtaining a reasonable shape estimate, even if it is considerable less tight than the previous scenario.

For the second part of the experiment (Figure 6.7), we considered a scenario where the target was moving along a path in the following way. First, the plane moved in a straight line starting at $\left[0,0\right]^\top$. Then, it turned in a circular arc spanning from $\left[500,0\right]^\top$ at $k = 150$ to $\left[500,-2000\right]^\top$ at $k = 750$. Finally, it moved once more in a straight line until $\left[0,-2000\right]^\top$ at $k = 900$. From the left column (Figure 6.7a, Figure 6.7c, and Figure 6.7e) we observe that both models had little trouble following the target, even considering that the constant velocity model could predict the change in rotation, but not the circular motion. However, once clutter was enabled (Figure 6.7b, Figure 6.7d, and Figure 6.7f), the source distribution for the RHM fails once more to be valid. In consequence, by $k = 800$ the RHM shape estimate (blue) had mostly diverged, with only the centroid being near the target. The NIM estimate, however, still could provide a reasonable estimate.

6.7 Conclusions

The key objective of this chapter was to find a mechanism to incorporate not only positive measurements, which tell us where the target is, but also negative observations, which let us know where the target cannot possibly be. Note that we differentiate between negative and absent measurements, i.e., we do not assume that not receiving data provides information about the target. We developed a likelihood function similar to SDMs capable of exploiting positive and negative observations, and by analyzing its behavior we showed that it was highly robust against occlusions. However, this first formulation lacked numerical stability, raising the need for alternative formulations which took ideas from the simplicity of PIMs. This led to the derivation of NIM-PIMs, a robust mechanism that was simple to evaluate, easy to implement, and could address the extent problem from traditional PIMs. The proposed ideas were evaluated with two experiments, which tested the reliability of NIM-PIMs in the presence of occlusions and clutter. In the first scenario, we showed that, unlike RHMs, NIM-PIMss made no assumptions about a source distribution, and thus, could compensate for missing measurements easily. In the second scenario, we illustrated how NIMs could make up for clutter, i.e., incorrectly segmented positive and negative measurements, while RHMs diverged even after enabling a gating mechanism. All of these results proved that incorporating negative measurements can improve the reliability, robustness, and performance of shape estimation.

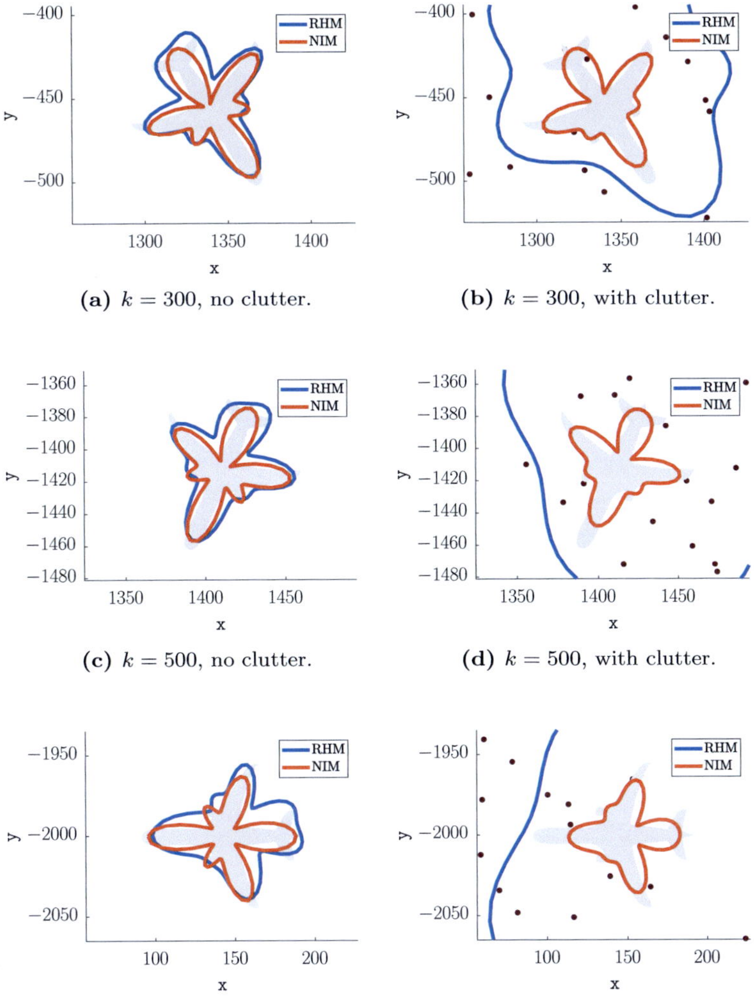

(a) $k = 300$, no clutter.
(b) $k = 300$, with clutter.
(c) $k = 500$, no clutter.
(d) $k = 500$, with clutter.
(e) $k = 800$, no clutter.
(f) $k = 800$, with clutter.

Figure 6.7: Snapshots of the experiment with a moving target. For the scenarios with clutter, example clutter measurements are shown in dark red.

CHAPTER 7

Modeling Extrusions

While previous chapters focused on two-dimensional shapes, we are now interested in extending our contributions into the three-dimensional world. This will allow the deployment of the proposed models in a wide variety of fields such as robotics, autonomous navigation, indoor localization and SLAM. In order to achieve this, we propose the use of *Extrusion Models*, a robust and straightforward construction mechanism which allows for the description of complex 3D shapes based on simple planar curves. As the emphasis on this chapter is on practical applications, when deriving mathematical formulations for these models, we will focus on how they respond to data from real-life, captured by off-the-shelf sensors such as Microsoft Kinect depth cameras. This chapter, which presents and extends ideas that the author published in [158], is structured as follows. First, we explain our motivation for this chapter in more detail. Then, we introduce a mathematical formulation for extrusions. After this, we derive extensions of the previously presented association models, in particular PIMs, RHMs, and NIMs, for work with extrusions. Finally, we present an evaluation of these concepts using real-life sensor data captured from daily life objects such as pencil cases, teapots and bottles.

7.1 Motivation

In previous chapters, we focused on EOT approaches that estimate targets as flat, two-dimensional shapes. Staying in two dimensions, even if the target being observed is three-dimensional, happens very commonly in practical scenarios and traditional literature. Historically, the main reason for this was the sensors being used. On the one hand, fields like aeronautics or maritime surveillance deal mostly with radar measurements, which yield a noisy silhouette of a target but are incapable of resolving more granular details [33]. Given that prior information on potentially available targets can be used to fill the missing information [109, 132, 133], three-dimensional data has usually not been deemed too important. On the other hand, complex shape estimation based on distance minimization has been generally related to cameras and other grid-based sensors, in fields such as robotics and autonomous driving. For these scenarios, a three-dimensional target is observed as a two-dimensional projection on a screen with relatively high resolution. Thus, computer vision techniques generally use contour curves [124] to describe the tracked object and then extrapolate three-dimensional data based on this information. The increasing ubiquity of depth sensors with low or moderate noise, however, allows for the direct incorporation of three-dimensional measurements into the estimation procedure, which in turn can provide much more accurate and robust results. This motivates the exploration of new techniques capable of exploiting all of this available information directly, while avoiding the usual pitfalls of unmanageably complex or inefficient estimation procedures.

While relatively uncommon when compared to their 2D counterparts, there are still a multitude of techniques in literature that deal with 3D targets. On the one hand, we observe that SDMs for simple shapes, such as ellipses [33], line segments [20], or rectangles (such as in Appendix 9.2.1), can be easily extended to three dimensions, but the usual problems of low robustness and numerical stability are also correspondingly increased. On the other hand, approaches based on GAMs or PIMs, such as those dealing with conics [38, 79], can also incorporate 3D measurements by adapting the distance function accordingly. For more complex targets, robust shape models need to take into account that, in most situations, individual sensors can only observe incomplete parts of the target. A common way to alleviate this issue is by exploting symmetries known a priori [149]. Otherwise, a different mechanism consists of trying to reconstruct the target non-parametrically [11, 131, 134] using captures from different angles. A critical weakness of reconstruction approaches, though, is that they assume that the target does not move, only the sensor. Furthermore, as their representation of the state is not parametric, the required memory to hold the acquired information can increase without bounds. Otherwise, for scenarios where the shape is known and only the pose needs to be found, the Iterative Closest Point [44, 135] method can be used.

(a) A: Paper roll. **(b)** B: Pencil case. **(c)** C: Teapot. **(d)** D: Wine bottle.

Figure 7.1: Four three-dimensional shapes observed in everyday life, which can be closely approximated as extrusions or general extrusions.

Nonetheless, approaches to estimate both the shape and pose of a moving three-dimensional target are scarce. In order to close this gap, we propose a mechanism called Extrusion Models, introduced in [158] and expanded in [56]. As previously mentioned, the key idea is to interpret complex 3D shapes as being constructed by shifting a simple, planar shape vertically, as can be illustrated in Figure 7.1. In this case, we observe that by displacing a circle (Figure 7.2a) along the z-axis, we can obtain a cylinder (Figure 7.2b). We denote objects constructed this way as *extrusions*. Furthermore, by applying additional transformations on the base shape as it is shifting, we can describe a larger variety of targets while retaining simple parametrizations. The end result is an estimator that retains the efficiency and robustness of two-dimensional shapes, while increasing accuracy by incorporating three-dimensional information. We will also show how the previously proposed association models, such as PIMs, RHMs and NIMs, can be easily extended to work with these shape models.

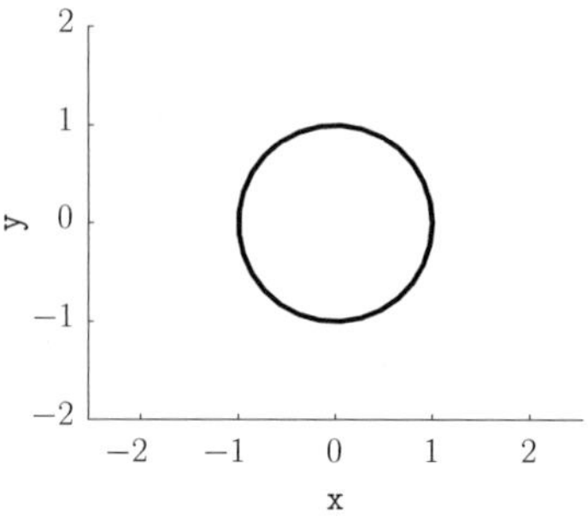

(a) Circular base shape.

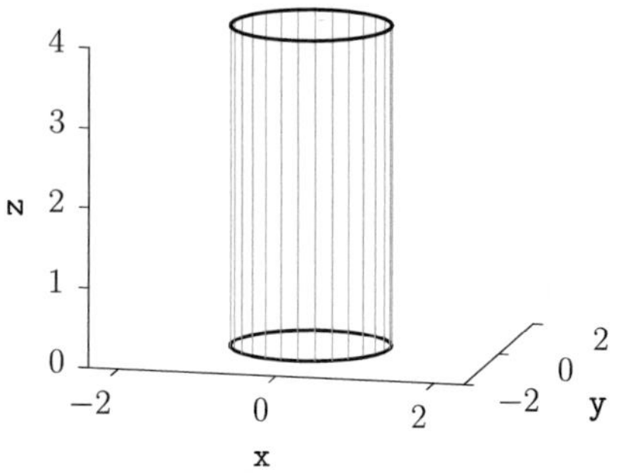

(b) Cylinder.

Figure 7.2: A circular base shape in the **xy**-plane is *extruded* into a cylinder by shifting it upwards.

7.2 General Extrusions

When deriving a formulation for extrusion models, it is useful to take into account the shapes that practical applications are likely to employ. Keeping in mind potential use in robotics and computer vision, we propose to focus on the figures illustrated in Figure 7.1. The shape in Figure 7.1a (denoted as Shape A) can be described as a cylinder, in a similar fashion as Figure 7.2b. An example parametrization for Figure 7.2b would be

$$\underline{\phi}_k(s_k, t_k) = \begin{bmatrix} \cos(s_k) \\ \sin(s_k) \\ \mathsf{h}_k \cdot t_k \end{bmatrix} \text{, for } s_k \in \left[0, 2\pi\right], t_k \in \left[0, 1\right] \text{ ,} \tag{7.1}$$

where the parameter t_k describes the shifting transformation along the axis z-axis, and h_k represents the height, which in the example case equals 4. From this example, two points stand out. First, we see that (7.1) describes only the lateral surface of the extrusion. We will focus on this part of the shape, as the bottom and top caps can be simply treated as two additional disks, as seen in [56]. Second, we note that the axis is a straight line orthogonal to the planar shape. This is an example of a *straight* extrusion, and for simplicity, in this chapter we will only consider this type of extrusions. Alternatives using a curved axis were explored in [161].

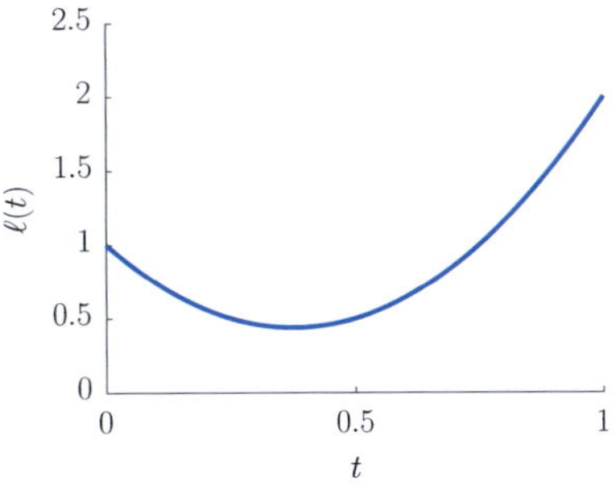

(a) Lateral function.

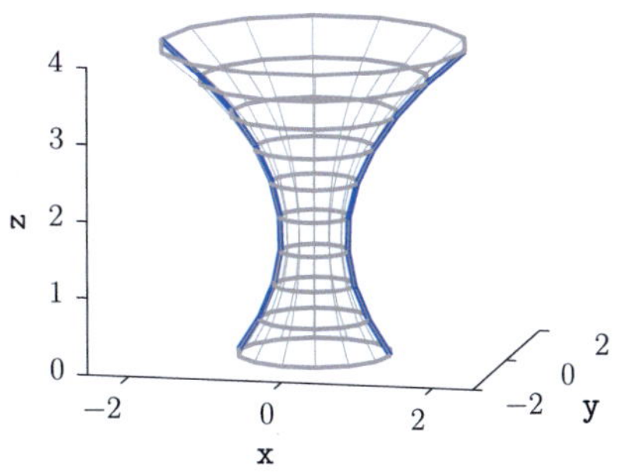

(b) General extrusion.

Figure 7.3: Construction of a three-dimensional shape as a general extrusion using a lateral function (light blue). By rotating it 90°, this shape can also be interpreted as a solid of revolution of the lateral function. The subindex k is omitted for legibility.

Shapes constructed this way can be used to approximate a variety of objects such as paper rolls or pens, or when using rectangles as the base shape, boxes or books, and many others. However, we can tweak this idea slightly to describe a wider range of objects more closely, in particular the remaining shapes in Figure 7.1. Looking at Figure 7.1b (Shape B), we can see that it can be constructed by taking a circular base shape and enlarging it horizontally as it moves upwards. In a similar way, Figure 7.1c (Shape C) and Figure 7.1d (Shape D) can be expressed as maintaining the original scale of the base shape until a certain point, then shrinking it. We denote this construction, based on shifting a planar shape in the z-axis while enlarging or shrinking it in the xy-plane, as *general extrusions* [158]. In order to derive a mathematical formulation of this idea, we will first introduce the concept of a *lateral function* $\ell_k(t_k) : [0,1] \to \mathbb{R}^+$, such as Figure 7.3a. This function determines the scaling applied on the base shape as it shifts. Thus, $\ell_k(0)$ tells us the coefficient used for scaling at the bottom, and $\ell_k(1)$ at the top. We can now describe a parametrization for the general extrusion in Figure 7.3b, in the form of

$$\underline{\phi}_k(s_k, t_k) = \begin{bmatrix} \ell_k(t_k) \cdot \cos(s_k) \\ \ell_k(t_k) \cdot \sin(s_k) \\ \mathsf{h}_k \cdot t_k \end{bmatrix} \text{, for } s_k \in [0, 2\pi], t_k \in [0,1] \;. \quad (7.2)$$

Note that, when the base shape is a circle, the result of a general extrusion is equivalent to the surface of a solid of revolution. For the sake of completeness, we will now describe a general parametrization for any base shape in an arbitrary pose. Let $\underline{\phi}_k^b(s_k) : \mathbb{R} \to \mathbb{R}^2$ be a parametrization of the two-dimensional base shape on the xy-plane, not necessarily a circle. Then, we obtain

$$\underline{\phi}_k(s_k, t_k) = \mathbf{R}_k \begin{bmatrix} \ell_k(t_k) \cdot \underline{\phi}_k^b(s_k) \\ \mathsf{h}_k \cdot t_k \end{bmatrix} + \underline{c}_k \text{, for } s_k \in \mathrm{S}_k, t_k \in \mathrm{T}_k \;, \quad (7.3)$$

where S_k is the set of possible values for s_k, and T_k is the domain of t_k, defined as $[0,1]$. Furthermore, the rotation matrix $\mathbf{R}_k$ and the translation vector $\underline{c}_k$ serve to determine the pose. As usual, all of these parameters are assumed to be encoded in the state vector $\underline{x}_k$.

7.3 Extending the Association Models to 3D

In the following subsections, we will extend the previously explored association models for use with general extrusions. These include Spatial Distribution Models (Extrusion SDMs), Partial Information Models (Extrusion PIMs), Random Hypersurface Models (Extrusion RHMs), and Negative Information Models (Extrusion NIMs).

7.3.1 Extrusion SDMs

The likelihood function for SDMs can be derived by extending (2.20) into three-dimensions, yielding

$$\begin{aligned}&\mathrm{p}(\underline{y}_k \mid \underline{x}_k)\\&= \int_{\mathrm{T}_k}\int_{\mathrm{S}_k} \mathcal{N}(\underline{y}_k - \underline{\phi}_k(s_k, t_k); \underline{0}, \mathbf{C}_k^v)\ \mathrm{p}(s_k, t_k \mid \underline{x}_k) \left\| \underline{\mathrm{n}}_k^{\phi}(s_k, t_k) \right\| \mathrm{d}s_k\, \mathrm{d}t_k \ ,\end{aligned}$$

where $\underline{\mathrm{n}}_k^{\phi}(s_k, t_k)$ represents the normal vector at the given point, defined in function of the partial derivatives as

$$\underline{\mathrm{n}}_k^{\phi}(s_k, t_k) := \frac{\partial \underline{\phi}_k(s_k, t_k)}{\partial s_k} \times \frac{\partial \underline{\phi}_k(s_k, t_k)}{\partial t_k} \ .$$

It can be seen that, in most cases, this expression is too complex to evaluate. An option, as mentioned in Section 2.4, is to assume that the source probability $\mathrm{p}(s_k, t_k \mid \underline{x}_k)$ is uniform on the shape. However, a more practical assumption for real-life experiments is to take into account the observation mechanisms of the most widely used sensors, i.e., laser scanners or depth cameras. For these devices, $\mathrm{p}(s_k, t_k \mid \underline{x}_k)$ is assumed to be uniform on the projected shape, i.e., the shape as it is visible on the sensor screen.

Note that, while it is possible to derive an accurate formulation for SDMs for a given sensor model, it is often the case that certain issues, such as artifacts or occlusions, cannot be reliably modeled at all. The problem is that these factors depend on properties such as the target material, ambient illumination, interference, and others, and many of these characteristics may change with time. As an example, we can consider Shape D from Figure 7.1d, and a corresponding capture from a depth camera in Figure 7.4. Based on the *screen view*, i.e., the two-dimensional image observed by the camera in Figure 7.4a, we can see that due to the glass material we cannot tell a priori which sources will produce a measurement. This effect can be confirmed in the *world view* showing the three-dimensional point cloud in Figure 7.4b. Because of this, as a general rule, the use of Extrusion SDMs is discouraged.

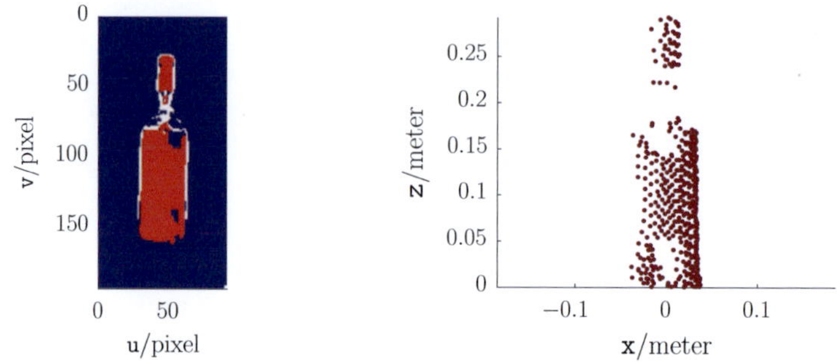

(a) Screen view with segmentation.

(b) World view.

Figure 7.4: Example capture of Shape D using a Kinect 2 depth camera: screen view (left) and world view (right). Measurements from the background are shown in blue, measurements in red belong to the target, while white gaps represent no measurements. Note that it is common to see unexpected gaps and incorrect segmentations, which means that the source distribution cannot be modeled a priori.

7.3.2 Extrusion GAMs and PIMs

GAMs and PIMs for extrusions do not differ substantially from the two-dimensional case (Section 2.5), as the usual shape functions such as the Euclidean or Mahalanobis distances can be easily extended to three dimensions. However, it should be taken into account that 3D objects generally require more information, and thus, they are more susceptible to noise or missing information. An egregious instance of this happens when a priori information about the shape is not available, and the lateral function is more detailed than necessary. An example can be seen in Figure 7.5a, where a cylinder (gray) was estimated using a polygonal lateral function (black), and where the shape function was the Euclidean distance. As only one or two support points are necessary, the remaining points should be more or less in a straight line, but they instead move inwards and outwards depending on the sensor noise.

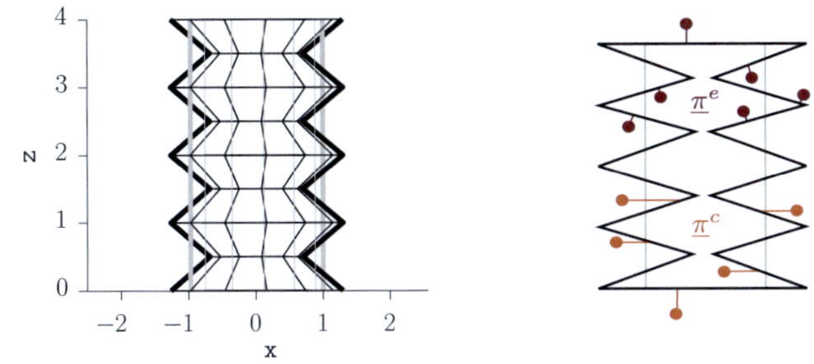

(a) Overfitting causing zigzag patterns. **(b)** Projection types.

Figure 7.5: Overfitting can happen when the complexity of the lateral function is higher than necessary (estimate in black, ground truth in gray). This issue can be alleviated by avoiding Euclidean projections (red lines) and using cylindrical projections (orange lines).

The origin of this artifact can be traced back to the Euclidean projection, sketched in Figure 7.5b. It can be seen that a zigzagging pattern can cover the red measurements better, as the corresponding Euclidean projections $\underline{\pi}_k^e(\,\cdot\,)$ (red lines) are closer to the noisy observations. This is an example of overfitting, where the estimated shape attempts to cover the received noisy measurements instead of filtering out the noise. Two approaches can be used to address this issue. On the one hand, a less complex lateral function can be used, but this requires a priori information that is not always available. While regularization could be employed, this introduces the issue of selecting an appropriate coefficient, which is not straightforward as mentioned previously. On the other hand, a better solution is to use *cylindrical projections* $\underline{\pi}_k^c(\,\cdot\,)$, seen in orange in Figure 7.5b, which are an extension of radial projections suitable for extrusions. The key idea of this approach is that the projection is assumed to be the point in the shape that intersects the line connecting the measurement with the extrusion axis (orange line). This discourages parts of the estimate from getting to close or too far from the extrusion axis, yielding flatter and smoother shapes. Furthermore, as this projection always happens 'horizontally', this also greatly reduces the search space for the projection, allowing the shape function to be evaluated in constant time independent of the complexity of the lateral function. Note that, in case that the measurement is above or below the shape (bottom orange circle or top red circle), the cylindrical projection becomes identical to the Euclidean projection. In addition, the use of cylindrical projections assumes that the shape being extruded is star-convex.

A measurement equation for Extrusion GAMs can be obtained by using the cylindrical distance, derived as the Euclidean distance to the cylindrical projection, i.e.,

$$\varphi_k^c(\underline{p}_k) := \left\| \underline{p}_k - \underline{\pi}_k^c(\underline{p}_k) \right\| .$$

for $\underline{p}_k \in \mathbb{R}^3$. In turn, this yields

$$\begin{aligned} 0 &= \varphi_k^c(\underline{y}_k - \underline{v}_k) \\ &\approx \left\| \underline{y}_k - \underline{v}_k - \underline{\pi}_k^c(\underline{y}_k) \right\| \\ &= h(\underline{x}_k, \underline{y}_k, \underline{v}_k) . \end{aligned}$$

A signed cylindrical distance function can then be derived by checking whether the argument is inside the shape. Based on these ideas, a PIM can also be obtained in a straightforward way. Note that constructing level-sets for PIM-LSet (Section 3.5) is not a difficult task, but evaluating the three-dimensional Gaussian integral generally lacks numerical stability. For this reason, we recommend employing PIM-Gauss (Section 3.4) instead, which has been shown to yield good results even for non-Gaussian sensor noise. The topic of PIMs with extrusions is explored in more detail in [56]. Furthermore, a likelihood function can be derived from this measurement equation using the same approaches explained in Chapter 3. Finally, if the estimation scenario requires the extent problem to be addressed, mechanisms such as active models from Section 4.3 can be implemented with minimal effort.

7.3.3 Extrusion RHMs

While Extrusion PIMs are simpler and more efficient than Extrusion SDMs, they suffer from the same issue as filled shapes: the extent problem (see Chapter 4). The difficulty stems from the fact that, unless additional information is available from the top or bottom caps, a PIM-based estimator cannot know where the lateral surface ends or begins vertically. As was the case with two dimensions, a straightforward solution is the application of active models, which can be easily extended to work with Extrusion PIMs. In this section, however, we explore the idea of extending RHMs to work with extrusions, which can be easily achieved by interpreting the extrusion itself as the transformation mechanism[158, 57]. Based on (7.3), we obtain the slices

$$\mathcal{S}_k^x(t_k) = \left\{ \underline{\phi}_k(s_k, t_k); s_k \in \mathrm{S}_k \right\} ,$$

where the shift parameter $t_k \in \mathrm{T}_k$ becomes the transformation parameter. However, if we want to deploy Extrusion RHMs in a practical setting, first we need to address two challenges: finding an appropriate measurement equation and deriving a probability for t_k suitable for depth sensors.

Without loss of generality, we will make the following assumptions. First, we assume that the target pose is the identity, i.e., $\mathbf{R}_k = \mathbf{I}$ and $\underline{c}_k = \underline{0}$. If this is not the case, we can remove the transformation by using the pseudo-measurement

$$\underline{y}_k^* = (\mathbf{R}_k)^{-1} \cdot (\underline{y}_k - \underline{c}_k)$$

instead. Second, we also assume that the $\mathbf{xy}$ and the $\mathbf{z}$ components of $\underline{y}_k$ are independent from each other. This means we can rewrite $\underline{y}_k$ and $\mathbf{C}_k^v$ as

$$\underline{y}_k = \begin{bmatrix} y_k^{\mathrm{x}} \\ y_k^{\mathrm{y}} \\ y_k^{\mathrm{z}} \end{bmatrix} , \text{ and } \mathbf{C}_k^v = \begin{bmatrix} c_k^{\mathrm{xx}} & c_k^{\mathrm{xy}} & 0 \\ c_k^{\mathrm{yx}} & c_k^{\mathrm{yy}} & 0 \\ 0 & 0 & c_k^{\mathrm{zz}} \end{bmatrix} .$$

As shorthand, we introduce the three following terms

$$\underline{y}_k^{\mathtt{xy}} = \begin{bmatrix} y_k^{\mathtt{x}} \\ y_k^{\mathtt{y}} \end{bmatrix}$$

$$\underline{v}_k^{\mathtt{xy}} \sim \mathcal{N}\left(\underline{0}, \begin{bmatrix} c_k^{\mathtt{xx}} & c_k^{\mathtt{xy}} \\ c_k^{\mathtt{yx}} & c_k^{\mathtt{yy}} \end{bmatrix}\right) \text{ , and}$$

$$v_k^{\mathtt{z}} \sim \mathcal{N}\left(0, c_k^{\mathtt{zz}}\right) \ .$$

Third, for simplicity, we will assume that the base shape is a circle of radius 1, but the same ideas can be used for arbitrary base shapes. Based on these three assumptions, we obtain the measurement equation

$$\begin{bmatrix} 0 \\ y_k^{\mathtt{z}} \end{bmatrix} = \begin{bmatrix} \left\| \underline{y}_k^{\mathtt{xy}} - \underline{v}_k^{\mathtt{xy}} \right\| - \ell_k(t_k) \\ \mathsf{h}_k \cdot t_k + v_k^{\mathtt{z}} \end{bmatrix}$$
$$= \underline{h}(\underline{x}_k, \underline{y}_k, \underline{v}_k, t_k) \ ,$$

where, as usual in RHMs, t_k is treated as a new noise term. Notice that the first line is simply a GAM measurement equation for a circle of radius $\ell_k(t_k)$, while the second line is an extension of the $\mathtt{z}$ component in (7.2). Of course, a PIM can also be used for the $\mathtt{xy}$ component. Note that the $\mathtt{z}$ component may be inobservable in LRKFs, an issue previously mentioned by [122, 57], requiring the introduction of a quadratic extension[122]. Finally, as a consequence of the assumption of independence, the likelihood function for Extrusion RHMs can be obtained simply by multiplying the individual likelihoods corresponding to $\mathtt{xy}$ and $\mathtt{z}$.

The remaining task is to find the distribution of the transformation parameter $\mathrm{p}(t_k \,|\, \underline{x}_k)$. Once more, we can simply assume that t_k is distributed uniformly in T_k, but as mentioned in Section 7.3.1, it is much more interesting to consider how the shape is observed by a sensor such as a camera. If we assume that the target is being observed almost laterally as in Figure 7.1, then the resulting terms are very easy to derive and calculate. In particular, the area of the projected shape in the screen view can be described as

$$A_k = \mathsf{h}_k \cdot \int_{\mathrm{T}_k} 2\ell_k(t_k) \ \mathrm{d}t_k \ ,$$

or in other words, twice the area under the curve in Figure 7.3a scaled by the height. By only taking a subset of the available $t_k \in \mathrm{T}_k$, we can extend this expression into a cdf

$$\mathrm{P}(t_k^* < t_k \,|\, \underline{x}_k) = \frac{1}{A_k} \cdot \mathsf{h}_k \cdot \int_0^{t_k} 2\ell_k(t_k^*)\ \mathrm{d}t_k^* \ ,$$

where A_k acts as a normalization factor. Finally, by calculating the derivative of this cdf, we obtain the pdf for t_k as

$$\begin{aligned} \mathrm{p}(t_k \,|\, \underline{x}_k) &= \frac{2\mathsf{h}_k}{A_k} \cdot \ell_k(t_k) \\ &= \frac{\ell_k(t_k)}{\int_{\mathrm{T}_k} \ell_k(t_k^*)\ \mathrm{d}t_k^*} \ , \end{aligned} \tag{7.4}$$

or in other words, $\mathrm{p}(t_k \,|\, \underline{x}_k)$ is simply a normalized form of the lateral function. As in Section 5.4, a Gaussian approximation of this distribution can be obtained using moment matching.

7.3.4 Extrusion NIMs

NIMs, as proposed in Chapter 6, can be easily extended to three-dimensional shapes simply by adjusting the distance functions. However, as with the previous models, it is once again critical to take into account how commonly used sensors, such as depth cameras, observe the target. As we saw before, Figure 7.4 shows how Shape A from Figure 7.1a is measured. Thus, it can be said that measurements come in two variants: a 3D form $\underline{y}_k \in \mathbb{R}^3$ with type $y_k^{\mathcal{T}}$ which stems from the world in front of the camera (Figure 7.4b), and a 2D form $\underline{y}_k^s \in \mathbb{R}^2$ with type $y_k^{\mathcal{T},s}$ as observed on the sensor screen (Figure 7.4a). However, we need to take into account two issues. First, three-dimensional negative measurements are generally of little use. The problem is that, while they may appear next to the target in the screen view, in most cases they belong to the background, and thus, they are usually very far from the target in the world view. Thus, they give us very little information about where the target cannot be. Second, while we gain positive measurements both in the screen and the world view, this does not mean that we have twice the amount of information. This stems from the fact that positive measurements in the world view were calculated from their counterparts in the screen view. Due to the strong correlations involved, the use of both versions of the positive observations is not advisable. Thus, the use of negative measurements in 3D and positive measurements in 2D should be avoided.

Conversely, this means that we need to find a way to combine positive observations in 3D and negative observations in 2D. A possible course of action would be to try to bring both of them into the same space. This, however, is not necessarily a good idea. On the one hand, projecting the 3D measurements into 2D would mean we lose valuable depth information. On the other hand, we can interpret the negative observations in the screen space as 3D 'negative lines', but this would present more difficulties, as all of our proposed models only deal with point measurements. Furthermore, even if we optimally chose a point from this line, we would still employ only a fraction of the information available. Instead, we propose to use a hybrid association model which deals with the 3D and 2D measurements without any transformation. More concretely, we extend the NIM-PIMs presented in Section 6.4 by using the Extrusion PIMs from Section 7.3.2 for the 3D positive measurements, and the traditional PIMs from Chapter 3 for 2D negative measurements. The obtained results can be fused during estimation in the usual way, either by multiplying the likelihoods or by stacking the measurement equations vertically.

We are now left with the task of obtaining measurement equations for the 3D positive and 2D negative measurements. For the positive observations, we proceed in the same way as in Section 6.4, and extend the cylindrical distance function $\varphi_k^c(\underline{y}_k)$ into a form $\varphi_k^n(\underline{y}_k, y_k^\tau)$ that incorporates the measurement type. By plugging this result into (6.6), we obtain

$$\begin{bmatrix} 0 \\ y_k^\tau \end{bmatrix} = \begin{bmatrix} \varphi_k^n(\underline{y}_k, y_k^\tau) - \nu_k \\ \nu_k^\tau \end{bmatrix} \tag{7.5}$$
$$= \underline{h}(\underline{x}_k, \underline{y}_k, y_k^\tau, \nu_k, \nu_k^\tau) \ ,$$

where ν_k is the bias correction term, and ν_k^T describes the possible types the measurement could have taken for a given source.

A similar approach can be applied for the negative measurements in two dimensions, but first we must address the following two challenges. The first one is to find an efficient mechanism to project the shape corresponding to a given state $\underline{x}_k$ (such as Figure 7.6a) on the camera screen. Given that finding an exact formulation can be extremely time consuming, for this section we are interested in obtaining a simplified silhouette in the form of a polygonal chain (as in Figure 7.6b) that allows us to calculate the distance function very quickly. We will describe an abridged sketch of the algorithm we used. First, we define the term

$$\alpha_k = \max\left(-\underline{\kappa}_k^\top \cdot \underline{e}^{\mathbf{z}}, 0\right) \ ,$$

where $\underline{\kappa}_k$ is the camera direction, and $\underline{e}^{\mathbf{z}} := \left[0, 0, 1\right]^\top$ is the extrusion axis. This term, based on ideas from the field of graphical projection[136], tells us how 'squashed' a flat surface with normal $\underline{e}^{\mathbf{z}}$ becomes due to perspective projection for a given camera direction. Thus, if we are looking at the surface from above, it holds that $\alpha_k = 1$, i.e., it has a maximal size. However, if we are looking at it from the side, we obtain $\alpha_k = 0$, meaning that we only see a single line. The max operator serves to cull surfaces looking away from the camera. Based on this concept, we can construct a silhouette such as in Figure 7.6, by

1. first, constructing a semi-circle of radius $\ell_k(1)$ as the upper cap, scaled vertically by α_k,
2. then, placing two vertical instances of the lateral function, scaled vertically by $\sqrt{1 - \alpha_k^2}$,
3. and finally, placing a semi-circle of radius $\ell_k(0)$ as the lower cap, scaled vertically by α_k.

The resulting shape is then translated, rotated, and scaled depending on the estimated pose and the camera calibration. Two points stand out. On the one hand, we observe that in step 2 the squashing of the lateral function is different, given that the extrusion axis is oriented at a 90°

angle to the caps. On the other hand, note that this simplification only gives appropriate results as long as the extrusion is being seen more or less 'from the side'. If higher accuracy is needed, the exact silhouette edges can be obtained using techniques of computer vision such as [137].

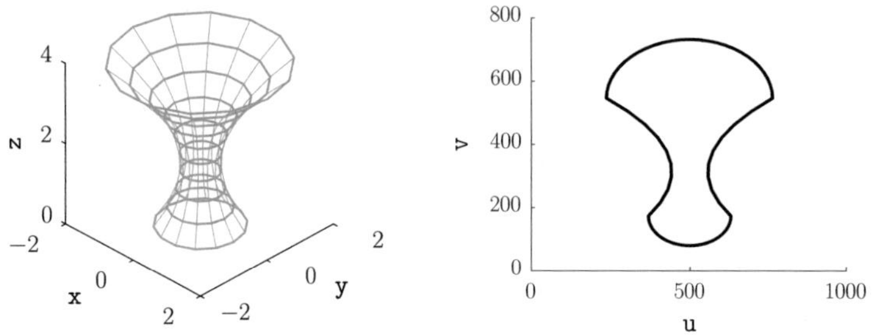

(a) 3D visualization of target.

(b) Simplified view from camera.

Figure 7.6: Example simplification of shape projection based on the lateral function and two semicircles, based on a camera with a resolution of 1000 × 800 pixels. Note that while this projection is easy to calculate, it is not exact, as can be seen by the lower part of the upper cap being described incorrectly.

The second challenge is to find an appropriate distance function for the negative measurements on the screen. We propose to use the same idea as with the cylindrical projection, i.e., the projection of a given point will always be on the line that connects it to the extrusion axis. As with 3D, this ensures an efficient evaluation of the shape function while removing zigzagging artifacts. This leads to a measurement equation which is functionally identical to (7.5), except that it uses the values corresponding to the screen instead, in the form of

$$\begin{aligned}\begin{bmatrix} 0 \\ y_k^{\tau,s} \end{bmatrix} &= \begin{bmatrix} \varphi_k^{n,s}(\underline{y}_k^s, y_k^{\tau,s}) - \nu_k^s \\ \nu_k^{\tau,s} \end{bmatrix} \\ &= \underline{h}(\underline{x}_k, \underline{y}_k^s, y_k^{\tau,s}, \nu_k^s, \nu_k^{\tau,s}) \ .\end{aligned}$$

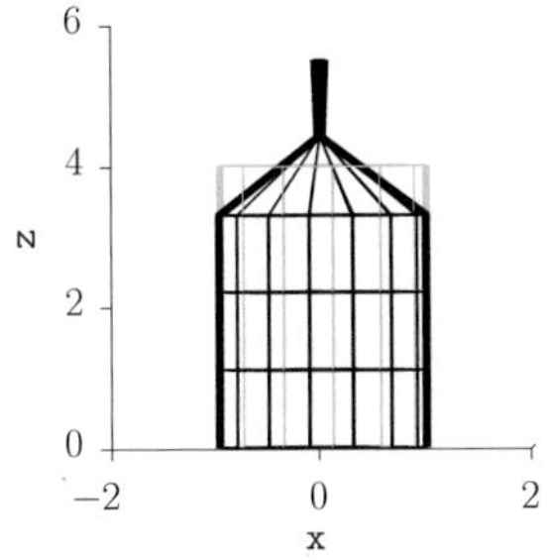

(a) Overfitting causing height artifact.

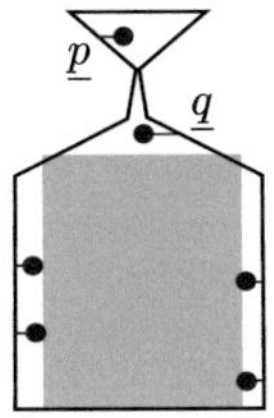

(b) Example measurements.

Figure 7.7: In cases of bad initialization, overfitting can cause a height artifact with parts of the estimate (black) 'dangling' above or below the target (gray). Negative measurements such as $\underline{q}$ generally solve these errors, but in case they are missing, observations like $\underline{p}$ may pull the height upwards.

At this point, we would like to discuss an uncommon artifact due to overfitting that arises in situations when the height has been vastly overestimated. In this case, we may end up in a situation such as Figure 7.7a, with a 'dangling' part of the shape that does not correspond to any part of the true target. This issue is problematic, as the estimator cannot correct this problem on its own, as can be explained based on the sketch in Figure 7.7b. In this scenario, we have six negative measurements around the ground truth (gray), which are projected onto the incorrect estimate (black). Unlike the four measurements in the bottom part, which pull the estimate towards the ground truth as expected, measurements such as $\underline{q}$ serve two tasks simultaneously: shrinking the radius horizontally, and correcting the height downwards. However, observations such as $\underline{p}$ serve the same purpose but in the opposite way, attempting instead to correct the estimate by pulling it upwards, making them particularly damaging. In consequence, after several timesteps, we end up with a thin 'tube' that cannot be corrected (see top of Figure 7.7a), as no negative or positive measurements end up being associated with these degenerated parts. Fortunately, this artifact is extremely rare and only happens in pathological situations, such as vastly incorrect initializations or jerky motions. Nonetheless, if it can be reasonably expected for this issue to appear, a straightforward solution is to temporarily apply a weak active model (Section 4.3) that slightly pushes the height down at each timestep.

7.4 Evaluation

The evaluation of the proposed extrusion models was based on real data captured using a Microsoft Kinect 2 device. The targets considered were those presented in Figure 7.1, as they are representative of shapes observed in daily life, which in turn can show the applicability of these concepts in tasks such as indoor navigation or autonomous systems. However, we omitted Shape A, as it can be approximated as a simple cylinder, for which several solutions already exist in literature [56, 57, 135, 43]. A detailed description of the treated shapes, also visualized in Figure 7.8, is as follows.

- **Shape B**, a pencil case, could be seen as an inverted truncated cone of height 13.5 cm, with upper radius 6.8 cm, and lower radius 4.3 cm (Figure 7.8a). The material was opaque and had good visibility.
- **Shape C**, a teapot, was approximately a cylinder with a truncated cone on top. Its total height was 18.5 cm, with upper radius 5.2 cm and lower radius 7.7 cm (Figure 7.8b). The material was moderately reflective, but had relatively good visibility.
- **Shape D**, a bottle, could be approximated as a sequence of a cylinder, a truncated cone, and another cylinder. Its height was 31 cm, its upper radius was 1.5 cm, and its lower radius was 3.6 cm (Figure 7.8c). The glass material was highly reflective. Furthermore, the shape was opaque in the lower parts and transparent in the upper parts, due to the liquid inside. Because of this, the visibility was unreliable and could not be modeled appropriately, as some parts of the shape were visible in some frames and invisible in others.

- **Shape D*** was the same bottle as Shape D, but covered in cardboard. For this reason, the dimensions of this shape were increased by 0.1 cm in all directions (Figure 7.8d). The visibility of the modified bottle was similar to the first two objects.

For the shape representation, we used a circle of radius 1 m as the base shape. The lateral function was represented as a polygonal function, i.e., $\ell_k(t_k)$ was continuous and piecewise linear. This type of function works as follows. We assume that there are N equidistant support points, where each support point $1 \leq i \leq N$ consists of a position $t_k^i := \frac{i-1}{N-1}$, and an associated radius r_k^i. Thus, it holds for every i that $\ell_k(t_k^i) = \mathsf{r}_k^i$, and the remaining values for $t_k \in [0,1]$ are linearly interpolated from the nearest support points. Figure 7.7a shows an example with $N = 6$ (i.e., 6 'layers'). However, for this evaluation, we chose a more complex lateral function with $N = 8$, as can be seen for example in Figure 7.9. This leads to a state in the form of

$$\underline{x}_k = \left[\underline{c}_k^\top, \underline{r}_k^\top, \mathsf{h}_k, \mathsf{r}_k^1, \cdots, \mathsf{r}_k^8\right]^\top ,$$

where $\underline{c}_k \in \mathbb{R}^3$ is the translation component, $\underline{r}_k \in \mathbb{R}^3$ is the rotation encoded with a Rodrigues transformation (as explained in Appendix 9.1), and h_k is the height.

In the following, we will describe two evaluation scenarios. On the one hand, the static evaluation considered multiple objects and then measured how closely the estimated dimensions were to the real shape. On the other hand, the dynamic evaluation dealt with a moving target, and determined how much the dimension errors changed depending on the motion of the observed object.

7.4.1 Static Evaluation

For the static evaluation, the setup was as follows. The considered objects were positioned on a table about 1 m from the camera, in order to maximize the number of measurements and minimize the amount of sensor artifacts. Being a depth camera, a Microsoft Kinect 2 device yields measurements based on two types of captures: a 2D image that can be segmented into positive and negative measurements, and a 3D point cloud that consists of only positive measurements. The transformation between 2D and 3D coordinates was taken from [145, 156, 56], which also indicate how to obtain the uncertainty $\mathbf{C}_k^v$ associated to each measurement $\underline{y}_k$. In order to determine which measurements belonged to the target, spatial gating and hue segmentation were used. We note that each frame can yield up to 10000 measurements, which is far more than what is needed for a good estimate. Because of this, we only used 1000 positive and 2000 negative measurements, spread along 100 timesteps (i.e., 10 positive and 20 negative measurements per timestep), selected at random. Given that this introduces a degree of non-determinism into the estimation, we compared the results of 30 runs. Note that this nonstandard approach is only for the sake of evaluation, and a practical application aiming to obtain the best possible results should employ all available information at any given time.

(a) Shape B. **(b)** Shape C. **(c)** Shape D. **(d)** Shape D*.

Figure 7.8: Example capture of Shape B, Shape C, and Shape D introduced in Figure 7.1, as observed by a Microsoft Kinect 2 device. Sizes are to scale relative to each other. We omit Shape A due to its simplicity. Furthermore, we introduce Shape D*, which is the same glass bottle used for Shape D but covered in cardboard, in order to improve its sensor visibility. Note that, no matter the material, every shape contains gaps and outliers.

The following association models were evaluated,

- *Extrusion PIMs with active models* (PIM+A) from Section 7.3.2, with a small regularization coefficient of $\mathsf{c}_k = 10^{-3}$,
- *Extrusion RHMs* (RHM) from Section 7.3.3, employing a Gaussian approximation of (7.4), and

- *Extrusion NIMs* (NIM) from Section 7.3.4.

Note that all models used 3D positive measurements, but only NIM employed 2D negative observations in addition to that. The estimator we chose was the S^{2}KF [88], with a total of 150 state samples. The initial state for the estimator, specifically its mean $\hat{\underline{x}}_0$ and its covariance matrix $\mathbf{P}_0$, were set as follows. The mean $\hat{\underline{x}}_0$ was selected to represent a very small cylinder of height 3 cm and with all radii set to 1 cm, which can be seen to be much smaller than any of the considered shapes. This means that the active model proposed for NIM was not necessary. The initial rotation was set to the identity, and the translation was set as the mean of the measurements received in the first frame. The initial covariance matrix was set to $\mathbf{P}_0 = 10^{-6} \cdot \mathbf{I}$. As no motion was assumed, the system equation was

$$\underline{x}_{k+1} = \mathbf{A}_k^{reg}(\mathsf{c}_k) \cdot \underline{x}_k + \underline{w}_k \ .$$

For PIM+A, the system matrix $\mathbf{A}_k^{reg}$ incorporated the effect of the regularization coefficient, while for RHM and NIM, it was simply the identity. Furthermore, the process noise $\underline{w}_k$ was assumed to be Gaussian distributed with zero-mean and covariance matrix $\mathbf{Q}_k = 10^{-8} \cdot \mathbf{I}$.

We start with Shape D, as it is the most difficult target from the proposed shapes. The results from PIM+A and NIM can be seen in Figure 7.9. The left column shows the screen view of the target after segmentation, with negative measurements in blue, positive in red, and missing measurements in white. It can be seen that the segmentation is extremely unreliable, with many sections inside the shape being detected as negative, and a significant contour of missing measurements around the target. It is also noteworthy that the region below the neck of the bottle mostly lacks positive measurements. This can be confirmed on the right column, which shows the 3D positive measurements in the world view. Nonetheless, the estimates are moderately correct. In the first row we observe the PIM+A estimates, which underestimate the true size due to the regularization coefficient. Still, the resulting shape is still approximately that of a bottle. Note that the projection of PIM+A on the segmented image in Figure 7.9a is only for visualization, as this association model does not use any 2D information.

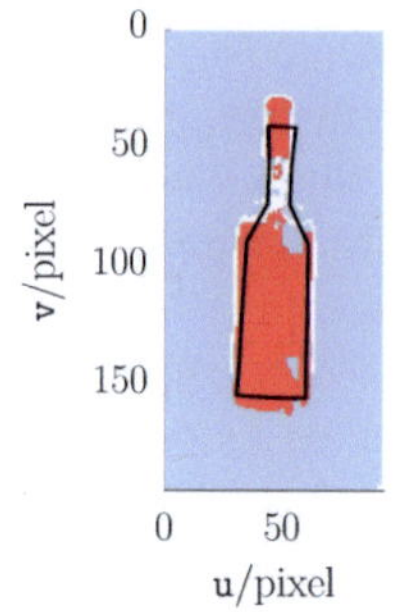

(a) Screen view - PIM+A.

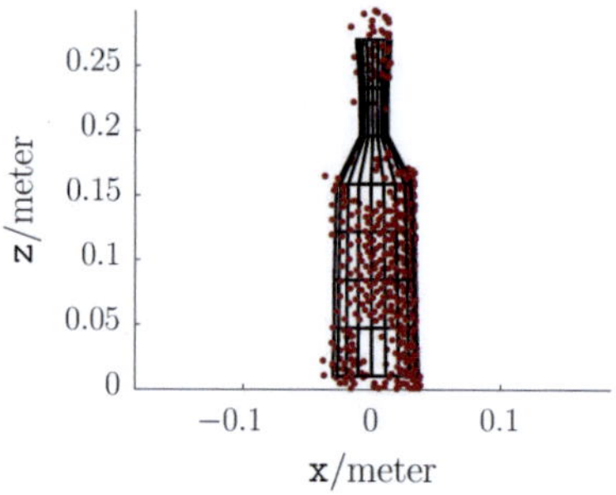

(b) World view - PIM+A.

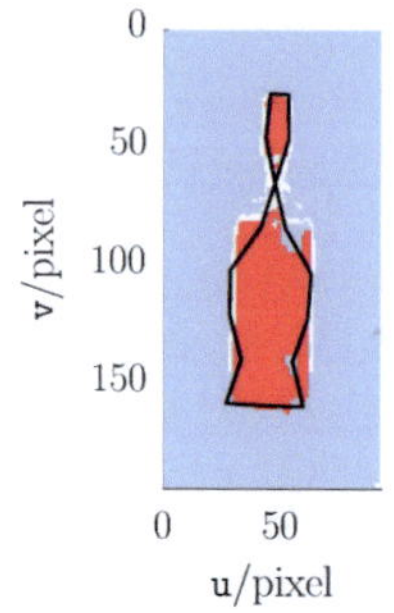

(c) Screen view - NIM.

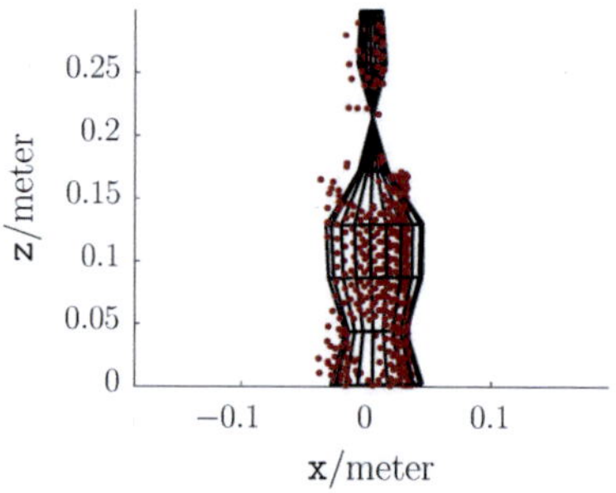

(d) World view - NIM.

Figure 7.9: Estimates for Shape D using Extrusion PIMs with active models and Extrusion NIMs. The left column shows the screen view, including positive (red) and negative (blue) measurements. A projection of the shape estimate is displayed in black. The right column illustrates the same estimates in the world view. Example measurements in dark red.

The results of NIM can be seen in the second row, where it is obvious that the result is less bottle-shaped. This can be explained based on the negative measurements from Figure 7.9b, especially around the neck, which incorrectly push the estimate towards the inside. However, the height was still estimated almost correctly, averaging around 30 cm (ground truth was 31 cm). Note that, based on Figure 7.9b, we can see that this is the best height estimate that can be achieved, as the resulting shape completely covers the observed target vertically. The incorrect height can be explained instead as an artifact of the spatial segmentation procedure, given that the lower parts of the shape needed to be clamped away in order to avoid spurious measurements from the table.

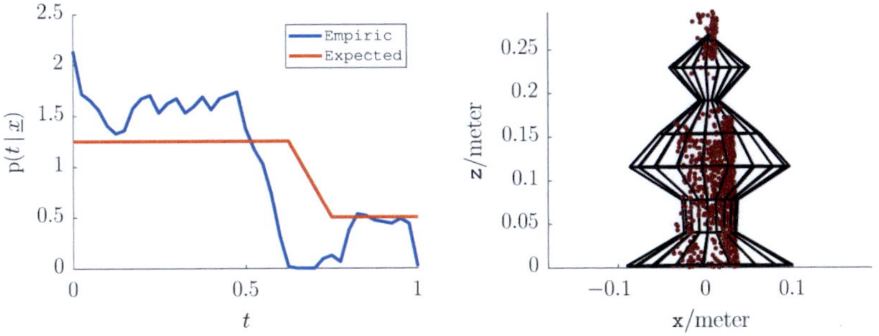

(a) Distribution of t_k. **(b)** World view of RHM estimate.

Figure 7.10: Empiric and expected distributions of the shifting parameter t_k for Shape D, and an estimate using an Extrusion RHM. Due to the difficulty of obtaining a proper distribution of t_k, and the high amount of outliers, both Extrusion RHMs and ARHMs generally produce unreliable results when the shape complexity is high.

However, there were several problems with obtaining a robust RHM estimate for Shape D. The main difficulty with this task was obtaining a reasonable distribution for t_k when using Kinect sensors, given the high amount of gaps and outliers. As a reminder, a lack of a source distribution was the main reason not to employ Extrusion SDMs. It appears that, unfortunately, this issue is also present in RHMs, as can be evidenced in Figure 7.10a. Here, we show the empiric distribution of observed t_k values (in blue), based on the point cloud shown in red in Figure 7.10b. We can see how this pdf vaguely follows the same contour as the theoretical distribution we expected from (7.4) (in red), but nonetheless differs considerably from it. During estimation, we can see the negative effects of this disparity (Figure 7.10b). The observed shape (in black) is not only incorrect in the height, but also diverges dramatically in the radii, leaving the translation as the only correctly estimated parameter. Thus, it cannot be said that Extrusion RHMs were a success for this evaluation, not even after extending it into an ARHM by applying a considerable regularization force.

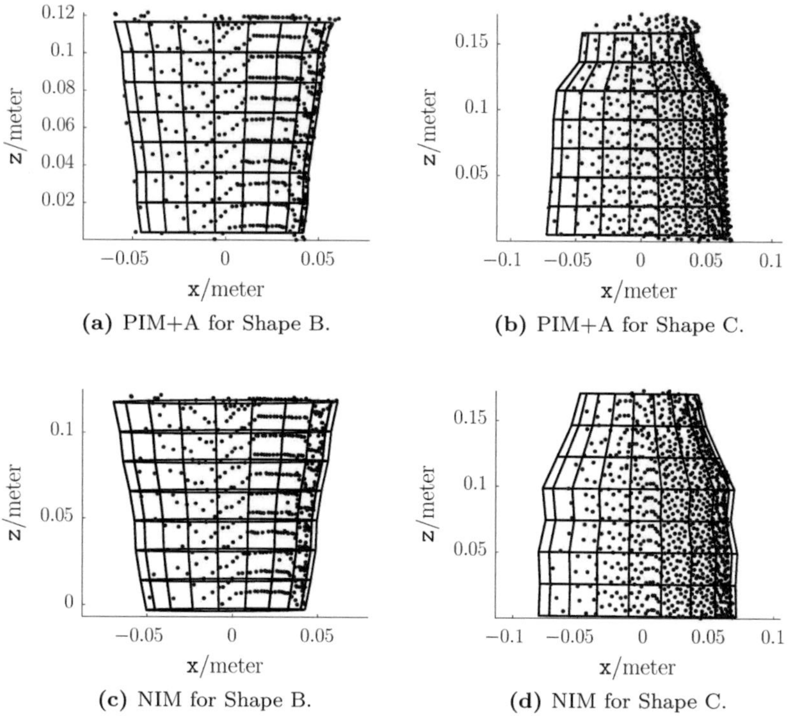

Figure 7.11: World view of the results for Shape B and Shape C, using PIM+A and NIM. Estimates in black, example measurements in dark red.

In this context, it must be taken into account that RHMs that employ similar ideas to extrusions have worked correctly in the past [56, 57, 158], and thus, we feel obligated to give an explanation for why RHMs do not work correctly here. While [57] also worked with Kinect point clouds, it dealt only with a cylinder, i.e., a height and a radius, and the simplicity of that model is also the source of its robustness. In [158], a very similar form of Extrusion RHMs were considered, but the used synthetic data had little noise and no gaps or outliers. Finally, in [56], the ground shape of the extrusion was estimated as a star-convex approximation, while also using Kinect data. However, the parameters of the lateral function were not being estimated, and thus, the effect of an incorrect distribution of t_k were not as egregious. This comparison also illustrates the conditions under which Extrusion RHMs can work, i.e., when the measurement quality is proportional to the shape complexity. Nonetheless, it should be pointed out that PIM+A and NIM can both survive these low information scenarios without much trouble.

As the final part of the static evaluation, we present the results for Shape B and C using PIM+A and NIM as shown in Figure 7.11. We observe that, by virtue of the lateral function employing 8 support points, the shape model is too complex for the rather simple shapes. Nonetheless, the negative effects of overfitting are almost completely absent, even across different runs. The lateral function for Shape B is virtually straight in both association models, with few indentations, and even for Shape C the lower part of the shape can be approximately seen to be cylindrical. Still, it can be seen that the resistance to overfitting for PIM+A is higher. Where NIM succeeds is in the height estimation, where we can observe that PIM+A is consistently smaller than it should as a result of the active model. Of course, it could be argued that this is the result of using an incorrect regularization coefficient. However, addressing this issue would require the manual work of finding an appropriate c_k for each scenario and each shape, which is a difficult task if no prior information is known. It is also an adjustment that NIM does not demand.

7.4.2 Dynamic Evaluation

For the dynamic evaluation, we wanted to show a scenario that happens quite frequently in daily life, which is a bottle serving a glass. The capture, using the modified bottle from Shape D*, lasted approximately 240 frames (corresponding to 8 seconds), and consisted of three parts (see setup in Figure 7.12). First, for frames 1 until about 80, the bottle was still. Then, for frames 80 – 120, the bottle was moved forward 20 cm and rotated so that it points vertically. For frames 120 – 160, the bottle was moved backwards and rotated to its original pose. Finally, for frames 160 – 240, the target remained still once more. In order to separate positive and negative measurements, hue segmentation and spatial gating was used, but due to the moving target the results were not as reliable as in the static evaluation. Because of this, outliers that belonged to other parts of the scene were sometimes misinterpreted as being part of the shape. In order to address this, the same gating mechanism based on the state uncertainty from Section 6.6.2 was applied here. An important question in this context was how to categorize the hand as seen for example in Figure 7.12c. Usually, measurements from nearby objects are treated as negative, but the problem here is that each 2D measurement actually represents a line in 3D, and thus, stating that an observation is negative implies that the object cannot be at any point of the unprojected line. However, as can be seen in the setup images, it is often the case that the target is located behind a part of the hand, and thus, marking those regions as negative would case the estimate to break in that part of the shape. For this reason, those measurements were marked as indeterminate instead.

For the dynamic evaluation, most of the parameters were set in the same way as the static evaluation. However, the state was modified to incorporate a constant velocity motion model in the form of

$$\underline{x}_k = \left[\underline{c}_k^\top, \underline{r}_k^\top, \mathsf{h}_k, \mathsf{r}_k^1, \cdots, \mathsf{r}_k^8, \underline{\dot{c}}_k^\top, \underline{\dot{r}}_k^\top\right]^\top ,$$

where the new parameter $\underline{\dot{c}}_k$ represents the translational velocity, and $\underline{\dot{r}}_k$ the rotational velocity. The measurement equation is extended to

$$\underline{x}_{k+1} = \mathbf{F}_k \cdot \mathbf{A}_k^{reg}(\mathsf{c}_k) \cdot \underline{x}_k + \underline{w}_k ,$$

where $\mathbf{F}_k$ is a system matrix that scales the velocities by the elapsed time and adds them to the translation and the rotation. The evaluated association models being evaluated were PIM+A and NIM.

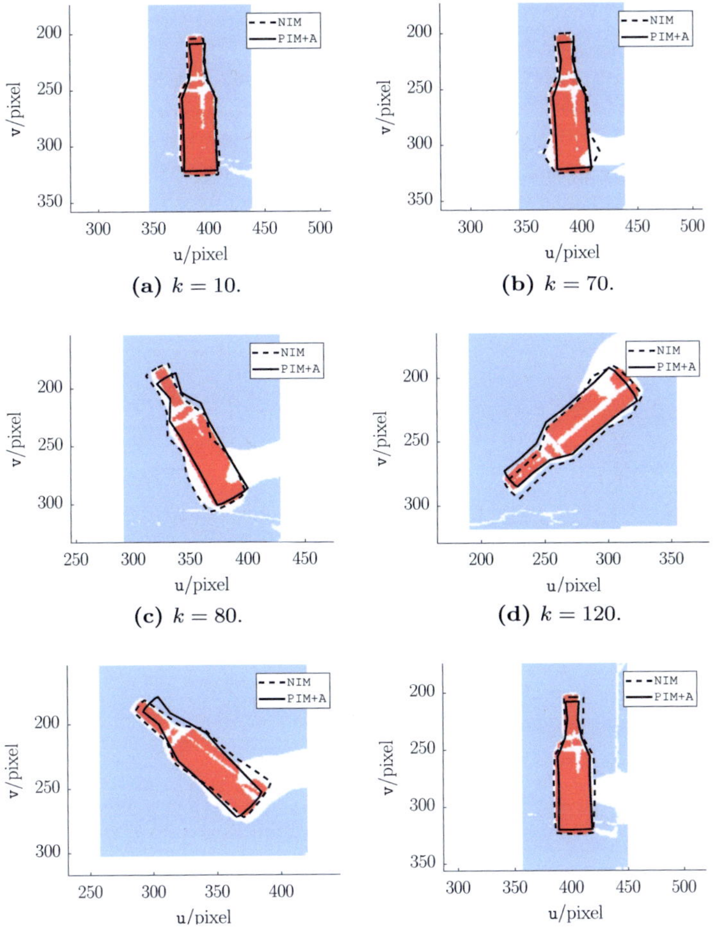

(a) $k = 10$. (b) $k = 70$.

(c) $k = 80$. (d) $k = 120$.

(e) $k = 140$. (f) $k = 175$.

Figure 7.12: Setup and screen view for the dynamic evaluation, where Shape D* was taken from the table, rotated and translated, and then put back in its original position. The segmentation shows positive measurements in red, negative in blue, indeterminate (incl. hand) in white. Estimates in black represent the mean of 30 runs. Note that PIM+A did not use two-dimensional information, and is presented only for comparison.

The results of the evaluation can be seen in Figure 7.12, Figure 7.13, and Figure 7.14. In Figure 7.12 we can see the screen projections of the estimates for selected timesteps. In a similar way as with the static evaluation, it becomes clear that PIM+A underestimates the height, again as a consequence of the active model. It also occasionally lags behind the NIM, which can explained from the fact that the latter works with more information given the additional incorporation of negative observations.

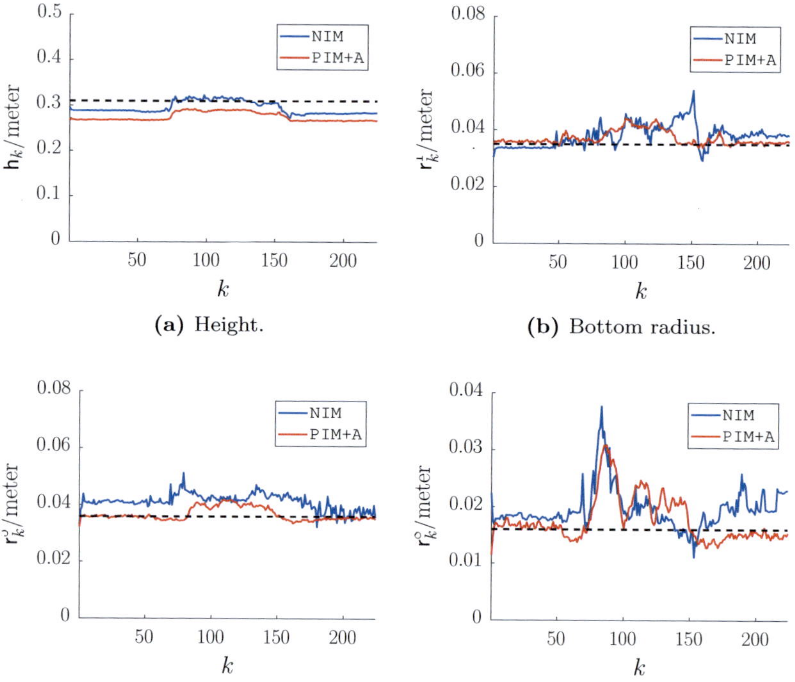

(a) Height. (b) Bottom radius.

(c) Middle radius. (d) Top radius.

Figure 7.13: Results of the dynamic evaluation for the bottom radius, the middle radius, the top radius, and the height. NIM in blue, PIM+A in red, ground truth in dashed black line. Values represent the mean of 30 runs.

However, a very interesting artifact happens due to the lack of measurements around the shape, in particular as the hand measurements were marked as indeterminate. It can be seen in Figure 7.12c that the NIM, instead of yielding a tight fit around the positive measurements, becomes actually slightly inflated, appearing to incorporate the white gap. This makes sense when taking into account that it is the task of negative measurements to shrink an incorrect radius, and in the regions where no measurements are present, the estimator cannot know whether the shape is there or not. While this effect is usually harmless, it can damage otherwise accurate estimates, as can be seen in Figure 7.12b and Figure 7.12e, where part of the bottle is inflated around the hand region.

A better assessment of the estimation accuracy can be found in Figure 7.14. The height, shown in Figure 7.13a, distinctly portrays the three stages of the experiment. PIM+A, due to the regularization, is constantly smaller than the ground truth, i.e., 31.1 cm. (dashed black line). Of interest is the fact that NIM, usually unbiased in relation to the height, was below the ground truth most of the time, but became correct when the bottle was being held in the air. This result makes sense when taking into account the spatial gating artifact previously mentioned in the static evaluation, where the lower part of the bottle was clamped away in order to avoid noisy measurements from the table below it. Thus, we can see that the moment the bottle is lifted from the table, the height estimate immediately becomes correct. The stages can also be more or less recognized in the bottom radius (Figure 7.13b), where the estimate becomes disturbed the moment the hand appears in $k = 60$, and remains so until the bottle is released at about $k = 180$. As in the static evaluation, PIM+A was more reliable in the radius estimation, and NIM was slightly biased due to the contour of invalid measurements. A similar result can be seen in the middle radius in Figure 7.13c. The top radius, however, was considerably more noisy, due to its smaller size and to being the point in the shape that moved the most. The highest disturbances appeared when the bottle started moving and when it stopped, as the motion model could not take into account this change. Nonetheless, it can be seen that both models were capable of approximating the moving bottle in an appropriate way at every moment.

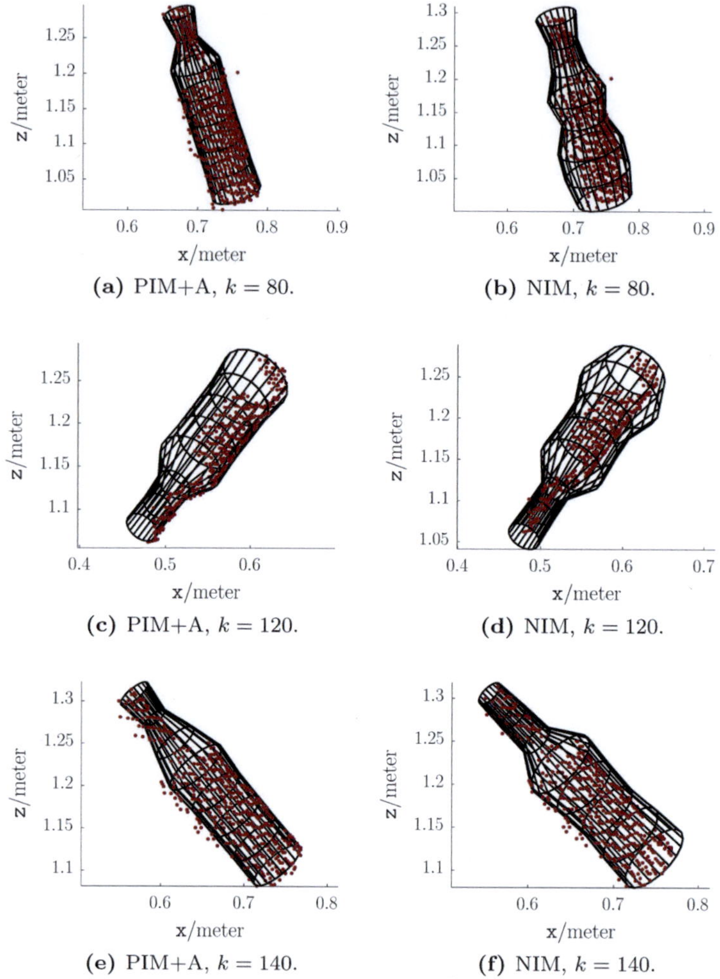

(a) PIM+A, $k = 80$.

(b) NIM, $k = 80$.

(c) PIM+A, $k = 120$.

(d) NIM, $k = 120$.

(e) PIM+A, $k = 140$.

(f) NIM, $k = 140$.

Figure 7.14: World view of the results of the dynamic evaluation for selected timesteps, showing the moment when the bottle was being grabbed (first row), the moment when it was being pointed down (second row), and when it was being pulled back (third row). Estimates represent the mean of 30 runs. Sample measurements in red, estimates in black.

Finally, we can see the estimation results for selected timesteps in Figure 7.14. In the first row we can see the bottle as it is being lifted, showing how the NIM estimate was slightly distorted due to the presence of the hand. Furthermore, neither model was particularly disturbed by the outlier to the right of the shape. In the second row we observe that both models were able to follow the rotation without much trouble. Finally, in the third row the high measurement noise becomes evident, but even then, both estimates can be seen to be extremely close.

7.5 Conclusions

The objective of this chapter was to extend the previously presented association models in order to estimate three-dimensional targets. A simple mechanism for this extension was in the form of extrusions, where a flat base shape is shifted vertically to construct a 3D object. For example, a rectangle can be shifted to construct a cuboid, or a circle to produce a cylinder. We further elaborated on this idea and proposed general extrusions, which apply a scaling transformation on the base shape as it is being shifted. This allowed the description of shapes like truncated cones, or in a more general sense, solids of rotation. We explored four association models for extrusions, with a particular focus on adapting them for use in depth sensors to ensure their applicability in the real world. We derived a likelihood function for SDMs, but observed that the necessity for an accurate model for the sensor distribution made such an approach unreliable. Extrusion GAMs and PIMs, on the other hand, were much simpler to implement, but we proposed the use of cylindrical projections instead of Euclidean distances in order to avoid artifacts of overfitting. Extrusion RHMs were also straightforward to extend, but we pointed out the importance of finding an appropriate distribution for the shifting parameter. For Extrusion NIMs, we faced the challenge that the sensors did not directly provide negative measurements in three dimensions. In order to address this, we exploited the fact that depth sensors provide two types of captures: a two-dimensional image (screen view), and a three-dimensional point cloud (world view). Thus, we presented a hybrid mechanism that simultaneously incorporated 2D negative measurements from the screen view and 3D positive measurements from the world view.

For the evaluation, we explored three shapes: a pencil case, a teapot, and a bottle. When estimating the target shapes in a static scenario without motions, we observed that the results for Extrusion RHMs were disappointing, even when applying active models with appropriate regularization coefficients. This proved the weakness of probabilistic techniques such as SDMs and RHMs, which can tolerate incorrect distributions only if the measurement quality is proportional to the shape complexity, which was not the case in these scenarios. It should be pointed out, however, that Extrusion PIMs with active models and Extrusion NIMs produced very accurate results for all shapes under the same circumstances. For the dynamic evaluation, we moved a bottle as if serving a cup. Both the PIM with active model and the NIM could follow the shape without problem. However, issues with the segmentation produced a small bias in the NIM, occasionally causing the width of the bottle to be overestimated. Based on these results, we can say that Extrusion PIMs and NIMs can be used in practical applications with minimum implementation and deployment effort.

CHAPTER 8

Conclusions

The main topic of this thesis was extended object tracking. Traditionally, literature in this topic has treated targets as a single point without extent or orientation, as a result of the low sensor resolution that tracking applications have historically dealt with. However, as technology advanced and sensor resolution increased, multiple measurements per scan became available, which could be used to estimate the pose and shape of the target more accurately. This shape information could, in turn, be employed in many applications ranging from localization and classification to navigation and mapping, in a variety of disciplines such as autonomous driving, entertainment, robotics, and many others. However, incorporating this information is not straightforward, especially for the following reasons. First, the observed measurements are noisy, and thus, it is difficult to know where on the shape they originated. This task is also made difficult by the fact that we may be missing observations from parts of the shape, due to occlusions or because the sensor can only see one side of the target. Second, lack of a priori information means that flexible shape models are needed, which must be capable of describing a variety of shapes even with an inappropriate initialization. Third, there are many situations where only few measurements with low quality can be obtained, and thus, we need to find the optimal way to exploit all the information available from the sensor. In this thesis, we proposed several mechanisms to address these three challenges, and examined their strengths and weaknesses with multiple experiments. Furthermore, as a way to prove their applicability in practical scenarios, we developed extensions to allow them to incorporate three-dimensional information, and evaluated them using real-world data. In the following, we present a brief summary of our contributions, and an outline for future work.

8.1 Summary

Dealing with noisy data, in particular for shape fitting, can be problematic, given that the measurement noise makes it difficult to associate a measurement to the source that generated it. In consequence, as the noise level increases, so do errors in the association, which in turn leads to estimation bias. Partial Information Models aims to address this issue, proving a mechanism to derive a probabilistic bias correction term by analyzing how the distance function behaves around a source. Still, previous work on this topic has focused on describing the correction term using a Gaussian approximation, which becomes unreliable in cases of high noise, or when occlusions are present In this thesis, we proposed the use of **Level-set Partial Information Models**, which can calculate the correction term with arbitrary accuracy independent of the noise term. This improved reliability, however, required the construction of level-sets, which may be difficult to obtain for arbitrary non-convex shapes. The evaluations using circles and rectangles proved how the proposed approach could yield improved results over similar techniques in literature, in particular for situations with extremely high noise and occlusions, addressing conclusively the first challenge.

The next contribution focused on flexible modeling techniques for filled shapes able to deal with little a priori information and high measurement noise. An important difficulty was how to describe the shape interior, as the usual approach used in literature was based on scaling the boundary inwards, which only worked appropriately for star-convex shapes. Our solution was in the form of **Level-set Active Random Hypersurface Models**, which employed level-sets of the distance function as the transformation mechanism. In order to parameterize the shape boundary, we chose a polygonal representation, as it allowed for an easy calculation of the distance function. However, the increased flexibility caused a lack of robustness when the target shape was less complex than the polygonal boundary, which could in extreme cases lead to overfitting and divergence. We solved this issue with a regularization mechanism inspired by ideas from active contours, which consisted of softly correcting the shape each timestep by making each vertex act like a spring that pulled its neighbors. The advantages of this approach, which demonstrated how our contribution addressed the second challenge, were illustrated in a two-part evaluation. On the one hand, the static evaluation proved that our contribution had no trouble describing a variety of non-convex shapes even when initialized as a circle. On the other hand, the dynamic evaluation highlighted the robustness of our approach when estimating a constantly changing target with a dynamic model that included translations, rotations, and shape morphing. The results proved that our models remained accurate even when little a priori information was available.

Next, we wanted to study a mechanism to maximize the amount of information incorporated from sensor data. In particular, we focused on the fact that devices such as RGB and depth cameras observe not only the target, but also other objects in its surroundings. These 'negative' measurements, usually discarded as clutter, are also valuable, as they give us information about where the object cannot be. Furthermore, given that they are generally more numerous than 'positive' measurements that stem from the target, they can be extremely beneficial in scenarios with low information or occlusions. We proposed a probabilistic model capable of incorporating both negative and positive measurements called **Negative Information Models**, and extended it using ideas of shape fitting in order to increase its robustness. We also explored a mechanism to take into account the possibility of measurement clutter. A preliminary experiment with a static target demonstrated the ability of the proposed model to overcome high measurement noise and occlusions, conclusively addressing the third challenge. Then, an evaluation with a non-convex moving target and high clutter showed how NIM estimates could yield accurate results even in situations where RHMs easily diverged.

While the previously explored ideas focused on two-dimensional shapes, there are several applications in fields such as robotics or indoor navigation that need to incorporate information about three-dimensional shapes. Doing so required us to extend our proposed models into 3D, while retaining their robustness and without increasing their complexity. In order to achieve this, we proposed **Extrusion Models**, a straightforward mechanism to describe complex shapes by interpreting them as the result of vertically 'shifting' a planar shape. We studied several formulations of these models in order to see how they dealt with sensor data from depth cameras, where issues such as artifacts, outliers, and missing information are common. Association models based on probabilistic assumptions, such as RHMs, proved to be unreliable due to the difficulty in approximating how sources were distributed on the target. Furthermore, Negative Information Models required a slight reformulation due to the fact that there were no direct three-dimensional negative measurements available. Instead, a hybrid approach was taken, combining 2D negative measurements from the depth image with 3D positive observations drawn from the point cloud. An extensive evaluation was implemented, estimating the shape and pose of objects commonly seen in daily life, such as bottles, teapots, and a pencil case. We saw how our proposed contributions, even with the presence of numerous outliers and occlusions, could effortlessly yield accurate pose estimates of a moving target.

8.2 Outlook

While we believe that our contributions represent substantial advances in the field of extended object tracking, we cannot say in any meaningful way that the topic is closed, and there are several open questions remaining which yield opportunities for further research. We will now enumerate potential topics which deserve further consideration.

- Sensors such as depth cameras produce measurements with extremely high noise when the observed target is very far away. There is, however, no reliable mechanism in literature to model the distribution of this noise. This is an ideal scenario to test how Level-set PIMs behave in a real-world experiment.
- When dealing with Level-set ARHMs, we assumed that the amount of polygon vertices was known a priori. There is no intrinsic need for this assumption, and a different formulation can be explored which slowly increases the shape complexity until an optimum is found.
- In the many formulations of ARHMs, the regularization coefficient was selected manually depending on the scenario. It may be useful to develop a generic algorithm to calculate a coefficient depending on factors such as shape complexity, measurement uncertainty and process noise.
- Our discussion of Extrusion Models focused on circular base shapes. However, a more advanced approach would be to estimate the base shape in addition to the lateral function using Level-set ARHMs. This would drastically increase the amount of required information, which may need a more careful consideration of the measurement quality provided by the depth sensors.
- The evaluation of Extrusion Models dealt exclusively with Microsoft Kinect sensors. A larger variety of devices could be employed to conclusively prove the suitability of these models for arbitrary data.
- It would be useful to explore mechanisms to incorporate our contributions into a multiple target tracking framework.

CHAPTER

9

Assorted Expressions and Formulas

In order to preserve legibility in the previous chapters, we found it necessary to remove some of the less relevant expressions and formulas. Many of them are common knowledge in literature, while others may be too technical and detract from the reading flow. For the sake of completeness, we present them in this appendix instead.

9.1 Expressions for Rotations

When working with pose estimation, for example in Chapter 5, Chapter 6, and Chapter 7, it is necessary to describe the target rotation in a concise way. When dealing with two dimensions, only a scalar angle $\alpha_k \in \mathbb{R}$ is necessary. A rotation matrix can be obtained using

$$\mathbf{R}\left(\alpha_k\right) := \begin{bmatrix} \cos(\alpha_k) & -\sin(\alpha_k) \\ \sin(\alpha_k) & \cos(\alpha_k) \end{bmatrix} .$$

For three dimensions, however, there are multiple mechanisms to represent a rotation. Of interest for this thesis is the Rodrigues representation, which exploits the fact that any rotation can be described in function of an angle θ_k and an axis $\underline{\mathsf{k}}_k = \left[\mathsf{k}_k^{\mathsf{x}}, \mathsf{k}_k^{\mathsf{y}}, \mathsf{k}_k^{\mathsf{z}}\right]^\top$ with $\|\underline{\mathsf{k}}_k\| = 1$. We can then encode the rotation uniquely using the vector $\underline{r}_k = \theta_k \cdot \underline{\mathsf{k}}_k$.

Mathematically, the rotation matrix corresponding to $\underline{r}_k$ can be obtained from

$$\mathbf{R}(\underline{r}_k) = \mathbf{I} + \sin(\theta_k) \cdot \mathbf{K}(\underline{\mathsf{k}}_k) + (1 - \cos(\theta_k)) \cdot \mathbf{K}(\underline{\mathsf{k}}_k) \cdot \mathbf{K}(\underline{\mathsf{k}}_k) \ ,$$

where the auxiliary matrix $\mathbf{K}$ is defined as

$$\mathbf{K}(\underline{\mathsf{k}}_k) := \begin{bmatrix} 0 & -\mathsf{k}_k^{\mathrm{z}} & \mathsf{k}_k^{\mathrm{y}} \\ \mathsf{k}_k^{\mathrm{z}} & 0 & -\mathsf{k}_k^{\mathrm{x}} \\ -\mathsf{k}_k^{\mathrm{y}} & \mathsf{k}_k^{\mathrm{x}} & 0 \end{bmatrix} .$$

Note that this auxiliary matrix is simply an alternative representation of the cross product, i.e., for any vector $\underline{b} \in \mathbb{R}^3$ it holds that $\mathbf{K}(\underline{\mathsf{k}}_k) \cdot \underline{b} = \underline{\mathsf{k}}_k \times \underline{b}$. For both cases, it always holds that

$$\mathbf{R}(\underline{r}_k)^{-1} = \mathbf{R}(\underline{r}_k)^\top = \mathbf{R}(-\underline{r}_k) \ .$$

9.2 Expressions for Association Models

In this section, we will show the derivation of an assortment of algorithms and functions required for estimation using SDMs and GAMs, as explained in Chapter 2. These approaches are part of the contribution of this thesis, and were originally proposed as auxiliary functions for Level-set PIMs[160], Level-set ARHMs[156], and NIMs [159, 161].

9.2.1 Likelihood for SDMs based on Filled Rectangles

In this subsection, we will derive the expression $\mathrm{p}(\underline{y}_k \,|\, \underline{x}_k)$ for an SDM that describes a filled rectangle with uniform source distribution, first proposed in [159, 161]. Let the target related to $\underline{x}_k$ be the a rectangle with center $\underline{c}_k$, rotated by angle α_k, with dimensions w_k and h_k. An example parametrization using the argument $\underline{s}_k = \left[s_{k,1}, s_{k,2}\right]^\top$ would be

$$\underline{\phi}_k(\underline{s}_k) = \underline{c}_k + \mathbf{R}\left(\alpha_k\right) \cdot \begin{bmatrix} \mathsf{w}_k \cdot s_{k,1} \\ \mathsf{h}_k \cdot s_{k,2} \end{bmatrix} ; s_{k,1} \in \left[-\tfrac{1}{2}, \tfrac{1}{2}\right], s_{k,2} \in \left[-\tfrac{1}{2}, \tfrac{1}{2}\right] .$$

Furthermore, let $\underline{y}_k$ be a measurement with isotropic noise covariance matrix $\mathbf{C}_k^v = \sigma_v^2 \cdot \mathbf{I}$. Then, by transforming the coordinate system to make the rectangle axis-aligned and centered on the origin, we obtain the pseudo-measurement $\underline{y}_k^*$ as

$$\underline{y}_k^* = \begin{bmatrix} y_k^{\mathrm{x}} \\ y_k^{\mathrm{y}} \end{bmatrix} := \mathbf{R}\left(-\alpha_k\right) \cdot \left(\underline{y}_k - \underline{c}_k\right) .$$

As it holds that $s_1, s_2 \sim \mathcal{U}(-\frac{1}{2}, \frac{1}{2})$, it follows that

$$\mathrm{p}(\underline{y}_k \,|\, \underline{x}_k) = \frac{1}{\mathsf{w}_k \cdot \mathsf{h}_k} \cdot \mathrm{G}\left(y_k^{\mathrm{x}}, \frac{\mathsf{w}_k}{2}, \sigma_v^2\right) \cdot \mathrm{G}\left(y_k^{\mathrm{y}}, \frac{\mathsf{h}_k}{2}, \sigma_v^2\right) ,$$

with

$$\mathrm{G}\left(z, a, \sigma_v^2\right) := \frac{1}{2}\left(\operatorname{erf}\left(\frac{a-z}{\sqrt{2}\sigma_v}\right) - \operatorname{erf}\left(\frac{-a-z}{\sqrt{2}\sigma_v}\right)\right) .$$

The proof for this follows from the fact that s_1 and s_2 are independent, and the noise covariance matrix is isotropic and invariant under the transformations. Thus, we see that

$$\begin{aligned}
&\mathrm{p}(\underline{y}_k \,|\, \underline{x}_k) \\
&= \frac{1}{\|\mathcal{S}_k^x\|} \int\limits_{\mathcal{S}_k^x} \mathcal{N}(\underline{y}_k - \underline{z}_k; \underline{0}, \sigma_v^2 \cdot \mathbf{I}) \, \mathrm{d}\underline{z}_k \\
&= \frac{1}{\mathsf{w}_k \cdot \mathsf{h}_k} \int\limits_{-\frac{\mathsf{w}_k}{2}}^{\frac{\mathsf{w}_k}{2}} \int\limits_{-\frac{\mathsf{h}_k}{2}}^{\frac{\mathsf{h}_k}{2}} \mathcal{N}(\underline{y}_k^* - \begin{bmatrix} s_1 \\ s_2 \end{bmatrix}; \underline{0}, \sigma_v^2 \cdot \mathbf{I}) \, \mathrm{d}s_2 \, \mathrm{d}s_1 \\
&= \frac{1}{\mathsf{w}_k \cdot \mathsf{h}_k} \left(\int\limits_{-\frac{\mathsf{h}_k}{2}}^{\frac{\mathsf{h}_k}{2}} \mathcal{N}(y_k^{\mathrm{x}} - s_1; 0, \sigma_v^2) \, \mathrm{d}s_1 \right) \left(\int\limits_{-\frac{\mathsf{w}_k}{2}}^{\frac{\mathsf{w}_k}{2}} \mathcal{N}(y_k^{\mathrm{y}} - s_2; 0, \sigma_v^2) \, \mathrm{d}s_2 \right) \\
&= \frac{1}{\mathsf{w}_k \cdot \mathsf{h}_k} \cdot \mathrm{G}\left(y_k^{\mathrm{x}}, \frac{\mathsf{w}_k}{2}, \sigma_v^2\right) \cdot \mathrm{G}\left(y_k^{\mathrm{y}}, \frac{\mathsf{h}_k}{2}, \sigma_v^2\right) .
\end{aligned}$$

9.2.2 Likelihood for SDMs based on a Line Segment

In this subsection, we will derive the expression $\mathrm{p}(\underline{y}_k \,|\, \underline{x}_k)$ for an SDM that describes a line segment with uniform source distribution, used in [160]. Let the target related to $\underline{x}_k$ be the line segment with endpoints $\underline{a}_k$ and $\underline{b}_k$, with parametrization

$$\underline{\phi}_k(s) = \underline{a}_k + s_k \cdot (\underline{b}_k - \underline{a}_k) \text{ for } s_k \sim \mathcal{U}(0,1)$$

Furthermore, let $\underline{y}_k$ be a measurement with isotropic noise covariance matrix $\mathbf{C}_k^v$, not necessarily isotropic. It follows that

$$\mathrm{p}(\underline{y}_k \,|\, \underline{x}_k) = \frac{1}{\|\underline{b}_k - \underline{a}_k\|} \cdot \mathrm{L}\left(\underline{y}_k, \underline{a}_k, \underline{b}_k, \mathbf{C}_k^v\right) ,$$

where $\mathrm{L}\left(\underline{y}_k, \underline{a}_k, \underline{b}_k, \mathbf{C}_k^v\right)$ is the integral of the distribution $\mathcal{N}\left(\underline{y}_k, \mathbf{C}_k^v\right)$ over the path $\left[\underline{a}_k, \underline{b}_k\right]$, i.e.,

$$\mathrm{L}\left(\underline{y}_k, \underline{a}_k, \underline{b}_k, \mathbf{C}_k^v\right) := \int_0^1 \mathcal{N}(\underline{a}_k + s_k\ (\underline{b}_k - \underline{a}_k) - \underline{y}_k; \underline{0}, \mathbf{C}_k^v)\, \|\underline{b}_k - \underline{a}_k\|\, \mathrm{d}s_k\,.$$

This expression can be solved in closed-form. First, we define

$$\begin{aligned} n_0 &:= (\underline{b}_k - \underline{a}_k)^\top (\mathbf{C}_k^v)^{-1} (\underline{b}_k - \underline{a}_k) \\ n_1 &:= 2\,(\underline{b}_k - \underline{a}_k)^\top (\mathbf{C}_k^v)^{-1} \left(\underline{y}_k - \underline{a}_k\right) \\ n_2 &:= \left(\underline{y}_k - \underline{a}_k\right)^\top (\mathbf{C}_k^v)^{-1} \left(\underline{y}_k - \underline{a}_k\right) . \end{aligned}$$

This allows us to obtain the parameters

$$\begin{aligned} \sigma^* &:= \frac{1}{\sqrt{n_0}} \\ \mu^* &:= -\frac{n_1}{2n_0} \\ \kappa &:= \frac{\|\underline{b}_k - \underline{a}_k\|}{2\sqrt{2\pi \det\left(\mathbf{C}_k^v\right)}} \cdot \sigma^* \cdot \exp\left(-\frac{1}{2}\left(n_2 - \frac{n_1^2}{4n_0}\right)\right) . \end{aligned}$$

The final result is

$$\mathrm{L}\left(\underline{y}_k, \underline{a}_k, \underline{b}_k, \mathbf{C}_k^v\right) = \kappa \cdot \left(\operatorname{erf}\left(\frac{1+\mu^*}{\sqrt{2}\sigma^*}\right) - \operatorname{erf}\left(\frac{\mu^*}{\sqrt{2}\sigma^*}\right)\right) .$$

9.2.3 Logarithm of a Difference of Error Functions

When working with estimators based on SDMs, it is often the case that we require the $\log(\,\cdot\,)$ form of the corresponding likelihood for numerical stability. We observe that the difference of $\operatorname{erf}(\,\cdot\,)$ terms appears frequently in these expressions. Because of this, it makes sense to explore a robust implementation of the function

$$\ell(a, b) = \log\left(\operatorname{erf}(a) - \operatorname{erf}(b)\right) .$$

This can be achieved using the scaled error complementary function $\operatorname{erfcx}(\,\cdot\,)$, available in modern statistics libraries and frameworks such as MATLAB. An implementation is shown in Algorithm 1.

Algorithm 1: Calculate logDiffErf.

input : a, b, where $a > b$
if $a \cdot b \geq 0$ **then**
  $\ell \leftarrow \log\left(\operatorname{erf}(a) - \operatorname{erf}(b)\right)$;
else
  if $a < 0$ **then**
    $\alpha \leftarrow -b$;
    $\beta \leftarrow -a$;
  else
    $\alpha \leftarrow a$;
    $\beta \leftarrow b$;
  $\ell \leftarrow \log\left(\operatorname{erfcx}(\beta) - \operatorname{erfcx}(\alpha) \cdot \exp\left(\beta^2 - \alpha^2\right)\right) - \beta^2$;
output : ℓ

9.2.4 Most Likely Source in a Line Segment and a Polygon

In many applications, such as PIMs from Chapter 3, it is necessary to obtain the source $\underline{z}_k^m$ in a given shape that most likely generated a measurement $\underline{y}_k$. In the following, we present an analytic solution for a line segment connecting two points $\underline{a}_k$ and $\underline{b}_k$, first presented in [156]. This segment is parametrized as

$$\underline{\phi}_k(s_k) = \underline{a}_k + s_k \cdot (\underline{b}_k - \underline{a}_k) \text{ for } s_k \in [0,1] \ .$$

It follows that the most likely source for this segment is $\underline{z}_k^m = \underline{a}_k + s_k^m \cdot (\underline{b}_k - \underline{a}_k)$, for

$$s_k^m := \underset{0 \leq s \leq 1}{\arg\min} \left(\underline{y}_k - \underline{\phi}_k(s)\right)^\top (\mathbf{C}_k^v)^{-1} \left(\underline{y}_k - \underline{\phi}_k(s)\right) \ .$$

This is a convex function whose minimum can be found using standard calculus techniques. The closed-form solution is

$$s_k^m = \text{clamp}\left(\frac{\left(\underline{y}_k - \underline{a}_k\right)^\top (\mathbf{C}_k^v)^{-1} (\underline{b}_k - \underline{a}_k)}{(\underline{b}_k - \underline{a}_k)^\top (\mathbf{C}_k^v)^{-1} (\underline{b}_k - \underline{a}_k)}\right) ,$$

where $\text{clamp}(t) := \max(\min(t,1),0)$. Similarly, the most likely source in a polygon path can be obtained by iterating through all polygon segments and finding the most likely source among the results of Section 9.2.4. Based on this, an algorithm to calculate the most likely source in a polygon is given in Algorithm 2.

9.2.5 Gaussian Integral over a Polygon Path

We will now discuss an approach to calculate the integral of a Gaussian pdf centered on the measurement source $\underline{z}_k$ with covariance matrix $\mathbf{C}_k^v$ over the given polygon. We observe that the derivation of this integral is very easy, as it is extremely similar to the one introduced in Section 9.2.2. By simply using the function $\mathrm{L}(\cdot\,,\cdot\,,\cdot\,,\cdot)$, we obtain a concise closed-form solution as shown in Algorithm 3.

Algorithm 2: Calculate the most likely source in a polygon.

---

input : Polygon $\{\underline{p}_k^1, \cdots, \underline{p}_k^n\}$, measurement $\underline{y}_k$ with noise covariance matrix $\mathbf{C}_k^v$

output : $\underline{z}_k^m$

$d_k^m \leftarrow \infty$;

for $j = 1$ **to** n **do**

  $\underline{z}_k^j \leftarrow$ Calculate most likely source from segment $\underline{p}_k^j$ and $\underline{p}_k^{j+1}$;

  $d_k^j \leftarrow \left(\underline{y}_k - \underline{z}_k^j\right)^\top (\mathbf{C}_k^v)^{-1} \left(\underline{y}_k - \underline{z}_k^j\right)$;

  if $d_k^j < d_k^m$ **then**

    $\underline{z}_k^m \leftarrow \underline{z}_k^j$;

    $d_k^m \leftarrow d_k^j$;

Algorithm 3: Calculate the Gaussian integral over a polygon.

---

input : Polygon $\{\underline{p}_k^1, \cdots, \underline{p}_k^n\}$, measurement source $\underline{z}_k$ with noise covariance matrix $\mathbf{C}_k^v$

output : ℓ_k

$\ell_k \leftarrow 0$;

for $j = 1$ **to** n **do**

  $\ell_k \leftarrow \ell_k + \mathrm{L}\left(\underline{z}_k, \underline{p}_k^j, \underline{p}_k^{j+1}, \mathbf{C}_k^v\right)$

9.3 Propagation of a Pdf over a Function

We will now briefly review two mechanisms to propagate uncertainties over nonlinear functions, necessary in particular for models based on PIMs from Chapter 3.

First, we consider the function

$$\underline{\phi}_k = \underline{\Phi}_k(\underline{\nu}_k) ,$$

where $\underline{\nu}_k$ is a random variable whose probability function is described by $\mathrm{p}(\underline{\nu}_k)$. Assuming $\underline{\Phi}_k$ is bijective, the resulting pdf of $\underline{\phi}_k$ can be written as

$$\mathrm{p}(\underline{\phi}_k) = \mathrm{p}(\underline{\nu}_k) \cdot \left|\det\left(\mathbf{J}_k^{\Phi}(\underline{\nu}_k)\right)\right|^{-1} ,$$

where $\mathbf{J}_k^{\Phi}(\underline{\nu}_k)$ represents the Jacobian matrix of the function $\underline{\Phi}_k(\underline{\nu}_k)$. Otherwise, if $\underline{\Phi}_k$ is not bijective, obtaining a closed-form solution for $\mathrm{p}(\underline{\phi}_k)$ may be difficult. Assuming that $\mathrm{p}(\underline{\nu}_k)$ is Gaussian, solutions for basic operations such as affine transformations or quadratic forms are available. Otherwise, only approximations are possible. Algorithm 4 briefly describes an approach presented in [148] to calculate the first and second moments of $\mathrm{p}(\underline{\phi}_k)$, i.e., the mean $\hat{\underline{\phi}}_k$ and covariance matrix $\mathbf{C}_k^{\phi}$, given a set of samples that approximates the distribution of $\mathrm{p}(\underline{\nu}_k)$. The resulting distribution can be written as $\mathrm{p}(\underline{\phi}_k) \approx \mathcal{N}(\underline{\phi}_k; \hat{\underline{\phi}}_k, \mathbf{C}_k^{\phi})$.

9.4 Recursive Estimation using LRKFs

This section briefly describes the update step of Linear Regression Kalman Filters (LRKFs), which are extensions of the well-known Kalman filters for nonlinear measurement equations, and were widely employed in this thesis, for example in Chapter 5, Chapter 6, and Chapter 7. We assume that we are given a state $\underline{x}_k$ with mean $\hat{\underline{x}}_k$ and covariance matrix $\mathbf{P}_k$. As a review, a Kalman filter considers a linear measurement equation and a

Algorithm 4: Calculate propagated moments.

input : Function $\underline{\Phi}_k$, samples with weights $\{\underline{\nu}_k^j, W_k^j\}_{j=1}^{n_v}$

for $j = 1$ **to** n_v **do**

  $\underline{\phi}_k^j \leftarrow \underline{\Phi}_k(\underline{\nu}_k^j)$;

$\hat{\underline{\phi}}_k \leftarrow \sum_{j=1}^{n_v} W_k^j \cdot \underline{\phi}_k^j$;

$\mathbf{C}_k^\phi \leftarrow \sum_{j=1}^{n_v} W_k^j \cdot \left[\underline{\phi}_k^j - \hat{\underline{\phi}}_k\right]\left[\underline{\phi}_k^j - \hat{\underline{\phi}}_k\right]^\top$;

output: $\hat{\underline{\phi}}_k$, $\mathbf{C}_k^\phi$

linear system equation

$$\begin{aligned} \underline{y}_k &= \mathbf{H}_k \cdot \underline{x}_k + \underline{v}_k \ , \\ \underline{x}_{k+1} &= \mathbf{F}_k \cdot \underline{x}_k + \underline{w}_k \ . \end{aligned}$$

The update step for Kalman Filters can be found in Algorithm 5, and their prediction step can be seen in Algorithm 6. Both steps can be extended to consider an implicit nonlinear measurement equation and a nonlinear system equation, i.e.,

$$\begin{aligned} \underline{0} &= \underline{h}_k(\underline{x}_k, \underline{y}_k, \underline{v}_k, \underline{t}_k) \ , \\ \underline{x}_{k+1} &= \underline{a}_k(\underline{x}_k, \underline{w}_k) \ . \end{aligned}$$

The general update step can be found in Algorithm 7, and the analogous prediction step can be seen in Algorithm 8. A gating mechanism for LRKFs is presented in Algorithm 9.

9.5 Related Work

In order to validate the approaches presented in this thesis, for example Chapter 5 and Chapter 6, it is necessary to compare them to existing techniques in literature. In this section, we will describe a brief implementation of shape estimation using Random Matrices, and shape representations using Fourier series and Gaussian processes.

Algorithm 5: Direct measurement update step for LRKFs.

input : predicted state mean $\hat{\underline{x}}_k^p$ and covariance matrix $\mathbf{P}_k^p$, measurement $\underline{y}_k$ with noise covariance matrix $\mathbf{C}_k^v$ and measurement matrix $\mathbf{H}_k$.

$\mathbf{S}_k \leftarrow \mathbf{C}_k^v + \mathbf{H}_k \cdot \mathbf{P}_k^p \cdot \mathbf{H}_k{}^\top$;

$\mathbf{K}_k \leftarrow \mathbf{P}_k^p \cdot \mathbf{H}_k{}^\top \cdot (\mathbf{S}_k)^{-1}$;

$\hat{\underline{x}}_k^e \leftarrow \hat{\underline{x}}_k^p + \mathbf{K}_k \cdot \left(\underline{y}_k - \mathbf{H}_k \cdot \hat{\underline{x}}_k^p\right)$;

$\mathbf{P}_k^e \leftarrow \mathbf{P}_k^p - \mathbf{K}_k \cdot \mathbf{S}_k \cdot \mathbf{K}_k{}^\top$;

output : $\hat{\underline{x}}_k^e, \mathbf{P}_k^e$

Algorithm 6: Direct prediction step for LRKFs.

input : estimated state mean $\hat{\underline{x}}_k^e$ and covariance matrix $\mathbf{P}_k^e$, system noise covariance matrix $\mathbf{C}_k^w$, system matrix $\mathbf{F}_k$.

$\hat{\underline{x}}_{k+1}^p \leftarrow \mathbf{F}_k \cdot \hat{\underline{x}}_k^e$;

$\mathbf{P}_{k+1}^p \leftarrow \mathbf{F}_k \cdot \mathbf{P}_k^e \cdot \mathbf{F}_k{}^\top + \mathbf{C}_k^w$;

output : $\hat{\underline{x}}_{k+1}^p, \mathbf{P}_{k+1}^p$

Algorithm 7: Sample-based measurement update step for LRKFs.

input : predicted state mean $\hat{\underline{x}}_k^p$ and covariance matrix $\mathbf{P}_k^p$,
measurement $\underline{y}_k$,
prior state samples with weights $\{\underline{\chi}_k^j, W_k^j\}_{j=1}^{n_x}$,
measurement noise samples with weights $\{\underline{v}_k^j, W_k^j\}_{j=1}^{n_x}$,
shape noise samples with weights $\{\underline{t}_k^j, W_k^j\}_{j=1}^{n_x}$.

for $j = 1$ **to** n_x **do**
  $\underline{\varphi}_k^j \leftarrow \underline{h}_k(\underline{\chi}_k^j, \underline{y}_k, \underline{v}_k^j, \underline{t}_k^j)$;

$\hat{\underline{\varphi}}_k \leftarrow \sum_{j=1}^{n_x} W_k^j \cdot \underline{\varphi}_k^j$;

$\mathbf{C}_k^{\varphi} \leftarrow \sum_{j=1}^{n_x} W_k^j \cdot \left[\underline{\varphi}_k^j - \hat{\underline{\varphi}}_k\right] \left[\underline{\varphi}_k^j - \hat{\underline{\varphi}}_k\right]^\top$;

$\mathbf{C}_k^{x\varphi} \leftarrow \sum_{j=1}^{n_x} W_k^j \left[\underline{\chi}_k^j - \hat{\underline{x}}_k^p\right] \left[\underline{\varphi}_k^j - \hat{\underline{\varphi}}_k\right]^\top$;

$\mathbf{K}_k \leftarrow \mathbf{C}_k^{x\varphi} \cdot (\mathbf{C}_k^{\varphi})^{-1}$;

$\hat{\underline{x}}_k^e \leftarrow \hat{\underline{x}}_k^p + \mathbf{K}_k \cdot \hat{\underline{\varphi}}_k$;

$\mathbf{P}_k^e \leftarrow \mathbf{P}_k^p - \mathbf{K}_k \cdot \mathbf{C}_k^{\varphi} \cdot \mathbf{K}_k{}^\top$;

output : $\hat{\underline{x}}_k^e, \mathbf{P}_k^e$

Algorithm 8: Sample-based prediction step for LRKFs.

input : estimated state samples with weights $\{\underline{\chi}_k^j, W_k^j\}_{j=1}^{n_x}$,
system noise samples with weights $\{\underline{w}_k^j, W_k^j\}_{j=1}^{n_x}$.

for $j = 1$ **to** n_x **do**
  $\underline{\mathbf{x}}_k^j \leftarrow \underline{a}_k(\underline{\chi}_k^j, \underline{w}_k^j)$;

$\hat{\underline{x}}_{k+1}^p \leftarrow \sum_{j=1}^{n_x} W_k^j \cdot \underline{\mathbf{x}}_k^j$;

$\mathbf{P}_{k+1}^p \leftarrow \sum_{j=1}^{n_x} W_k^j \cdot \left(\underline{\mathbf{x}}_k^j - \hat{\underline{x}}_{k+1}^p\right) \left(\underline{\mathbf{x}}_k^j - \hat{\underline{x}}_{k+1}^p\right)^\top$;

output : $\hat{\underline{x}}_{k+1}^p, \mathbf{P}_{k+1}^p$

Algorithm 9: Gating step for LRKFs.

input : measurement mean $\hat{\underline{\varphi}}_k$ with covariance matrix $\mathbf{C}_k^{\varphi}$, gating parameter γ_k .

$C \leftarrow \left(\hat{\underline{\varphi}}_k^{\top} (\mathbf{C}_k^{\varphi})^{-1} \hat{\underline{\varphi}}_k \right) < \gamma_k$;

output : Boolean value C

9.5.1 Tracking Extended Objects using Random Matrices

In this subsection, we will present an implementation of the approach introduced by [33] to track elliptic approximations of extended targets with random matrices. The state consists of the pair $\left[\underline{x}_k^c, \mathbf{X}_k\right]$, where $\underline{x}_k^c$ determines the position of the target's centroid, and $\mathbf{X}_k$ is a $d \times d$ matrix which models the elliptic target extent, described as

$$\mathcal{S}_k^e = \{\underline{p}_k \in \mathbb{R}^d \,|\, \underline{p}_k^{\top} \cdot \mathbf{X}_k^{-1} \cdot \underline{p}_k \leq s_k\} \ ,$$

where $s_k \in \mathbb{R}$ is an arbitrary scaling factor, usually 1, and d is the dimension of the measurement space. The state uncertainty is described by the pair $\left[\mathbf{P}_k, \nu_k\right]$, where $\mathbf{P}_k$ is the covariance matrix of $\underline{x}_k^c$, and ν_k represents both the number of observed measurements and the extent uncertainty. The update step can be found in Algorithm 10. The prediction step, which assumes a linear system equation $\underline{x}_k^{c,p} = \mathbf{F}_k \cdot \underline{x}_k^{c,e} + \underline{w}_k$, a change in time ΔT_k, and a 'forgetting' factor τ_k, can be found in Algorithm 11.

9.5.2 Representing a Boundary with Fourier Series

We will now derive a radial function $r_k^f(\theta_k)$ to describe the boundary of a target using Fourier series, as presented in [27, 162, 153, 28]. A Fourier series of degree n is defined using a series of coefficients $\left[a_k^0, a_k^1, b_k^1, \cdots, a_k^n, b_k^n\right]^{\top}$, generally estimated as part of the state. The

Algorithm 10: Update step.

input : $\underline{x}_k^p$,$\mathbf{P}_k^p$,ν_k^p,$\mathbf{X}_k^p$, $\mathbf{H}_k$
Measurements $\mathcal{Y}_k = \{\underline{y}_{k,1}, \ldots, \underline{y}_{k,n}\}$ with noise covariance matrix $\mathbf{C}_k^v$
output: $\underline{x}_k^e$,$\mathbf{P}_k^e$,ν_k^e,$\mathbf{X}_k^e$

$\hat{\underline{y}}_k \leftarrow \frac{1}{n} \sum_{i=1}^{n} \underline{y}_{k,i}$;
$\mathbf{C}_k^y \leftarrow \sum_{i=1}^{n} \left(\underline{y}_{k,i} - \hat{\underline{y}}_k\right) \left(\underline{y}_{k,i} - \hat{\underline{y}}_k\right)^\top$;
$\mathbf{Y}_k \leftarrow \mathbf{X}_k^p + \mathbf{C}_k^v$;
$\mathbf{S}_k \leftarrow \mathbf{H}_k \cdot \mathbf{P}_k^e \cdot \mathbf{H}_k{}^\top + \frac{1}{n}\mathbf{Y}_k$;
$\mathbf{K}_k^x \leftarrow \mathbf{P}_k^e \cdot \mathbf{H}_k{}^\top \cdot \mathbf{S}_k{}^{-1}$;
$\mathbf{X}_k^{p,s} \leftarrow \text{chol}\,(\mathbf{X}_k^p)$;
$\mathbf{S}_k^s \leftarrow \text{chol}\,(\mathbf{S}_k)$;
$\mathbf{Y}_k^s \leftarrow \text{chol}\,(\mathbf{Y}_k)$;
$\mathbf{N}_k^s \leftarrow \mathbf{X}_k^{p,s} \cdot (\mathbf{S}_k^s)^{-1} \cdot \left(\hat{\underline{y}}_k - \mathbf{H}_k \cdot \underline{x}_k^p\right)$;
$\mathbf{N}_k \leftarrow \mathbf{N}_k^s \cdot \mathbf{N}_k^{s\top}$;
$\mathbf{K}_k^X \leftarrow \mathbf{X}_k^{p,s} \cdot (\mathbf{Y}_k^s)^{-1}$;
$\underline{x}_k^e \leftarrow \underline{x}_k^p + \mathbf{K}_k^x \cdot \left(\hat{\underline{y}}_k - \mathbf{H}_k \cdot \underline{x}_k^p\right)$;
$\mathbf{P}_k^e \leftarrow \mathbf{P}_k^p - \mathbf{K}_k^x \cdot \mathbf{S}_k \cdot \mathbf{K}_k^{x\top}$;
$\nu_k^e \leftarrow \nu_k^p + n$;
$\mathbf{X}_k^e \leftarrow \left(\nu_k^p \cdot \mathbf{X}_k^p + \mathbf{N}_k + \mathbf{K}_k^X \cdot \mathbf{C}_k^y \cdot \mathbf{K}_k^{X\top}\right) / \nu_k^e$;

Algorithm 11: Prediction step.

input : $\underline{x}_k^e$,$\mathbf{P}_k^e$,ν_k^e,$\mathbf{X}_k^e$, $\mathbf{F}_k$, τ_k, ΔT_k
output: $\underline{x}_k^p$,$\mathbf{P}_k^p$,ν_k^p,$\mathbf{X}_k^p$

$\underline{x}_k^p \leftarrow \mathbf{F}_k \cdot \underline{x}_k^e$;
$\mathbf{P}_k^p \leftarrow \mathbf{F}_k \cdot \mathbf{P}_k^e \cdot \mathbf{F}_k{}^\top + \mathbf{C}_k^w$;
$\nu_k^e \leftarrow d + \exp\left(-\Delta T_k/\tau_k\right)(\nu_k^p - d)$;
$\mathbf{X}_k^e \leftarrow \mathbf{X}_k^p$;

radial function takes the form

$$r_k^f(\theta_k) := \frac{a_k^0}{2} + \sum_{j=1}^{n} a_k^j \cdot \cos(j\theta_k) + b_k^j \cdot \sin(j\theta_k) .$$

Note that, equivalently, this expression can be written as

$$r_k^f(\theta_k) = \frac{a_k^0}{2} + \sum_{j=1}^{n} \sqrt{(a_k^j)^2 + (b_k^j)^2} \cdot \sin(j\theta_k + \mathrm{atan2}(a_k^j, b_k^j)) .$$

Thus, the radial function is simply a series of translated and scaled $\sin(\,\cdot\,)$ curves superimposed on top of each other. This also serves to demonstrate that an explicit shape rotation parameter is, in principle, unobservable, as any rotation can be expressed as a different shape by adjusting the Fourier coefficients.

9.5.3 Representing a Boundary with a Gaussian Process

In this section we will derive a radial function $r_k^f(\theta)$ to describe the boundary of a target using ideas from Gaussian processes, as presented in [29]. First, we need to define the covariance function

$$k(\theta_1, \theta_2) = \sigma_f^2 \cdot \exp\left(-\frac{2}{l^2} \sin\left(\frac{\theta_1 - \theta_2}{2} \right)^2 \right) + \sigma_r^2 ,$$

where σ_f^2 represents the variance of the prior signal amplitude, σ_r^2 is the variance of the mean function, and l is the standard deviation hyperparameter of the Gaussian process. We will now proceed to extend this function to accept multiple values simultaneously. Let

$$\underline{\theta_1} = \left[\theta_1^1, \cdots, \theta_1^n\right]^\top , \text{ and}$$
$$\underline{\theta_2} = \left[\theta_2^1, \cdots, \theta_2^m\right]^\top$$

be two arbitrary input vectors. We now define

$$K(\underline{\theta}_1, \underline{\theta}_2) = \begin{bmatrix} k\left(\theta_1^1, \theta_2^1\right) & \cdots & k\left(\theta_1^1, \theta_2^m\right) \\ \vdots & \ddots & \vdots \\ k\left(\theta_1^n, \theta_2^1\right) & \cdots & k\left(\theta_1^n, \theta_2^m\right) \end{bmatrix} .$$

For this function, [29] proposes the default parameters $\sigma_r^2 = 4$, $\sigma_f^2 = 4$, and $l = \frac{\pi}{4}$.

Given a covariance function, a Gaussian process boundary of degree n is defined using a series of coefficients $\underline{a}_k = \left[a_k^1, \cdots, a_k^n\right]^\top$, generally estimated as part of the state, and a series of support angles $\underline{u}_k = \left[u_k^1, \cdots, u_k^n\right]^\top$ for $u_k^j \in \left[0, 2\pi\right]$. The radial function takes the form

$$r_k^g(\theta_k) := K(\theta_k, \underline{u}_k) \cdot K(\underline{u}_k, \underline{u}_k)^{-1} \cdot \underline{a}_k .$$

Note that it holds that $r_k^f(u_k^j) = a_k^j$ for $1 \leq j \leq n$. As part of the Gaussian process, each angle also has an associated radial uncertainty

$$\Sigma_k^u(\theta_k) := \sigma_r^2 + \sigma_f^2 - K(\theta_k, \underline{u}_k) \cdot K(\underline{u}_k, \underline{u}_k)^{-1} \cdot K(\theta_k, \underline{u}_k)^\top ,$$

which should be taken into account as part of the measurement noise. For the support angles, [29] proposes a uniform distribution in the range $\left[0, 2\pi\right]$, i.e., $u_k^j = 2\pi \cdot \frac{j}{n}$.

Bibliography

[1] K. Granstrom and M. Baum, "Extended object tracking: Introduction, overview and applications," *arXiv preprint arXiv:1604.00970*, 2016.

[2] J. D. Kendrick, P. Maybeck, and J. Reid, "Estimation of aircraft target motion using orientation measurements," *IEEE Transactions on Aerospace and Electronic Systems*, no. 2, pp. 254–260, 1981.

[3] R. N. Jazar, "Vehicle dynamics," *Theory and Applications. Riverdale, NY: Springer Science+ Business Media*, 2008.

[4] Y. Bar-Shalom and T. Fortmann, *Tracking and Data Association.* Mathematics in Science and Engineering Series, Academic Press, 1988.

[5] Y. Bar-Shalom, P. K. Willett, and X. Tian, *Tracking and data fusion.* YBS publishing, 2011.

[6] K. Kastella and M. Biscuso, "Tracking algorithms for air traffic control applications," *Air Traffic Control Quarterly*, vol. 3, no. 1, pp. 19–43, 1995.

[7] I. Hwang, H. Balakrishnan, and C. Tomlin, "State estimation for hybrid systems: applications to aircraft tracking," *IEE Proceedings-Control Theory and Applications*, vol. 153, no. 5, pp. 556–566, 2006.

[8] S. Brusch, S. Lehner, T. Fritz, M. Soccorsi, A. Soloviev, and B. van Schie, "Ship surveillance with terrasar-x," *IEEE Transactions on Geoscience and Remote Sensing*, vol. 49, pp. 1092–1103, March 2011.

[9] G. Vivone and P. Braca, "Joint probabilistic data association tracker for extended target tracking applied to x-band marine radar data," *IEEE Journal of Oceanic Engineering*, vol. 41, pp. 1007–1019, Oct 2016.

[10] Q. Zhu, L. Chen, Q. Li, M. Li, A. Nüchter, and J. Wang, "3d lidar point cloud based intersection recognition for autonomous driving," in *2012 IEEE Intelligent Vehicles Symposium*, pp. 456–461, June 2012.

[11] R. A. Newcombe, S. Izadi, O. Hilliges, D. Molyneaux, D. Kim, A. J. Davison, P. Kohli, J. Shotton, S. Hodges, and A. Fitzgibbon, "Kinectfusion: Real-time dense surface mapping and tracking," in *IEEE ISMAR*, IEEE, October 2011.

[12] O. Drummond, S. Blackman, and K. Hell, "Multiple sensor tracking of clusters and extended objects," in *Technical Proceedings*, 1988.

[13] O. E. Drummond, S. S. Blackman, and G. C. Pretrisor, "Tracking clusters and extended objects with multiple sensors," *Signal and Data Processing of Small Targets 1990*, vol. 1305, no. 1, pp. 362–375, 1990.

[14] K. Granström, A. Natale, P. Braca, G. Ludeno, and F. Serafino, "Gamma gaussian inverse wishart probability hypothesis density for extended target tracking using x-band marine radar data," *IEEE Transactions on Geoscience and Remote Sensing*, vol. 53, no. 12, pp. 6617–6631, 2015.

[15] G. Vivone, P. Braca, K. Granström, A. Natale, and J. Chanussot, "Converted measurements random matrix approach to extended target tracking using x-band marine radar data," in *Information Fusion (Fusion), 2015 18th International Conference on*, pp. 976–983, IEEE, 2015.

[16] J. W. Koch, "Bayesian Approach to Extended Object and Cluster Tracking using Random Matrices," *IEEE Transactions on Aerospace and Electronic Systems*, vol. 44, pp. 1042–1059, July 2008.

[17] M. Feldmann and D. Fränken, "Tracking of Extended Objects and Group Targets using Random Matrices – A New Approach," *Proceedings of the 11th International Conference on Information Fusion (Fusion 2008)*, pp. 1–8, July 2008.

[18] M. Baum and U. D. Hanebeck, "Tracking a Minimum Bounding Rectangle based on Extreme Value Theory," in *Proceedings of the 2010 IEEE International Conference on Multisensor Fusion and Integration for Intelligent Systems (MFI 2010)*, (Salt Lake City, Utah, USA), Sept. 2010.

[19] M. Baum and U. D. Hanebeck, "Tracking an Extended Object Modeled as an Axis-Aligned Rectangle," in *4th German Workshop on Sensor Data Fusion: Trends, Solutions, Applications (SDF 2009), 39th Annual Conference of the Gesellschaft für Informatik e.V. (GI)*, (Lübeck, Germany), Oct. 2009.

[20] K. Gilholm and D. Salmond, "Spatial Distribution Model for Tracking Extended Objects," *IEE Proceedings on Radar, Sonar and Navigation*, vol. 152, no. 5, pp. 364–371, 2005.

[21] A. Elfes, "Using occupancy grids for mobile robot perception and navigation," *Computer*, vol. 22, no. 6, pp. 46–57, 1989.

[22] F. Fleuret, J. Berclaz, R. Lengagne, and P. Fua, "Multicamera people tracking with a probabilistic occupancy map," *Pattern Analysis and Machine Intelligence, IEEE Transactions on*, vol. 30, pp. 267–282, Feb 2008.

[23] A. Elfes, "Occupancy grids: A stochastic spatial representation for active robot perception," in *Proceedings of the Sixth Conference on Uncertainty in AI*, vol. 2929, 1990.

[24] K. Granström, S. Reuter, D. Meissner, and A. Scheel, "A multiple model phd approach to tracking of cars under an assumed rectangular shape," in *Information Fusion (FUSION), 2014 17th International Conference on*, pp. 1–8, IEEE, 2014.

[25] M. Baum, *Simultaneous tracking and shape estimation of extended objects.* KIT Scientific Publishing, 2014.

[26] M. Baum and U. D. Hanebeck, "Extended Object Tracking with Random Hypersurface Models," *arXiv preprint: Systems and Control (cs.SY), Draft accepted for publication in IEEE Transactions on Aerospace and Electronic Systems*, Apr. 2013.

[27] M. Baum and U. D. Hanebeck, "Shape Tracking of Extended Objects and Group Targets with Star-Convex RHMs," in *Proceedings of the 14th International Conference on Information Fusion (Fusion 2011)*, (Chicago, Illinois, USA), July 2011.

[28] L. Sun, J. Lan, and X. R. Li, "Extended target tracking using star-convex model with nonlinear inequality constraints," in *Control Conference (CCC), 2012 31st Chinese*, pp. 3869–3874, July 2012.

[29] N. Wahlstrom and E. Ozkan, "Extended target tracking using gaussian processes," *Signal Processing, IEEE Transactions on*, vol. 63, no. 16, pp. 4165–4178, 2015.

[30] M. Baum and U. D. Hanebeck, "Extended Object Tracking with Random Hypersurface Models," *IEEE Transactions on Aerospace and Electronic Systems*, vol. 50, pp. 149–159, Jan. 2014.

[31] K. Granstrom, P. Willett, and Y. Bar-Shalom, "An extended target tracking model with multiple random matrices and unified kinematics," in *Information Fusion (Fusion), 2015 18th International Conference on*, pp. 1007–1014, July 2015.

[32] J. Lan and X. R. Li, "Tracking of maneuvering non-ellipsoidal extended object or target group using random matrix," *IEEE Transactions on Signal Processing*, vol. 62, pp. 2450–2463, May 2014.

[33] M. Feldmann, D. Franken, and W. Koch, "Tracking of Extended Objects and Group Targets Using Random Matrices," *IEEE Transactions on Signal Processing*, vol. 59, pp. 1409–1420, Apr. 2011.

[34] U. Orguner, "A Variational Measurement Update for Extended Target Tracking With Random Matrices," *IEEE Transactions on Signal Processing*, vol. 60, pp. 3827 –3834, July 2012.

[35] P. Lancaster and K. Salkauskas, "Curve and surface fitting. an introduction," *London: Academic Press, 1986*, vol. 1, 1986.

[36] W. Gander, G. H. Golub, and R. Strebel, "Least-squares fitting of circles and ellipses," *Bulletin of the Belgian Mathematical Society Simon Stevin*, vol. 3, no. 5, pp. 63–84, 1996.

[37] P. L. Rosin, "A Note on the Least Squares Fitting of Ellipses," *Pattern Recognition Letters*, vol. 14, no. 10, pp. 799 – 808, 1993.

[38] M. Baum and U. D. Hanebeck, "Fitting Conics to Noisy Data Using Stochastic Linearization," *Measurement*, pp. 1–6, 2011.

[39] M. Baum, V. Klumpp, and U. D. Hanebeck, "A Novel Bayesian Method for Fitting a Circle to Noisy Points," in *Proceedings of the 13th International Conference on Information Fusion (Fusion 2010)*, (Edinburgh, United Kingdom), 2010.

[40] L. Sun, X. Li, and J. Lan, "Extended object tracking based on support functions and extended gaussian images," in *Information Fusion (FUSION), 2013 16th International Conference on*, July 2013.

[41] J.-l. Yang, P. Li, and H.-w. Ge, "Extended target shape estimation by fitting b-spline curve," *Journal of Applied Mathematics*, vol. 2014, 2014.

[42] N. J. Mitra, M. Pauly, M. Wand, and D. Ceylan, "Symmetry in 3d geometry: Extraction and applications," *Computer Graphics Forum*, vol. 32, no. 6, 2013.

[43] T. Okatani and K. Deguchi, "On bias correction for geometric parameter estimation in computer vision," in *Computer Vision and Pattern Recognition, 2009. CVPR 2009. IEEE Conference on*, pp. 959–966, IEEE, 2009.

[44] Z. Zhang, "Iterative point matching for registration of free-form curves and surfaces," *International journal of computer vision*, vol. 13, no. 2, pp. 119–152, 1994.

[45] S. Rusinkiewicz and M. Levoy, "Efficient variants of the icp algorithm," in *3-D Digital Imaging and Modeling, 2001. Proceedings. Third International Conference on*, pp. 145 –152, 2001.

[46] T. Mallick, P. P. Das, and A. K. Majumdar, "Characterizations of noise in kinect depth images: A review," *IEEE Sensors Journal*, vol. 14, pp. 1731–1740, June 2014.

[47] C. V. Nguyen, S. Izadi, and D. Lovell, "Modeling kinect sensor noise for improved 3d reconstruction and tracking," in *2012 Second International Conference on 3D Imaging, Modeling, Processing, Visualization Transmission*, pp. 524–530, Oct 2012.

[48] T. Whelan, M. Kaess, M. Fallon, H. Johannsson, J. Leonard, and J. McDonald, "Kintinuous: Spatially extended kinectfusion," 2012.

[49] S. Thrun, "Learning occupancy grids with forward models," in *Intelligent Robots and Systems, 2001. Proceedings. 2001 IEEE/RSJ International Conference on*, vol. 3, pp. 1676–1681, IEEE, 2001.

[50] S. M. Seitz and C. R. Dyer, "Photorealistic scene reconstruction by voxel coloring," *International Journal of Computer Vision*, vol. 35, no. 2, pp. 151–173, 1999.

[51] J. C. Carr, R. K. Beatson, J. B. Cherrie, T. J. Mitchell, W. R. Fright, B. C. McCallum, and T. R. Evans, "Reconstruction and representation of 3d objects with radial basis functions," in *Proceedings of the 28th annual conference on Computer graphics and interactive techniques*, pp. 67–76, ACM, 2001.

[52] P. Jenke, M. Wand, M. Bokeloh, A. Schilling, and W. Straßer, "Bayesian point cloud reconstruction," in *Computer Graphics Forum*, vol. 25, pp. 379–388, Wiley Online Library, 2006.

[53] R. B. Rusu and S. Cousins, "3D is here: Point Cloud Library (PCL)," in *IEEE International Conference on Robotics and Automation (ICRA)*, (Shanghai, China), May 9-13 2011.

[54] Z. Zhang, "Parameter estimation techniques: a tutorial with application to conic fitting," *Image and Vision Computing*, vol. 15, no. 1, pp. 59 – 76, 1997.

[55] B. Leibe, N. Cornelis, K. Cornelis, and L. Van Gool, "Dynamic 3d scene analysis from a moving vehicle," in *Computer Vision and Pattern Recognition, 2007. CVPR'07. IEEE Conference on*, pp. 1–8, IEEE, 2007.

[56] F. Faion, *Tracking Extended Objects in Noisy Point Clouds with Application in Telepresence Systems.* Dissertation, Karlsruhe Institute of Technology (KIT), ISAS - Intelligent Sensor-Actuator-Systems Laboratory, Referent: U. D. Hanebeck, Korreferent: Priv.-Doz. Dr. Wolfgang Koch, Karlsruhe Series on Intelligent Sensor-Actuator-Systems 19, 2015. ISBN 978-3-7315-0517-4.

[57] F. Faion, M. Baum, and U. D. Hanebeck, "Tracking 3D Shapes in Noisy Point Clouds with Random Hypersurface Models," in *Proceedings of the 15th International Conference on Information Fusion (Fusion 2012)*, (Singapore), July 2012.

[58] B.-n. Vo, M. Mallick, Y. Bar-shalom, S. Coraluppi, R. Osborne, R. Mahler, and B.-t. Vo, "Multitarget tracking," *Wiley Encyclopedia of Electrical and Electronics Engineering*, 2015.

[59] Y. Bar-Shalom and X.-R. Li, "Multitarget-multisensor tracking: principles and techniques," *Storrs, CT: University of Connecticut, 1995.*, 1995.

[60] S. Blackman and R. Popoli, "Design and analysis of modern tracking systems(book)," *Norwood, MA: Artech House, 1999.*, 1999.

[61] Y. Bar-Shalom, T. Kirubarajan, and X.-R. Li, *Estimation with Applications to Tracking and Navigation.* New York, NY, USA: John Wiley & Sons, Inc., 2002.

[62] R. L. Streit and T. E. Luginbuhl, "Probabilistic multi-hypothesis tracking," tech. rep., DTIC Document, 1995.

[63] P. Willett, Y. Ruan, and R. Streit, "Pmht: problems and some solutions," *IEEE Transactions on Aerospace and Electronic Systems*, vol. 38, no. 3, pp. 738–754, 2002.

[64] M. J. Waxman and O. E. Drummond, "A Bibliography of Cluster (Group) Tracking," *Signal and Data Processing of Small Targets 2004*, vol. 5428, no. 1, pp. 551–560, 2004.

[65] K. Granström and U. Orguner, "A PHD Filter for Tracking Multiple Extended Targets Using Random Matrices," *IEEE Transactions on Signal Processing*, vol. 60, pp. 5657 –5671, nov. 2012.

[66] M. Wieneke and S. J. Davey, "Histogram pmht with target extent estimates based on random matrices," in *Information Fusion (FUSION), 2011 Proceedings of the 14th International Conference on*, pp. 1–8, IEEE, 2011.

[67] M. Wieneke and W. Koch, "A pmht approach for extended objects and object groups," *IEEE Transactions on Aerospace and Electronic Systems*, vol. 48, no. 3, pp. 2349–2370, 2012.

[68] K. Granstrom, C. Lundquist, and O. Orguner, "Extended target tracking using a gaussian-mixture phd filter," *IEEE Transactions on Aerospace and Electronic Systems*, vol. 48, no. 4, pp. 3268–3286, 2012.

[69] A. Yilmaz, O. Javed, and M. Shah, "Object Tracking: A Survey," *ACM Computing Surveys*, vol. 38, Dec. 2006.

[70] K.-S. Fu and J. Mui, "A survey on image segmentation," *Pattern recognition*, vol. 13, no. 1, pp. 3–16, 1981.

[71] H. Zhang, J. E. Fritts, and S. A. Goldman, "Image segmentation evaluation: A survey of unsupervised methods," *computer vision and image understanding*, vol. 110, no. 2, pp. 260–280, 2008.

[72] J. Freixenet, X. Muñoz, D. Raba, J. Martí, and X. Cufí, "Yet another survey on image segmentation: Region and boundary information integration," *Computer Vision—ECCV 2002*, pp. 21–25, 2002.

[73] A. Rivers, F. Durand, and T. Igarashi, "3D modeling with silhouettes," *ACM Transactions on Graphics*, vol. 29, p. 1, July 2010.

[74] F. Faion, M. Baum, and U. D. Hanebeck, "Silhouette Measurements for Bayesian Object Tracking in Noisy Point Clouds," in *Proceedings of the 16th International Conference on Information Fusion (Fusion 2013)*, (Istanbul, Turkey), July 2013.

[75] A. Blake and M. Isard, *Active contours: the application of techniques from graphics, vision, control theory and statistics to visual tracking of shapes in motion*. Springer Science & Business Media, 2012.

[76] M. Kass, A. Witkin, and D. Terzopoulos, "Snakes: Active contour models," *International Journal of Computer Vision*, vol. 1, no. 4, pp. 321–331, 1988.

[77] M. Baum, F. Faion, and U. D. Hanebeck, "Tracking Ground Moving Extended Objects using RGBD Data," in *Proceedings of the 2012 IEEE International Conference on Multisensor Fusion and Integration for Intelligent Systems (MFI 2012)*, (Hamburg, Germany), Sept. 2012.

[78] G. Kurz, P. Hegedus, G. Szabo, and U. D. Hanebeck, "Experimental Evaluation of Kinect and Inertial Sensors for Beating Heart Tracking," in *12. Jahrestagung der Deutschen Gesellschaft für Computer- und Roboterassistierte Chirurgie (CURAC13)*, (Innsbruck, Austria), Nov. 2013.

[79] K.-i. Kanatani, "Statistical bias of conic fitting and renormalization," *IEEE Transactions on Pattern Analysis and Machine Intelligence*, vol. 16, no. 3, pp. 320–326, 1994.

[80] K. Wyffels and M. Campbell, "Modeling and fusing negative information for dynamic extended multi-object tracking," in *Robotics and Automation (ICRA), 2013 IEEE International Conference on*, pp. 3176–3182, IEEE, 2013.

[81] W. R. Blanding, W. Koch, and U. Nickel, "Adaptive phased-array tracking in ecm using negative information," *IEEE Transactions on Aerospace and Electronic Systems*, vol. 45, no. 1, pp. 152–166, 2009.

[82] J. Hoffman, M. Spranger, D. Gohring, and M. Jungel, "Making use of what you don't see: negative information in markov localization," in *Intelligent Robots and Systems, 2005. (IROS 2005). 2005 IEEE/RSJ International Conference on*, pp. 2947–2952, Aug 2005.

[83] M. Baum and U. D. Hanebeck, "Random Hypersurface Models for Extended Object Tracking," in *2009 IEEE International Symposium on Signal Processing and Information Technology (ISSPIT)*, (Ajman, United Arab Emirates), pp. 178–183, Ieee, Dec. 2009.

[84] F. Scholz, "Maximum likelihood estimation," *Encyclopedia of Statistical Sciences*, 1985.

[85] M. S. Arulampalam, S. Maskell, N. Gordon, and T. Clapp, "A tutorial on particle filters for online nonlinear/non-gaussian bayesian tracking," *IEEE Transactions on Signal Processing*, vol. 50, Feb 2002.

[86] F. Gustafsson, F. Gunnarsson, N. Bergman, U. Forssell, J. Jansson, R. Karlsson, and P.-J. Nordlund, "Particle filters for positioning, navigation, and tracking," *IEEE Transactions on signal processing*, vol. 50, no. 2, pp. 425–437, 2002.

[87] J. Steinbring and U. D. Hanebeck, "Progressive Gaussian Filtering Using Explicit Likelihoods," in *Proceedings of the 17th International Conference on Information Fusion (Fusion 2014)*, (Salamanca, Spain), July 2014.

[88] J. Steinbring and U. D. Hanebeck, "LRKF Revisited: The Smart Sampling Kalman Filter (S^2KF)," *Journal of Advances in Information Fusion*, vol. 9, pp. 106 – 123, Dec. 2014.

[89] S. J. Julier and J. K. Uhlmann, "Unscented filtering and nonlinear estimation," *Proceedings of the IEEE*, vol. 92, Mar. 2004.

[90] O. Straka, J. Duník, and M. Simandl, "Randomized unscented kalman filter in target tracking," in *Information Fusion (FUSION), 2012 15th International Conference on*, pp. 503–510, July 2012.

[91] Y. Bar-Shalom, P. K. Willett, and X. Tian, *Tracking and Data Fusion: A Handbook of Algorithms.* YBS Publishing, 2011.

[92] X. R. Li and V. P. Jilkov, "Survey of maneuvering target tracking. part i. dynamic models," *IEEE Transactions on aerospace and electronic systems*, vol. 39, no. 4, pp. 1333–1364, 2003.

[93] R. P. Mahler, *Statistical multisource-multitarget information fusion.* Artech House, Inc., 2007.

[94] G. Ackerson and K. Fu, "On state estimation in switching environments," *Automatic Control, IEEE Transactions on*, vol. 15, no. 1, pp. 10–17, 1970.

[95] M. Baum, B. Noack, and U. D. Hanebeck, "Random Hypersurface Mixture Models for Tracking Multiple Extended Objects," in *Proceedings of the 50th IEEE Conference on Decision and Control (CDC 2011)*, (Orlando, Florida, USA), Dec. 2011.

[96] K. Gilholm, S. Godsill, S. Maskell, and D. Salmond, "Poisson Models for Extended Target and Group Tracking," in *SPIE: Signal and Data Processing of Small Targets*, 2005.

[97] H. A. Blom and Y. Bar-Shalom, "The interacting multiple model algorithm for systems with markovian switching coefficients," *Automatic Control, IEEE Transactions on*, vol. 33, no. 8, pp. 780–783, 1988.

[98] M. J. Waxman and O. E. Drummond, "A bibliography of cluster (group) tracking," in *Defense and Security*, pp. 551–560, International Society for Optics and Photonics, 2004.

[99] L. Mihaylova, A. Y. Carmi, F. Septier, A. Gning, S. K. Pang, and S. Godsill, "Overview of bayesian sequential monte carlo methods for group and extended object tracking," *Digital Signal Processing*, vol. 25, pp. 1–16, 2014.

[100] S. Bordonaro, P. Willett, Y. Bar-Shalom, M. Baum, and T. Luginbuhl, "Extracting speed, heading and turn-rate measurements from extended objects using the em algorithm," in *2015 IEEE Aerospace Conference*, pp. 1–12, IEEE, 2015.

[101] L. Hammarstrand, M. Lundgren, and L. Svensson, "Adaptive radar sensor model for tracking structured extended objects," *IEEE Transactions on Aerospace and Electronic Systems*, vol. 48, no. 3, pp. 1975–1995, 2012.

[102] D. Salmond and M. Parr, "Track maintenance using measurements of target extent," *Radar, Sonar and Navigation, IEE Proceedings*, vol. 150, pp. 389–395, Dec. 2003.

[103] Z. Zhong, H. Meng, and X. Wang, "Extended target tracking using an imm based rao-blackwellised unscented kalman filter," in *2008 9th International Conference on Signal Processing*, pp. 2409–2412, IEEE, 2008.

[104] A. Fitzgibbon, M. Pilu, and R. B. Fisher, "Direct least square fitting of ellipses," *Pattern Analysis and Machine Intelligence, IEEE Transactions on*, vol. 21, no. 5, pp. 476–480, 1999.

[105] D. Chaudhuri and A. Samal, "A simple method for fitting of bounding rectangle to closed regions," *Pattern recognition*, vol. 40, no. 7, pp. 1981–1989, 2007.

[106] Y. Bar-Shalom, F. Daum, and J. Huang, "The Probabilistic Data Association Filter," *IEEE Control Systems Magazine*, vol. 29, pp. 82–100, December 2009.

[107] R. Courant and F. John, *Introduction to calculus and analysis I*. Springer Science & Business Media, 2012.

[108] M. Baum, F. Faion, and U. D. Hanebeck, "Modeling the Target Extent with Multiplicative Noise," in *Proceedings of the 15th International Conference on Information Fusion (Fusion 2012)*, (Singapore), 2012.

[109] J. Lan and X. R. Li, "Joint tracking and classification of extended object using random matrix," in *Information Fusion (FUSION), 2013 16th International Conference on*, pp. 1550–1557, IEEE, 2013.

[110] F. C. Schweppe, *Uncertain dynamic systems*. Prentice Hall, 1973.

[111] M. S. Nixon, "Circle Extraction via Least Squares and the Kalman Filter," in *Proceedings of the 5th International Conference on Computer Analysis of Images and Patterns*, 1993.

[112] J. Porrill, “Fitting ellipses and predicting confidence envelopes using a bias corrected kalman filter,” *Image and Vision Computing*, vol. 8, no. 1, pp. 37 – 41, 1990.

[113] S. Umeyama, “Least-squares estimation of transformation parameters between two point patterns,” *IEEE Transactions on pattern analysis and machine intelligence*, vol. 13, no. 4, pp. 376–380, 1991.

[114] S. S. H. U. Gamage and J. Lasenby, “New least squares solutions for estimating the average centre of rotation and the axis of rotation,” *Journal of biomechanics*, vol. 35, no. 1, pp. 87–93, 2002.

[115] K. K. Talukdar and W. D. Lawing, “Estimation of the parameters of the rice distribution,” *The Journal of the Acoustical Society of America*, vol. 89, no. 3, pp. 1193–1197, 1991.

[116] Z. Zhang, “Parameter estimation techniques: a tutorial with application to conic fitting,” *Image and Vision Computing*, vol. 15, no. 1, pp. 59 – 76, 1997.

[117] N. Chernov, *Circular and Linear Regression: Fitting Circles and Lines by Least Squares.* CRC Press, 2010.

[118] J. A. Sethian, *Level set methods and fast marching methods: evolving interfaces in computational geometry, fluid mechanics, computer vision, and materials science*, vol. 3. Cambridge university press, 1999.

[119] S. Osher and R. Fedkiw, *Level set methods and dynamic implicit surfaces*, vol. 153. Springer Science & Business Media, 2003.

[120] G. Matheron, *Random sets and integral geometry.* John Wiley & Sons, 1975.

[121] M. Baum and U. D. Hanebeck, “Extended Object Tracking Based on Set-Theoretic and Stochastic Fusion,” *IEEE Transactions on Aerospace and Electronic Systems*, vol. 48, pp. 3103–3115, Oct. 2012.

[122] M. Baum, B. Noack, and U. D. Hanebeck, “Extended Object and Group Tracking with Elliptic Random Hypersurface Models,” in *Proceedings of the 13th International Conference on Information Fusion (Fusion 2010)*, (Edinburgh, United Kingdom), July 2010.

[123] M. Baum, M. Feldmann, D. Fränken, U. D. Hanebeck, and W. Koch, "Extended Object and Group Tracking: A Comparison of Random Matrices and Random Hypersurface Models," in *Proceedings of the IEEE ISIF Workshop on Sensor Data Fusion: Trends, Solutions, Applications (SDF 2010)*, (Leipzig, Germany), Oct. 2010.

[124] A. Blake and M. Isard, *Active Contours: The Application of Techniques from Graphics, Vision, Control Theory and Statistics to Visual Tracking of Shapes in Motion.* Secaucus, NJ, USA: Springer-Verlag New York, Inc., 1st ed., 1998.

[125] M. Jacob, T. Blu, and M. Unser, "Efficient energies and algorithms for parametric snakes," *IEEE Transactions on Image Processing*, pp. 1231–1244, 2004.

[126] X. Li and V. Jilkov, "A survey of maneuvering target tracking: Dynamic models," in *Proc. 2000 SPIE Conf. on Signal and Data Processing ...*, no. April, (Orlando, Florida, USA), 2000.

[127] H. Samet, *The design and analysis of spatial data structures*, vol. 199. Addison-Wesley Reading, MA, 1990.

[128] W. Koch, "On 'negative' information in tracking and sensor data fusion: Discussion of selected examples," in *Proceedings of the Seventh International Conference on Information Fusion*, vol. 1, pp. 91–98, IEEE Publ. Piscataway, NJ, 2004.

[129] W. Koch, "On exploiting 'negative' sensor evidence for target tracking and sensor data fusion," *Information Fusion*, vol. 8, no. 1, 2007.

[130] K. Wyffels and M. Campbell, "Negative observations for multiple hypothesis tracking of dynamic extended objects," in *American Control Conference (ACC), 2014*, pp. 642–647, IEEE, 2014.

[131] A. Laurentini, "The visual hull concept for silhouette-based image understanding," *Pattern Analysis and Machine Intelligence, IEEE Transactions on*, vol. 16, pp. 150–162, Feb 1994.

[132] A. Fasoula, H. Driessen, and P. Van Genderen, "Model-based Integrated HRR Object Tracking and Classification," in *12th International Conference on Information Fusion*, pp. 1006–1013, July 2009.

[133] D. Angelova and L. Mihaylova, "Joint Target Tracking and Classification with Particle Filtering and Mixture Kalman filtering using Kinematic Radar Information," *Digital Signal Processing*, vol. 16, no. 2, pp. 180 – 204, 2006.

[134] K. Grauman, G. Shakhnarovich, and T. Darrell, "A bayesian approach to image-based visual hull reconstruction," in *Computer Vision and Pattern Recognition, 2003. Proceedings. 2003 IEEE Computer Society Conference on*, vol. 1, pp. I–187–I–194 vol.1, June 2003.

[135] P. J. Besl and N. D. McKay, "Method for registration of 3-d shapes," in *Robotics-DL tentative*, pp. 586–606, International Society for Optics and Photonics, 1992.

[136] P. Maynard, *Drawing distinctions: the varieties of graphic expression.* Cornell University Press, 2005.

[137] A. Choudhury and S. G. Parker, "Ray tracing npr-style feature lines," in *Proceedings of the 7th International Symposium on Non-Photorealistic Animation and Rendering*, pp. 5–14, ACM, 2009.

Supervised Student Theses

[138] J. P. Gerlach. *Virtual-Reality-gestützte Simulation eines heterogenen Sensornetzwerkes für Tracking-Anwendungen.* Master thesis, Karlsruhe Institute of Technology, 2016.

[139] V. Kaiser. *Projection-Based Gating for Extended Objects.* Bachelor thesis, Karlsruhe Institute of Technology, 2014.

[140] J. McClelland. *Development of a Human-Computer-Interface for the e-Installation of Marc Lee's "10,000 Moving Cities – Same but Different".* Diploma thesis, Karlsruhe Institute of Technology, 2014.

[141] F. Pohl. *Erstellung und telepräsente Reinszenierung einer e-Installation am Beispiel von 10.000 Moving Cities.* Bachelor thesis, Karlsruhe Institute of Technology, 2016.

[142] F. Szeliga. *Augmented Reality Echtzeit-Lagetracking eines Smartphones für die Industrie 4.0.* Master thesis, Karlsruhe Institute of Technology, 2017.

[143] P. Weidel. *Sensoreinsatzplanung für Multi-Kinect-Netzwerke.* Minor thesis, Karlsruhe Institute of Technology, 2013.

Own Publications

[144] F. Faion, M. Dolgov, A. Zea, and U. D. Hanebeck. Closed-form Bias Reduction for Shape Estimation with Polygon Models. In *Proceedings of the 19th International Conference on Information Fusion (Fusion 2016)*, Heidelberg, Germany, July 2016.

[145] F. Faion, S. Friedberger, A. Zea, and U. D. Hanebeck. Intelligent Sensor-Scheduling for Multi-Kinect-Tracking. In *Proceedings of the 2012 IEEE/RSJ International Conference on Intelligent Robots and Systems (IROS 2012)*, pages 3993–3999, Vilamoura, Algarve, Portugal, Oct. 2012.

[146] F. Faion, P. Ruoff, A. Zea, and U. D. Hanebeck. Recursive Bayesian Calibration of Depth Sensors with Non-Overlapping Views. In *Proceedings of the 15th International Conference on Information Fusion (Fusion 2012)*, Singapore, July 2012.

[147] F. Faion, A. Zea, M. Baum, , and U. D. Hanebeck. Bayesian Estimation of Line Segments. In *Proceedings of the IEEE ISIF Workshop on Sensor Data Fusion: Trends, Solutions, Applications (SDF 2014)*, Bonn, Germany, Oct. 2014.

[148] F. Faion, A. Zea, M. Baum, and U. D. Hanebeck. Partial Likelihood for Unbiased Extended Object Tracking. In *Proceedings of the 18th International Conference on Information Fusion (Fusion 2015)*, Washington D. C., USA, July 2015.

[149] F. Faion, A. Zea, M. Baum, and U. D. Hanebeck. Symmetries in Bayesian Extended Object Tracking. *Journal of Advances in Information Fusion*, 10(1):13–30, June 2015.

[150] F. Faion, A. Zea, and U. D. Hanebeck. Reducing Bias in Bayesian Shape Estimation. In *Proceedings of the 17th International Conference on Information Fusion (Fusion 2014)*, Salamanca, Spain, July 2014.

[151] J. M. Morcillo, F. Faion, A. Zea, U. D. Hanebeck, and C. Y. R. von Trotha. e-Installation: Synesthetic Documentation of Media Art via Telepresence Technologies. *arXiv preprint: Other Computer Science (cs.OH)*, Aug. 2014.

[152] S. Özgen, F. Faion, A. Zea, and U. D. Hanebeck. A Non-Parametric Inference Technique for Shape Boundaries in Noisy Point Clouds. In *Proceedings of the 2017 IEEE International Conference on Multisensor Fusion and Integration for Intelligent Systems (MFI 2017)*, Daegu, Korea, Nov. 2017.

[153] J. Steinbring, M. Baum, A. Zea, F. Faion, and U. D. Hanebeck. A Closed-Form Likelihood for Particle Filters to Track Extended Objects with Star-Convex RHMs. In *Proceedings of the 2015 IEEE International Conference on Multisensor Fusion and Integration for Intelligent Systems (MFI 2015)*, San Diego, California, USA, Sept. 2015.

[154] A. Zea, F. Faion, M. Baum, and U. D. Hanebeck. Level-Set Random Hyper Surface Models for Tracking Non-Convex Extended Objects. In *Proceedings of the 16th International Conference on Information Fusion (Fusion 2013)*, Istanbul, Turkey, July 2013.

[155] A. Zea, F. Faion, M. Baum, and U. D. Hanebeck. Tracking Simplified Shapes Using a Stochastic Boundary. In *Proceedings of the Eighth IEEE Sensor Array and Multichannel Signal Processing Workshop (SAM 2014)*, A Coruña, Spain, June 2014.

[156] A. Zea, F. Faion, M. Baum, and U. D. Hanebeck. Level-set random hyper surface models for tracking non-convex extended objects. *IEEE Transactions on Aerospace and Electronic Systems*, 2017.

[157] A. Zea, F. Faion, and U. D. Hanebeck. Tracking Connected Objects Using Interacting Shape Models. In *Proceedings of the 17th International Conference on Information Fusion (Fusion 2014)*, Salamanca, Spain, July 2014.

[158] A. Zea, F. Faion, and U. D. Hanebeck. Tracking Extended Objects using Extrusion Random Hypersurface Models. In *Proceedings of the IEEE ISIF Workshop on Sensor Data Fusion: Trends, Solutions, Applications (SDF 2014)*, Bonn, Germany, Oct. 2014.

[159] A. Zea, F. Faion, and U. D. Hanebeck. Exploiting Clutter: Negative Information for Enhanced Extended Object Tracking. In *Proceedings of the 18th International Conference on Information Fusion (Fusion 2015)*, Washington D. C., USA, July 2015.

[160] A. Zea, F. Faion, and U. D. Hanebeck. Shape Tracking using Partial Information Models. In *Proceedings of the 2015 IEEE International Conference on Multisensor Fusion and Integration for Intelligent Systems (MFI 2015)*, San Diego, California, USA, Sept. 2015.

[161] A. Zea, F. Faion, and U. D. Hanebeck. Tracking Elongated Extended Objects Using Splines. In *Proceedings of the 19th International Conference on Information Fusion (Fusion 2016)*, Heidelberg, Germany, July 2016.

[162] A. Zea, F. Faion, J. Steinbring, and U. D. Hanebeck. Exploiting Negative Measurements for Tracking Star-Convex Extended Objects. In *Proceedings of the 2016 IEEE International Conference on Multisensor Fusion and Integration for Intelligent Systems (MFI 2016)*, Baden-Baden, Germany, Sept. 2016.

Karlsruhe Series on Intelligent Sensor-Actuator-Systems

Edited by Prof. Dr.-Ing. Uwe D. Hanebeck // ISSN 1867-3813

Band 1 **Oliver Schrempf**
Stochastische Behandlung von Unsicherheiten in kaskadierten dynamischen Systemen. 2008
ISBN 978-3-86644-287-0

Band 2 **Florian Weißel**
Stochastische modell-prädiktive Regelung nichtlinearer Systeme. 2009
ISBN 978-3-86644-348-8

Band 3 **Patrick Rößler**
Telepräsente Bewegung und haptische Interaktion in ausgedehnten entfernten Umgebungen. 2009
ISBN 978-3-86644-346-4

Band 4 **Kathrin Roberts**
Modellbasierte Herzbewegungsschätzung für robotergestützte Interventionen. 2009
ISBN 978-3-86644-353-2

Band 5 **Felix Sawo**
Nonlinear state and parameter estimation of spatially distributed systems. 2009
ISBN 978-3-86644-370-9

Band 6 **Gregor F. Schwarzenberg**
Untersuchung der Abbildungseigenschaften eines 3D-Ultraschall-Computertomographen zur Berechnung der 3D-Abbildungsfunktion und Herleitung einer optimierten Sensorgeometrie. 2009
ISBN 978-3-86644-393-8

Die Bände sind unter www.ksp.kit.edu als PDF frei verfügbar oder als Druckausgabe bestellbar.

Band 7 **Marco Huber**
Probabilistic Framework for Sensor Management. 2009
ISBN 978-3-86644-405-8

Band 8 **Frederik Beutler**
Probabilistische modellbasierte Signalverarbeitung zur instantanen Lageschätzung. 2010
ISBN 978-3-86644-442-3

Band 9 **Marc Peter Deisenroth**
Efficient Reinforcement Learning using Gaussian Processes. 2010
ISBN 978-3-86644-569-7

Band 10 **Evgeniya Ballmann**
Physics-Based Probabilistic Motion Compensation of Elastically Deformable Objects. 2012
ISBN 978-3-86644-862-9

Band 11 **Peter Krauthausen**
Learning Dynamic Systems for Intention Recognition in Human-Robot-Cooperation. 2013
ISBN 978-3-86644-952-7

Band 12 **Antonia Pérez Arias**
Haptic Guidance for Extended Range Telepresence. 2013
ISBN 978-3-7315-0035-3

Band 13 **Marcus Baum**
Simultaneous Tracking and Shape Estimation of Extended Objects. 2013
ISBN 978-3-7315-0078-0

Band 14 **Benjamin Noack**
State Estimation for Distributed Systems with Stochastic and Set-membership Uncertainties. 2014
ISBN 978-3-7315-0124-4

Band 15 **Jörg Fischer**
Optimal Sequence-Based Control of Networked Linear Systems. 2014
ISBN 978-3-7315-0305-7

Band 16 **Marc Reinhardt**
Linear Estimation in Interconnected Sensor Systems with Information Constraints. 2015
ISBN 978-3-7315-0342-2

Band 17 **Gerhard Kurz**
Directional Estimation for Robotic Beating Heart Surgery. 2015
ISBN 978-3-7315-0382-8

Band 18 **Igor Gilitschenski**
Deterministic Sampling for Nonlinear Dynamic State Estimation. 2016
ISBN 978-3-7315-0473-3

Band 19 **Florian Faion**
Tracking Extended Objects in Noisy Point Clouds with Application in Telepresence Systems. 2016
ISBN 978-3-7315-0517-4

Band 20 **Martin Klemm**
Intraoperative Planning and Execution of Arbitrary Orthopedic Interventions Using Handheld Robotics and Augmented Reality. 2018
ISBN 978-3-7315-0800-7

Band 21 **Antonio Kleber Zea Cobo**
Tracking Extended Objects with Active Models and Negative Measurements. 2019
ISBN 978-3-7315-0877-9
